TRANSNATIONAL ACTORS IN CENTRAL

AND EAST EUROPEAN TRANSITIONS

PITT SERIES IN RUSSIAN AND EAST EUROPEAN STUDIES

JONATHAN HARRIS, EDITOR

TRANSNATIONAL ACTORS IN CENTRAL AND EAST EUROPEAN TRANSITIONS

EDITED BY MITCHELL A. ORENSTEIN

STEPHEN BLOOM

AND NICOLE LINDSTROM

UNIVERSITY OF PITTSBURGH PRESS

Published by the University of Pittsburgh Press, Pittsburgh, Pa., 15260
Copyright © 2008, University of Pittsburgh Press
Manufactured in the United States of America
Printed on acid-free paper
10 9 8 7 6 5 4 3 2 1

Library of Congress Cataloging-in-Publication Data

Transnational actors in Central and East European transitions / edited by Mitchell
Orenstein, Stephen Bloom, and Nicole Lindstrom.
    p. cm.
Includes bibliographical references and index.
ISBN-13: 978-0-8229-4348-8 (cloth : alk. paper)
ISBN-10: 0-8229-4348-4 (cloth : alk. paper)
ISBN-13: 978-0-8229-5994-6 (pbk. : alk. paper)
ISBN-10: 0-8229-5994-1 (pbk. : alk. paper)
    1. Europe, Eastern—Politics and government—1989- 2. Europe, Central—Politics
and government—1989- 3. Former Soviet republics—Politics and government.
4. International agencies—Former communist countries. I. Orenstein, Mitchell A.
(Mitchell Alexander) II. Bloom, Stephen R., 1968- III. Lindstrom, Nicole.
    JN96.A58T75 2008
    320.947—dc22

                2008004513

CONTENTS

ACKNOWLEDGMENTS

The editors would like to acknowledge the support of the European Union Center of Excellence at Syracuse University, Syracuse University Center for European Studies, and Cornell University's Institute for European Studies for funding several seminars during 2005–2006 that enabled the authors of this volume to come together to discuss the development of this research agenda. These three centers at Syracuse and Cornell are supported by the European Union and a joint Title VI National Resource Center grant from the U.S. Department of Education. We owe a special thanks to Valerie Bunce and Davydd Greenwood at Cornell Institute for European Studies and to Peg Hermann at Syracuse's Moynihan Institute for helping to make this project a reality.

We wish to express our appreciation to the many scholars whose comments enriched these chapters and the volume as a whole, including Mark Baskin, David Black, Dominic Boyer, Valerie Bunce, Holly Case, Cheng Chen, Mikhail Filippov, Anna Grzymała-Busse, Richard Higgott, Abby Innes, Robert Kaufman, Jeff Kopstein, Sasha Milicevic, Cas Mudde, Renee de Nevers, Ambassador Martin Palouš, Craig Parsons, Eric Persons, Sharon Werning Rivera, Susan Rose-Ackerman, Hans Peter Schmitz, Olga Shevtsova, Rudy Sil, Bartosz Stanislawski, Diane Stone, Aleksandra Sznajder, Sidney Tarrow, Brian Taylor, Ramūnas Vilpišauskas, and Elaine Weiner. In addition, we wish to thank the graduate students from Cornell and Syracuse (and elsewhere) who contributed to the discussions leading up to this book: Lucia Antalova, Zaklina Marta Bogdanic, Mary Borissova, Todor Enev (University of Pennsylvania), Victor Gomez (University of Toronto), Petra Hejnova, Katya Kalandadze, Sooin Kim, Kathryn McGovern, Eric Olsen, Aleksandra Pastor, Tsveta Petrova, Aleksander Rekhtman, Azamat Sakiev, Elton Skendaj, and Haley Swedlund. We owe a special debt to Kathryn McGovern and Haley Swedlund at Syracuse University, who provided tremendous research and editorial assistance and prepared the manuscript for review. Thanks also to Elizabeth Isaman at Johns Hopkins University, who provided editorial assistance at later stages of this project. Finally, we wish to thank Peter Kracht, Jonathan Harris, Alberta Sbragia, and the editorial board at University of Pittsburgh

Press for moving this book forward to publication as well as to several anonymous reviewers for their thoughtful comments. Thanks also to Taylor and Francis and the board of *Review of International Political Economy*, which granted permission for us to republish Juliet Johnson's chapter that is a version of her article "Two-Track Diffusion and Central Bank Embeddedness: The Politics of Euro Adoption in Hungary and the Czech Republic, *Review of International Political Economy* 13, no. 3 (2006): 362–86.

LIST OF ABBREVIATIONS

CATW	Coalition Against Trafficking in Women
CDR	Democratic Convention of Romania
CNB	Czech National Bank
DPMNE	Democratic Party of Macedonian National Unity
EBRD	European Bank for Reconstruction and Development
ECB	European Central Bank
EMU	European Monetary Union
EU	European Union
FDI	foreign direct investment
GAATW	Global Alliance Against Trafficking in Women
HDF	Hungarian Defense Forces
ICTY	International Criminal Tribunal for the Former Yugoslavia
IGO	intergovernmental organization
IMF	International Monetary Fund
INGO	international nongovernmental organization
IO	international organization
IOM	International Organization on Migration
KLA	Kosovo Liberation Army
LAPMB	Liberation Army of Presevo, Medvedja, and Bujanovac
MAPP	Movement for the Abolition of Pornography and Prostitution
MoD	Ministry of Defense
MoF	Ministry of Finance
MSZP	Hungarian Socialist Party
NATO	North Atlantic Treaty Organization
NBH	National Bank of Hungary
NLA	National Liberation Army
NGO	nongovernmental organization
OECD	Organization for Economic Cooperation and Development
OSCE	Organization for Security and Co-operation in Europe
PCR	postcommunist reformer
PDSH	Democratic Party of Albanians
PPD	Party for Democratic Prosperity
RCP	Regional Clearing Point

SAP	Stabilization and Association Process
SDC	Swiss Agency for Development and Cooperation
SDSM	Social Democratic Union of Macedonia
SECI	Southeast European Cooperative Initiative
SFOR	Stabilization Force in Bosnia
SLD-PSL	Democratic Left Alliance-Polish Peasant Party
TIP	Trafficking in Persons
TVPA	Trafficking Victims of Protection Act
USAID	U.S. Agency for International Development
VMRO	Internal Macedonian Revolutionary Organization
WTO	World Trade Organization

TRANSNATIONAL ACTORS IN CENTRAL AND EAST EUROPEAN TRANSITIONS

1

A FOURTH
DIMENSION OF
TRANSITION

Mitchell A. Orenstein,

Stephen Bloom, and

Nicole Lindstrom

Transnational and nonstate actors have exerted a pervasive influence on postcommunist transitions in Central and East Europe. No aspect of politics has been untouched. To start with, transnational actors, including international governmental and nongovernmental organizations, corporations, foundations, and activist networks, have played a key role in processes of democratization in postcommunist Europe. When Russian President Vladimir Putin claimed that the Orange Revolution in Ukraine was fomented by outside forces, he appealed to xenophobic impulses and underestimated the domestic sources of protest. Yet no one could suggest that he was entirely wrong. In fact, a diverse mix of transnational actors was deeply involved, including United States aid agencies, the European Union (EU), and election observers of the Organization for Security and Co-operation in Europe (OSCE). The same could be said of the Rose Revolution in Georgia and the popular uprising in Kyrgyzstan that ousted President

Akaev. External actors have always influenced politics in Central and East Europe (Janos 2000; Rothschild 1974). But as Vachudova suggests in this volume, the diligence and ultimate success of external actors—particularly the EU—in influencing domestic change in the region is historically unprecedented.

In virtually any area of policy in Central and East European countries, one can find transnational actors assisting state reforms and societal organizations active in that area. International organizations and expert networks have provided critical aid to economic reform teams across postcommunist Europe starting in 1989. Recent studies have focused on transnational actor involvement in pension and social policy (Orenstein 2000; Sissenich 2006), minority rights (Kelley 2004), defense policy (Jacoby 2004), and across the areas included in the EU's body of laws and regulations, the *acquis communautaire*. Transnational actor influences are not restricted to state policy; they also extend deeply into postcommunist civil society. Aid organizations, international organizations, and transnational nongovernmental organizations (NGOs) like the Soros Foundation have played a substantial role in the development of local NGOs, civil associations, businesses, and social movements (Wedel 1998). Perhaps most dramatically, Bosnia and Herzegovina and the Republic of Kosovo were, at the time of this writing, mandates ruled in large part by transnational organizations such as the United Nations and the EU.

Despite growing interest in examining the role of transnational actors, many scholars have ignored, downplayed, or disputed their importance in Central and East Europe and elsewhere. Leading models of postcommunist transition, for instance, tend to emphasize the causal force of domestic variables such as domestic interest groups, political parties, institutional variation, and the like, often excluding transnational politics altogether. Others accept that transnational actors may dominate elite discourse in some areas, but have only minor significance on the ground. Scholars in the realist tradition insist that states, particularly powerful ones such as the United States or Germany, remain the leading actors in international society and that the impact of transnational actors is limited (Kennedy, this volume).

This book advances our understanding of Central and East European transitions by integrating a wealth of new research on transnational politics into the field of postcommunist politics. We do this first by reframing debates about the "dual" or "triple" transition to include a fourth aspect of postcommunist transition: the integration of new or newly independent nation-states into an international system marked by complex interdependence. Second, we show that careful analysis of the transnational dimension of transition requires attention to two central questions: how do transnational actors influence domestic politics and how much are they able to do. Third, we introduce a group of essays that make important empirical contributions to each of these research agendas. They represent competing perspectives that illustrate the terms of an emerging debate. Together, these essays advance an agenda that combines concern for both transnational and national dimensions of governance.

This effort to integrate transnational and domestic perspectives on postcommunist politics mirrors a broader trend in comparative and international politics. In recent years, a variety of scholars working in the fields of international relations and comparative politics have suggested that what used to be called "domestic" politics must include a systematic recognition of transnational influences (Orenstein and Schmitz 2006). Following developments in international relations theory and sociological institutionalism (Meyer et al. 1997; Strang and Soule 1998), comparative politics scholars have begun to collapse boundaries between international relations and comparative politics. This new transnational scholarship is characterized by five interlocking claims. First, it challenges the notion that there are one or two global trends transforming politics globally. Instead, the new transnationalism emphasizes multiple trends, including those in the field of governance and organization that are shaping outcomes differently in multiple contexts. Second, the new transnationalism focuses on a host of nonstate actors that have not been terribly significant in comparative politics scholarship before but are seen to have an increasing role in what used to be conceived of as "domestic" politics. Third, it recognizes that states themselves have transnational ties that go beyond the diplomatic realm. Slaughter (2004), for instance, emphasizes that a wide range of state agencies are now part of transnational governmental networks that increasingly develop norms that affect state behavior. Fourth, spheres of governance are being redefined away from hierarchical and territorial forms of governance and toward more networked forms of interaction in internationally contested policy arenas. Fifth, the new transnational scholarship takes both ideas and interests seriously. While influenced by constructivist scholarship in international relations, transnational scholarship in comparative politics has tended to show concern for both material interests and the construction of interests through norms, rather than pitting one set of explanations against another (Epstein 2005; Grabbe 2005). We seek to integrate these insights into the study of postcommunist transitions.

The Quadruple Transition

A key starting point for this project is the concept of transition itself. At the outset of transition in 1989, it was widely believed that postcommunist societies faced a challenging dual transition: a simultaneous move to capitalism and democracy. Przeworski (1991) and others (Dahrendorf 1990; Elster 1993) argued that creating new capitalist market economies and democratic political institutions were linked yet threatened to undermine one another. Democratic politics could put an end to economic reform. And economic dislocation could create a large body of economic losers who might vote against democracy in free elections. Using the J-curve to illustrate his point, Przeworski (1991) argued that voters could reject democracy at the polls if the postsocialist economic downturn was either too steep or too protracted. The potential incompatibility of the dual transition to market and democracy became a core issue in postcommunist transition theory.

Claus Offe (1997) broadened the scope of this debate by arguing that postcommunist societies actually faced a triple transition. Many postcommunist states were new or renewed nation-states. Their simultaneous move to nation-statehood, Offe hypothesized, could complicate efforts at democratization and economic reform, especially in multiethnic states. With the case of Weimar Germany in mind, Stephen Van Evera similarly argued that the economic dislocation that would follow the demise of state socialism could fuel nationalist mobilization and instigate ethnic war: "If economic conditions deteriorate, publics become more responsive to scapegoat myths, hence such myths are more believed, hence war is more likely" (1994, 30). Like the dual transition literature, the triple transition literature suggested that different aspects of transition had the potential to disrupt one another.

These problems of simultaneous reform caused scholars to analyze the optimal sequencing of various components of the triple transition. Some scholars argued for rapid economic reforms to take place before a democratic electoral reaction made such reforms impossible (Balcerowicz 1994;

Sachs 1993). Others took an opposite approach. Linz and Stepan (1992, 1996) cautioned that electoral institutions should be legitimated before serious economic reforms were introduced. They also stressed the importance that the proper sequencing of national and regional elections could play in the maintenance of national cohesion. Gorbachev's decision in 1990 to first hold elections to republican parliaments, Linz and Stepan argued, fostered secessionist pressures that eventually brought down the Soviet state. What these scholars had in common was a sense that different aspects of transition could undermine one another.

However, forecasts of the problems of dual and triple transitions proved overly pessimistic with regard to Central and East Europe. Greskovits went so far as to declare that "it now seems justified to write in the past tense: the breakdown literature has failed" (1998, 4). The simultaneous introduction of democratic political institutions, market economies, and nation-states went more smoothly than analysts had predicted. Contrary to the assumptions of the J-curve, the losers of economic reform did not turn against democratic political institutions. In fact, Steven Fish found a positive relationship between economic reform and democratization in postcommunist states. Countries that avoided democratic backsliding were generally those that implemented the most thoroughgoing economic liberalization (Fish 2001). Moreover, ethnic scapegoating and other manifestations of ethnonationalism failed to materialize during the postsocialist recession, despite the tremendous drop in living standards. In post-Soviet Latvia and Ukraine, economic reforms have been found to facilitate ethnic cooperation by breaking down the economic differentiation of ethnic groups cultivated during the Soviet period (Bloom 2004).

We believe that the central reason that the dual and triple transitions literatures failed to predict the relatively happy confluence of democratization, economic reform, and state building in Central and East Europe was that they ignored or underestimated a fourth dimension of transition: the role of transnational actors in the transition to complex interdependence in Europe. The process of integration of postcommunist states into not only the EU but also a whole range of international organizations, production networks, and international associations constituted a major, and initially ignored, dimension of transition. The geographical proximity of Central and East European states to the EU (Kopstein and Reilly 2000), as well as the simultaneous processes of transition and globalization, however, came to be seen as key variables in the analysis of postcommunist transitions.

The quadruple transition framework that we are advancing does not simply insert a neglected fourth component into the study of postcommunist transition. Rather, a quadruple transition framework suggests that the projects of nation-state building, democratization, and marketization have been embedded within transnational agendas and pressures, most importantly but not limited to those of the EU. The movement toward complex interdependence, we argue, helped to facilitate the simultaneous introduction of democratic political institutions, market economies, and nation-states. The Council of Europe, in coordination with the OSCE and the EU, carefully monitored the state of democracy throughout the region and, during political crises, dispatched teams to negotiate solutions that reinforced democratic political institutions (Pridham 2002). Transnational economic advisers influenced almost all areas of economic policy making, from privatization to monetary policy. Transnational economic assistance, such as the EU's PHARE and Tacis programs, however piecemeal, facilitated the efforts of foreign economic advisers and deepened their impact. A surprising 60 percent of the residents of Czechoslovakia were aware of the EU's PHARE program in 1991 (Central and Eastern Eurobarometer 1991). Transnational corporations also played a significant role in transition, with foreign firms gaining majority shares in banking, manufacturing, and other sectors in most Central and East European countries through the privatization process (see Epstein, this volume). As prospective members of the EU, postcommunist states were also more constrained than initially thought in their choice of minority policies. The EU required countries to develop national plans for combating ethnic discrimination, to ratify the Framework Convention for the Protection of National Minorities of the Council of Europe, and to implement a wide range of OSCE recommendations concerning the treatment of specific minorities (Kelley 2004). This motivated the ethnic majorities in these states to make credible commitments to protect minority rights (Fearon 1998). The quadruple transition framework rests on the observation that transnational integration limited the scope for disruptions and disjunctures that had been theorized between the various transition projects. At first ignored, transnational actors turned out to be the dark matter that held the various aspects of postcommunist transition together in Central and East Europe.

Transnational Actors in Postcommunist Politics

Any analysis of transnationalism should begin by defining the relevant terms. Transnationalism and transnational actors are used in a variety of ways in the academic literature. We take a broad definition here, considering transnational actors to include any intergovernmental organizations (IGOs), international nongovernmental organizations (INGOs), private enterprises, foundations, state bodies or associations that *act on policy in a transnational space*. IGOs consist of organizations such as the EU, Organization for Economic Cooperation and Development (OECD), World Bank, International Monetary Fund (IMF), OSCE, Council of Europe, and others, whose members are states and which seek to affect policy across multiple national boundaries. In addition, transnational actors include INGOs such as the Soros, Ford, and Mott Foundations that advocate or fund advocacy organizations operating in multiple states and policy areas, as well as issue-specific INGOs such Greenpeace, Transparency International, or Doctors without Borders. Transnational actors also work in coordination with bilateral and other state agencies that act as policy advocates and policy entrepreneurs in multiple states, such as the U.S. Agency for International Development (USAID) or the Swiss Agency for Development and Cooperation (SDC), as well as German party-based organizations such as Heinrich Böhl Stiftung. Finally, in any given issue area, proliferation of transnational actors can constitute a transnational policy community, issue network, or coalition (Rosenau 2003).

Transnational actors' agendas are not always clearly distinguished from those of states. A long literature has developed on the reasons that states delegate responsibilities to transnational and nonstate actors. Realist (Gilpin 2001) and neo-Marxist (Wade 2002) scholars argue that the actions of transnational actors are closely aligned with the priorities of powerful states. While this may be true, Barnett and Finnemore (2004) emphasize that there are a number of reasons to believe that international organizations act relatively independent of states. As typical bureaucracies, they seek to extend their own power and influence by stretching mandates into new areas and developing problem definitions and solutions that require new forms of activity, higher budgets, and greater independence. This helps to explain why few international organizations die, even after their initial mandate is completed. Transnational organizations, like all bureaucracies, can be creative at wrenching themselves free from strict hierarchical control by state sponsors. This relative independence of transnational actors applies especially to INGOs and NGOs, and to a lesser extent to state aid agencies or quasi-independent aid organizations that may represent policies grounded in a single party or bureaucratic constituency rather than the government in power.

Many recent studies of transnational influence in Central and East Europe have focused on the EU, for obvious reasons. The EU has been the most powerful transnational actor in postcommunist politics, wielding enormous influence over countries that placed a high premium on membership and were willing to accept almost any price to attain it (Grabbe 2006; Grzymała-Busse and Innes 2003; Moravcsik and Vachudova 2003). The EU is at once an international organization, representing the interests of its member states, and an autonomous actor in its own right, with agenda-setting power concentrated in Brussels. In terms of EU enlargement, the European Commission sought to build consensus around a policy goal not necessarily in the interest of all member states and powerful constituents by appealing to Europe's historic mission to reunite Europe around liberal democratic norms (see Schimmelfennig 2003; Sedelmeier 2005). On the part of would-be members, elite and popular desires to quickly "return" postcommunist states back to Europe guided the transition process and gave national elites much leeway in pushing through domestic reforms.

While the EU has been a powerful transnational actor in Central and East Europe, it is by no means the only one. This volume seeks to expand understanding of transnational actor influence beyond the EU. We include studies that emphasize the roles of the Catholic Church (Byrnes), international financial institutions (Johnson), and IGOs and NGOs (Lindstrom). This allows us to address areas of policy and politics beyond the narrow range of policy questions included in the *acquis communautaire*. Instead, we consider transnational influence on a wide variety of domains, such as party systems, public attitudes, interethnic relations, and the full range of postcommunist politics (see also Kelley 2004; Vachudova 2005). We also examine how the decision-making processes of the EU intersect with the agendas of other international organizations, networks, and coalitions. In defense policy, for instance, the North Atlantic Treaty Organization (NATO) was critically important (Epstein 2005; Jacoby 2004). In minority policy, the OSCE and Council of Europe played an important role (Hughes,

Sasse, and Gordon 2004; Kelley 2004; Kymlicka 1995). Analyses of bank privatization (Epstein, this volume) or central bank policy (Johnson, this volume) must consider how the European institutions complemented or conflicted with global financial institutions such as the World Bank or the IMF. Although many studies tend to emphasize the importance of a single organization like the EU, we show that in any given policy area multiple transnational actors are at play, often coordinating formally and informally to achieve maximum impact on postcommunist states and societies.

Integrating the study of transnational and national politics requires a multi-level research perspective. We focus on two separate but interrelated aspects of the relationship between transnational and national politics in Central and East Europe: how transnational actors seek to influence domestic politics, and how much influence transnational actors have at the national level. The contributors to this volume focus primarily either on mechanisms of transnational actor influence or on a critical evaluation of the extent of transnational actor influence.

How Do Transnational Actors Exert Influence?

Central to the emerging literature on transnational politics is the question of how transnational actors exert influence. The essays in this volume reflect two competing approaches: rationalist/materialist and constructivist. The rationalist/materialist tradition suggests that actors make choices based on a rational calculation of their material interests, while the constructivist tradition argues that ideas and issue frames also influence how actors perceive and construct their interests and behavior.

Studies drawing on rationalist approaches argue that conditionality mechanisms based on material interests and rewards can best explain domestic policy change in Central and East European states, particularly EU membership conditionality (Kelley 2004; Vachudova 2005). This external incentive model posits that when EU conditions are consistent and credible and domestic adoption costs are low, there is a high degree of domestic compliance (Schimmelfennig and Sedelmeier 2005). Milada Vachudova's essay takes a strong position in favor of rationalist/materialist interpretations.

Vachudova focuses on the EU as the "causal behemoth" of transnational influence in postcommunist politics. Given Central and East European states' overwhelming desire to reap the tremendous benefits of membership, the EU has managed to exert the greatest leverage of any transnational actor in shaping political change in the region. Anchoring her argument in the logic that material rewards create powerful incentives for states to comply with EU rules, Vachudova offers an explicitly rationalist framework for understanding transnational agenda setting. The European Commission, acting on behalf of EU member states, managed to influence political outcomes in the region through both passive and active leverage. Vachudova shows how in the early stages of transition, the attraction of EU membership itself—and the threat of exclusion—gave the EU passive leverage over aspiring members. Once the EU set out clear conditions and guidelines for membership, its leverage became more active, forcing states to comply with vast and intrusive entry requirements. The EU managed to make its active leverage more credible by taking advantage of the asymmetric interdependence between the EU and its weaker and poorer neighbors, as well as its enforcement mechanisms based on meritocracy. Vachudova suggests that while other transnational actors played a role in bringing about political change, namely NATO, the Council of Europe, and the OSCE, their leverage and influence relied on the EU providing legitimacy to the standards they set and creating material sanctions for violation of these standards.

In contrast to Vachudova's realism, several authors represented here engage with the constructivist tradition and seek to integrate the role of ideas into the study of transnational actor influence. They do this by disaggregating the state and transnational actors and studying the different ways actors approach particular policy agendas.

Nicole Lindstrom analyzes the role of ideational or cultural frames on policies toward antihuman trafficking policies in the Balkans. She notes that human trafficking has become an obsession of the international community, but there are at least four competing frames deployed in international discussions: a migration frame, a law-enforcement frame, an economic frame, and a human rights frame. These frames each suggest different policy responses, different targets, and different objectives. Lindstrom concedes that state interests remain important, because it is ultimately powerful states that determine the choice of frame to be deployed in an issue area. In the case of human trafficking, the EU has advocated a migration approach, while the United States emphasizes law enforcement, and these choices have made a difference. But the ideas that animate the problem definitions also have an independent influence. Lindstrom's account is nuanced in that it allows for the possibility that framing choices will change over time. Her account also suggests that policy obsessions (or campaigns) by diffuse networks of transnational actors may have negative or unintended consequences.

Chapters by Jacoby, Johnson, and Epstein combine arguments based on material incentives and ideational influence in innovative ways. Wade Jacoby seeks to bridge the rationalist/constructivist divide by studying the coalitions that form between transnational and domestic actors. This "coalition approach" to the study of transnational influence has the benefit of providing a finer-grained analysis of cross-border collaborations and their impacts (Jacoby 2006). Jacoby shows that transnational actors may have different levels and types of influence depending on the configuration of existing domestic actors and their ideas. While some may act as "veto players," others act as "vehicles" of transnational actor agendas. In particular, Jacoby suggests that transnational actors influence policy by allying with domestic groups that have historically been on the losing end of policy battles, or what he calls "minority traditions" in domestic politics. Transnational actors leverage their resources to turn domestic political losers into winners, thus gaining substantial influence on policy. In this way, the material resources of transnational actors are deployed to advance particular ideological agendas. Jacoby shifts the emphasis away from whether rational or ideational explanations are better by combining elements of both in a perspective that focuses on deciphering particular mechanisms of influence. He also provides a whole new language for thinking about transnational actor interventions through this "coalition approach."

Juliet Johnson contributes further to combining the realist and constructivist perspectives with an essay on two-track diffusion. While previous analysts have emphasized either normative suasion or material coercion as mechanisms of transnational actor influence, Johnson argues that both mechanisms may operate in any given area, affecting different groups differently. For instance, she argues that Central European central bankers tended to be heavily socialized into liberal economic norms, so heavily that their enthusiasm for the adoption of the euro, for instance, outstripped what many economists thought reasonable from the perspective of state interest. Other actors who had supported European integration out of interests and incentives but did not necessarily share the liberal zeal of central bankers, came to oppose quick adoption of the euro. Johnson concludes that the reasons actors adopt policy positions matter, since changes in incentives (or norms) may affect different actors differently over time, in this case preventing the embeddedness of policies. Johnson's contribution further suggests the importance of analyzing transnational actor influence not only on states but also on interest groups within states. This can lead to a finer grained analysis of the influence of transnational actors. It puts further weight on substantial differences between normative and incentive-based compliance.

Rachel Epstein emphasizes that international organizations can shift the terms of debate on policy in multiple states, but their influence is contingent on their ability to mobilize politically positioned domestic reformers. Such an argument is clearly consistent with that of Jacoby and the coalition approach. Epstein focuses her attention, however, on how transnational actors mobilize such support. Transnational actors successfully implement their agendas only when they are able to build domestic resonance for their policies. In this way, the content of policy ideas helps to determine the power of transnational actors. She puts forward three main reasons why transnational actors may mobilize domestic actor support: uncertainty of domestic actors about which policies to support, desire for social recognition, and perceived credibility of transnational agendas and policies. Where domestic actors have strongly formed countervailing preferences, Epstein would not expect to see compliance with transnational actor agendas. However, where domestic policy makers are not firmly wedded to alternative ideas, and indeed may be seeking solutions to significant policy problems, transnational actors may play a powerful role. Epstein also places great importance on the individual and group desire for social recognition by transnational actors. If policy makers care about the judgments of transnational actors, they may behave differently than if they are indifferent to them. Finally, the perceived credibility of transnational policies matters.

Epstein illustrates these arguments through a detailed discussion of debates over bank privatization in Central and East Europe. She argues that policy makers in Poland and Hungary were far more receptive to transnational actor agendas than their counterparts in Romania, since Romania had less interest in membership in various European clubs and simply ignored transnational actor advice that would have moved the country toward privatization and sale of banking assets to foreigners. Epstein thus moves toward a theory of why different social groups may accept or reject transnational actor advice.

These authors have found substantial support for the view that transnational actors affect policy in Central and East Europe. Further, they have identified a variety of mechanisms of influence and have begun to uncover when certain actors and mechanisms are important and when they are less so. They build on a broad literature in international relations theory on the role of transnational actors that shows the extent and type of international influence and domestic institutions to be key determinants of domestic change (Risse-Kappen 1995). By bringing this debate into the field of transition studies, these essays make a major contribution to the literature by illustrating how transnational actors have structured the opportunities and norms of transition.

How Influential Are Transnational Actors?

While a burgeoning literature has demonstrated the significant influence of transnational actors and considered the mechanisms of this influence, many scholars in comparative politics and international relations remain less convinced of the relevance of this research agenda. Some critics in the realist tradition argue that states remain the central determining actors in international relations and that international organizations act in the interest of leading states and their hegemonic interests. Skeptics of the transnational research agenda suggest that the influence of transnational actors still depends crucially on the cooperation of local actors who dominate national politics, from governing elites to powerful domestic constituencies. The influence of transnational actors is thus significantly constrained by domestic political institutions and interests and often amounts to small potatoes. Moreover, by neglecting to fully address the realities of domestic politics, transnational actors' actions can result in unintended consequences. Another criticism of the role of transnational actors is the reaction hypothesis. Many scholars have argued that the growing influence of transnational actors and the policies that they spread, including neoliberal economic policy, democratization, and cultural globalization, fuel nationalist and other particularist reactions. The campaigns of Zapatista, leader Subcommander Marcos, and the French sheepherder turned peasant leader José Bové, whose fight against the World Trade Organization (WTO) landed him in jail on charges of bombing a McDonald's restaurant, serve as vivid examples of what Benjamin Barber calls Jihad versus McWorld. Samuel Huntington's *The Clash of Civilizations* (1996) suggests that if members of non-Western civilizations previously emulated the West, today they are more likely to form reactive identities in opposition to it.

To what extent can these critiques of transnational politics be applied to postcommmunist Europe? Some analysts have argued that democratization and economic reform efforts encouraged by international organizations in the postcommunist countries have not only failed but also fueled domestic reaction. Jack Snyder, in considering the relationship between democratization and nationalism, argues that in newly democratic countries, politicians are rewarded for playing the nationalist card in the nascent and highly imperfect marketplace of ideas. Slobodan Milošević in Serbia and Franjo Tudjman in Croatia exemplify this trend (Mansfield and Snyder 2005; Snyder 2000; Snyder and Ballentine 1996). Susan Woodward (1995), also writing on the Balkans, claims Western-imposed structural adjustment policies were the root cause of nationalism in the former Yugoslavia. These measures, Woodward argues, led to heightened competition among the Yugoslav elite, producing incentives for the politicians of the wealthier republics, namely Slovenia and Croatia, to secede.

One may similarly hypothesize that as the EU has reached deeply into domestic society, reshaping much of the legal infrastructure of the new member states in its image, it has challenged the role of many national politicians, who are no longer the final arbiter in many decision-making arenas. That governing elites, some of whom fought for national independence, would not want to relinquish this newly won sovereignty to external entities does not seem surprising. The largely undemocratic (or at the very least nontransparent) manner in which the EU accession process has been conducted has provided additional incentives for local elites to adopt anti-EU reactive positions. With a casual glance at the findings of Eurobarometer surveys, one finds a sizable population of Euroskeptics in most new member states. It is only logical that local elites would capitalize on such anti-EU sentiment. Robert Rohrschneider, Stephen Whitefield, and their colleagues' analysis of public opinion surveys on EU integration noted growing Euro skepticism in East Central Europe as accession drew closer, as well as negative positions on key policies and values underpinning integration, including the foreign ownership of property and basic market values (2006). This suggests that transition to transnational interdependence may indeed foment nationalist reactions.

We should not assume, however, that politicians who seek to mobilize domestic resistance will be successful. As Gagnon's work shows, many politicians have either failed in their attempts at playing the nationalist card or their actions have been intended to demobilize rather than mobilize national groups (1996, 2004). Some of the EU enlargement-related issues are highly technical in nature and, as a result, may be difficult for domestic politicians to frame effectively. The appeal of domestic reaction has also been more varied than assumed by scholars. While many Serbs joined militias, others avoided the draft (Milicevic 2004). It is worth adding that the reaction against the supposed foreign roots of Ukraine's Orange Revolution failed miserably, whereas Putin's naked interference in Ukraine's domestic affairs, which included appearances before each round of the election, appeared to backfire (Karatnycky 2005). Liudmila Yanukovych, who may have ended up in the proverbial historical dustbin, instead became the butt of numerous jokes in Ukraine. Her reactive diatribe against the foreign financing of the demonstrations on Independence Square, which supposedly included the provision of American felt boots and narcotics-laced oranges, not only flopped but became the target of a popular dance remix. What is more Soviet than felt boots?

The broad currents of criticism of transnational actor influence—the "small potatoes" camp, the "reaction" camp, and the "realist" camp—are not irrelevant to the study of transnational actors because they present important objections to this line of analysis that can be useful in the development of the field. Contributors to this volume consider the highly contingent nature of the interplay between transnational and national politics in postcommunist Europe and the multiple unintended consequences of transnational actors' influence.

Timothy Byrnes, for example, presents a mixed view of the influence of transnational actors, showing that their influence can be muted by domestic politics. In particular, Byrnes questions how effective the Roman Catholic Church has been in advancing its transnational agenda. He finds limited results and roots his explanation in the structure of the church as an organization. Pope John Paul II did develop and seek to spread a coherent agenda for the future of Europe that included integration of Central and East European states into the EU, a reinvigoration of spiritual traditions in Europe, recognition of the Christian nature of Europe, and protection of life. This agenda was not always easy to pursue within the national churches of the region. Since national church leaderships in Poland, Slovakia, Hungary, and Croatia have been tied closely to nation-building projects in those countries, the transnational church was not always able to supersede those agendas. The church failed in its attempt to create better ties between Slovaks and Hungarians in Slovakia, for instance, or to influence the Croat church to support peace in the Balkans. Byrnes shows how the church's efforts backfired in these and other cases. An unintended consequence of the church's intervention in the Balkans was it being perceived as a bulwark of Croat national sentiment, a position Pope John Paul II had hoped to avoid.

Hislope similarly questions the transformative influence of transnational actors in his study of the impact of transnational anticorruption agendas in Macedonia. While he documents a widespread obsession or campaign by transnational actors against corruption, Hislope argues that corruption had a far more positive side than transnational actors perceive: it is the glue that held together a country otherwise beset by ethnic conflict. Interaction through bribes and corrupt activity was the only way rival Albanian and Macedonian political and business leaders could cooperate. Party competition, he clearly illustrated, did not lead to cooperation but to extreme competition and possibly to conflict and ethnic cleansing. Hislope showed that transnational actors have been ineffective in rooting out corruption in Macedonia, and, should they ever be effective, they would have the unintended consequence of undermining another major transnational objective: protection of ethnic peace. This conclusion points to the seeming inconsistency between different transnational actor agendas. Because transnational actors are not part of a single government, but rather a loose configuration of different organizations pursuing distinct policy campaigns or obsessions, it is possible that consistency is not the strong suit of transnational actors across different policy areas. Hislope's study also suggests that when transnational actors encounter deeply embedded cultural practices with strong domestic support, they can have only limited impact. Transnational actors need domestic partners and may not always find them.

David Ost's essays provides compelling support for both the realist and reaction critiques of the influence of transnational actors in his study of Polish foreign policy debates since the fall of communism. He finds that Poland's decision to adopt a pro-U.S. foreign policy stems mainly from a desire to check the power of the EU, with Poland effectively playing one transnational influence—that of NATO and U.S. interests more generally—off transnational influences coming from the EU. Why would Polish decision makers want to check the EU at the same time that they are trying to enter it?

Ost offers two main arguments for this seemingly paradoxical decision by Poland to pursue an independent foreign policy. First, the Polish elite, following the logic of political realism, increasingly feared that the EU masked the interests of leading states, especially France and Germany. Citing parallels to the interwar era and earlier historical periods when Poland was carved up by dominant powers, Ost shows how the strong voices coming from Old Europe fueled fears within the Polish elite that Poland's national interests would not be considered within the EU. Second, Polish decision makers adopted a pro-U.S. stance—and initially supplied one of the larger contributions of troops to Iraq—in reaction to the asymmetrical and deeply humiliating nature of the EU accession process. During the accession process, Polish politicians and intellectuals were not asked their opinions, but instead simply told to implement all of the *acquis communautaire*. When the opportunity arose to take an independent action, in this case supporting the U.S. decision to invade Iraq, Polish political actors reacted to the humiliations of accession by choosing an independent foreign policy in line with that of the United States. Ost also points out that the Polish decision to stand up to its Western European partners might have interesting unintended consequences. While some within the Polish elite initially feared the decision to adopt a pro-U.S. stance would hurt Polish interests within the EU, Polish defiance may have strengthened Poland's hand in later negotiations with the EU, guaranteeing it more rather than fewer goodies from Brussels.

The realist critique of the transnational politics literature is found in Michael Kennedy's chapter. Kennedy argues that transnational actor influence is embedded in broader geopolitical trends and belongings, features of the international system not readily apparent in the middle-range theory perspective of the transnational actor literature. Kennedy analyzes military and energy security issues in Central and East Europe and argues that in these policy areas, the dominant actors are still states that seek to protect their fundamental interests. Transnational actors are less important, and, indeed, the impact of transnational actors has to be seen in the context of a transition culture rooted in the Western powers' growing sphere of influence. Kennedy's argument notes important limits to transnational actor influence and suggests that it needs to be understood in the specific geopolitical context of post–cold war Central and East Europe. Outside such a context, defined by the rise of Western powers and the retreat of the Soviet Union, transnational actor influence may be limited.

Together with simultaneous processes of democratization, marketization, and nation-state building, postcommunist states are in the midst of a "fourth" transition to complex interdependence. The key issues in an emerging research agenda on transnational actors in postcommunist politics are these: How do transnational actors seek to affect state policy? By what mechanisms and modes of influence? And how much influence are they able to wield? Under what conditions can they be expected to be effective or not? These questions provide a useful starting point for a future research agenda in postcommunist politics. A quadruple transition framework helps to account for the anomalies of the triple transition literature and provides deeper insight into the domestic politics of accession than one that inquires into either the domestic or transnational projects alone.

The chapters in this volume do not adopt a unified approach to the analysis of transnational influence. Instead, they represent a range of perspectives that constitute an important emerging debate on the importance of transnational actors in Central and East European transitions.

2

THE EUROPEAN

UNION

THE CAUSAL BEHEMOTH
OF TRANSNATIONAL
INFLUENCE ON
POSTCOMMUNIST POLITICS

Milada Anna Vachudova

Since 1989, the democratization of East Central Europe has brought un-precedented attention to the role of transnational actors in shaping domestic political change. Throughout history, external actors have impacted domestic politics—through military, diplomatic, and economic influence or interference. But the democratization of East Central Europe brought a sea change in the apparent diligence, perseverance, and success with which transnational actors have promoted particular policies in the context of advocating one overarching regime type, liberal democracy.[1]

The end of the cold war removed the main justification for Washington to support authoritarian regimes in the third world, confining Moscow's support for such regimes to its immediate periphery. Regime change in East Central Europe took place on the very highly institutionalized European continent, where many established international organizations and other transnational actors were well placed to develop strategies for promoting components of liberal democracy—though the extent, time frame, and track record of these strategies has varied greatly. The revolutions of 1989 in East Central Europe—especially in Poland, Hungary, and the former Czechoslovakia—were about emulating Western democracy and economic prosperity. The Western model of liberal democracy, the rule of law, and market capitalism was deeply internalized by members of the opposition before the regime began to change in 1989 (see Dienstbier 1990; Kis 1989; Michnik 1985). Thus some local elites were subject to transnational influence and advice even as they were actively seeking it out.

East Central European states democratized not just on a densely institutionalized continent, but also on the borders of the world's most deeply integrated and rule-constrained international organization, the EU. As a regional hegemon, the EU is unique: European states subject to its (mainly economic) power can aspire to join it. In historical perspective, a seat at the EU table and the protection of EU rules represent a huge reversal of fortune for the weak states of East Central Europe, traditionally abused and exploited in tandem by Berlin and Moscow (and those farther south, by Rome and Athens). In the early years, Polish, Hungarian, and Czechoslovakian dissidents-turned-political leaders designated EU membership as the culmination of their democratic revolutions because of a feeling of cultural and political affinity, in addition to the economic and security benefits of membership (Geremek 1990). Eventually, the motivation that took center stage was the imperative of joining the EU to deliver growing economic prosperity.

Against this backdrop, political change in postcommunist states has created fascinating puzzles about the relative importance of domestic and external factors in explaining policy shift and regime change outcomes. The complexity of these puzzles is deepened by the interaction of domestic and external factors over time. Scholars have demonstrated that transnational influence on key domestic actors, such as political parties, ruling elites, and public officials, can profoundly shape policy making. Under certain domestic conditions, transnational influence can even help determine regime type by pushing states from one trajectory of political change to another.

The EU has had by far the greatest impact of any transnational actor in shaping the course of political change in East Central European states since 1989. The EU has achieved its supreme position of transnational influence because it has had an outstanding reward—membership—to offer states that establishes a functioning liberal democracy and market economy. This reward has been conditional on satisfying a wide range and quantity of requirements while advancing through the EU's preaccession process. The simplest way to understand EU leverage is that the tremendous benefits of joining the EU create incentives for political elites to satisfy the vast requirements of membership. In comparison, other international organizations and external actors have, individually, much less to offer—and have asked for much less in return.

This is not to say, however, that other transnational actors do not have substantial influence in certain policy areas, on certain governments, and at certain times—as many of the other chapters in this volume aptly demonstrate. Today we see a convergence toward liberal democracy among those states that have become, over time, credible candidates for EU membership. This convergence is no doubt the cumulative outcome of the activities of many different domestic *and* external actors working toward similar goals. But the incentives of attaining EU membership are, I argue, the driving force of this convergence. Indeed, the EU's leverage has directly amplified the influence of other transnational actors in two important ways: First, the EU has formally "outsourced" compliance with standards on democracy and the protection of minority rights to other actors. Second, the powerful incentives to move forward in the EU's preaccession process have increased the interest of politicians, bureaucrats, and political parties in learning from an array of external actors about the content of a Western or EU-compatible political and economic agenda.

Anchored in the logic that material rewards create incentives for compliance with EU rules, this is a rationalist argument that engages a debate that has emerged in the international relations literature between so-called rationalist and constructivist approaches. Both seek to identify the specific mechanisms that translate international influence into change: change in the behavior of domestic elites and change in broader domestic outcomes. Studies in the rationalist camp generally argue that mechanisms based on material interests and rewards explain the lion's share of policy change owing to international influence.[2] Studies in the constructivist camp argue that other, cognitive mechanisms based on the power of norms and the desire for approbation from Western actors must *also* be taken into account to understand fully the timing and content of externally driven domestic change (Epstein 2005b; Gheciu 2005; Grabbe 2006). To give an example, rationalists point to strategic learning from transnational actors on the part of East European elites (Vachudova 2005), while constructivists expect to find social learning that is not based on the expectation of political or economic gain (see Epstein 2005c). Regardless of which theoretical lens is used, these mechanisms are, in my opinion, the most exciting area of research concerning external influence on domestic change. Indeed, to capture the complexity of how such mechanisms work in different domestic contexts, it may be advisable to set "competition" between these two theoretical lenses aside (Jacoby 2004).

International relations theory poses another, more elemental puzzle. Holding the international (or systemic) environment constant, there is great variation in the response to external incentives of domestic actors across countries and across time (see Vachudova 2005). In the 1990s, for example, there was substantial variation in the eagerness of governing elites to satisfy the requirements of EU membership, even though the security and economic benefits of joining were tremendous and largely uniform for all of them. For systemic international relations scholars this is puzzling, because states should react to opportunities and threats in the international system in the same way, regardless of regime type.

Instead, postcommunism has revealed unambiguously that regime type matters profoundly: the behavior of postcommunist states on the international stage is determined by the domestic fortunes of different configurations of domestic interests. Put simply, the character of ruling elites and powerful institutions determines the tenor of a country's foreign as well as domestic policy. The prospect of EU membership brings this into sharp relief: joining the EU is a foreign policy goal that requires sweeping compliance with EU requirements in the conduct of domestic policy making. For ruling elites whose sources of domestic power include authoritarianism, extreme nationalism, or exploitation of a partially reformed market economy, the costs of compliance with EU rules have been too great (Vachudova 2005).

Given the diversity of elites and institutions controlling postcommunist polities, the variation in domestic reform trajectories among just the East Central European states has been tremendous—and this is multiplied many times over for the entire postcommunist region (Bunce 1999; Cameron 2001; Ekiert 2003; Fish 2005). In response, a lively debate in the comparative politics literature has asked what domestic factors put postcommunist states on such different paths of transition after 1989. Comparative politics scholars have generally explained this divergence by identifying variation in the legacies of the communist (and precommunist) period, and showing how they determined which constellation of elites and institutions were most powerful at the moment of regime change and in the decisive early transition years.[3]

The findings of this comparative politics literature are critical: In order to hypothesize about how transnational actors shape policy decisions and broader regime outcomes, it is imperative to build on a theory or group of theories that specify how domestic conditions and actors shape political change over time. It is worth emphasizing that all external influence is mediated by—and must work through—domestic actors and institutions. If a scholar does not specify the main domestic determinants of policy or regime outcomes, it is difficult if not impossible to hypothesize about how external influence may be changing these outcomes.

Simpler theory building that largely excluded external factors was fortunately possible in the early years (roughly 1989–1994), when domestic policies and regime outcomes appeared almost entirely domestically driven. The EU had yet to design a deliberate policy for exercising its leverage on aspiring member states (what I call active leverage), while the strategies of other transnational actors were at best piecemeal. Subsequently, explaining variation has become a two-level game with two moving targets. Variation in the character of transnational influence coexists with variation in domestic conditions in the target states, and both are changing not only over time but also in reaction to each other.

It is no longer possible to study a polity's transition to democracy and a market economy in isolation of the concurrent project of that polity joining the EU and interacting with a host of transnational actors in Europe's very busy and highly institutionalized geopolitical, economic, social, and cultural space. Comparative politics scholars need to consider a host of transnational influences when studying domestic politics in any region of the world today (see Orenstein and Schmitz 2006), but such influences are arguably most consequential on the European continent.

Still, a distinction must be made between studies of overall regime outcomes and of specific policy areas. Among policy areas, the variation in outside influence is tremendous. In some areas, such as social policy, healthcare, urban planning, and taxation (all very close to the heart of the voting public), transnational influence may be so diffuse, discordant, or sporadic as to ultimately have little or no causal significance.

By 2005 there was a decrease in the amount of regime diversity among East Central Europe and Western Balkan states. Among the EU's new members, candidates, and future candidates, there are no longer authoritarian regimes, and even the most difficult countries are making progress toward liberal democracy (though in Serbia this progress is tenuous at best) (Vachudova 2006). In this they are diverging from other postcommunist states in the post-Soviet space, where the trend is toward greater regime diversity and more authoritarian outcomes (Cameron 2005). While convergence among EU candidates provides circumstantial evidence for the EU's liberal democratic and therefore homogenizing effect, it also reveals great variation in the timing, speed, and character of EU-driven reforms across countries and across policy areas that scholars have only begun to explain. The main puzzles are ultimately the same for both comparative politics and international relations scholars, and for both studies of EU candidates and the entire postcommunist region: Under what domestic conditions and through which mechanisms do international actors have a causal impact on domestic political change? If the obstacle of authoritarian government is removed, what domestic and transnational factors explain the considerable residual variation in the speed and content of reform?

The dynamics of qualifying for EU membership make the EU's leverage powerful. In analyzing the mechanisms that translate EU leverage into regime as well as policy change, I will situate my arguments in the larger debate on the impact of EU enlargement and compare the EU's leverage with the influence of other international organizations on the ground in postcommunist Europe. By outsourcing the evaluation of its candidates and by creating incentives for local elites to learn about Western practices, the EU preaccession process amplifies the influence of a wide range of other transnational actors. I confine my analysis to states that are candidates or proto-candidates for EU membership.

The Relationship between the EU and the Candidate States

The relationship between the EU and aspiring member states is hierarchical; but it is based on incentives, not coercion, and it ends with new members having a seat at the EU table. States seek to join the EU in order to mitigate the power asymmetry between the EU and any small, weak country on or near its borders. The process of qualifying for EU membership does amplify this asymmetry, as the acceding state must adopt all EU rules and satisfy additional political and economic requirements of membership. What is striking, however, is that through membership—and the pooling of sovereignty that membership entails—bordering states end up with greater geopolitical and economic power, and arguably more say over domestic policy in areas related to the internal market than they would have if they remained outside of the EU.

I have created the concepts of "passive" and "active" leverage to separate theoretically the kinds of influence that the EU can have on states that wish to join it. By "passive leverage" I mean the attraction of EU membership, and by "active leverage" I mean the deliberate conditionality exercised in the EU's preaccession process.

PASSIVE LEVERAGE

The EU's passive leverage is the attraction of EU membership, absent any deliberate policies toward prospective members. It is the traction that the EU has on the domestic politics of credible candidate states merely by virtue of its existence and its usual conduct. The track record of passive leverage alone in shaping domestic policies in aspiring members is limited, but it is the foundation of the EU's active leverage.

The EU's passive leverage is based on the political and economic benefits of membership, and also on the costs of exclusion. The political benefits of EU membership include a voice in EU affairs and also the protection of EU rules. For weak states on the EU's borders, joining the EU regulates relations with powerful neighbors by way of a desirable set of clear and well-established rules. The rules of institutions strengthen the norm that principles of conduct must be generalized to all members, favoring weaker states. For the EU's postcommunist neighbors, one of the main motivations for seeking the protection of EU rules was early vulnerability to EU protectionism.

The economic benefits of EU membership are manifold, centering on inclusion in the internal market, transfers of know-how, and transfers from the EU budget. Entering the EU is expected to raise domestic output and growth rates by stimulating entrepreneurship, foreign direct investment (FDI), and technology transfers. Studies indicate that because of raised investor confidence, FDI inflows have been concentrated in those postcommunist states that were at the front of the queue to join the EU. Locking the applicants into the EU legal and regulatory frameworks also promises to improve administrative capacity and, all together, facilitate fuller insertion into the EU and global economy—thereby bringing substantial opportunities for higher returns to the national budget over the long run. While the financial transfers from the EU budget for the newest members have been modest, they are still economically significant, especially for Bulgaria and Romania.

The EU's passive leverage is also created by the overall cost of being excluded from the EU. This cost is largely determined by the way that the EU treats nonmember states. For the EU's neighbors, market access for agricultural and other sensitive goods remains restricted, while all other exports to the EU run the ongoing risk of incurring various forms of contingent protection. This takes on unusual importance given the sheer size of the EU market and the striking poverty of the proximate alternatives, particularly of the post-Soviet market. For those that fail to enter an enlarging EU along with their neighbors, there are also other economic consequences. A steady flow of aid, expertise, and FDI is diverted away from states that do not join the EU toward those that do. The costs of exclusion can weigh heavily on relatively rich states as well as poor ones. Walter Mattli has shown that economic integration can cause three kinds of negative externalities for states left outside: trade diversion, investment diversion, and aid diversion. These costs help explain the applications for EU membership of rich West European states as well as relatively poor states from postcommunist Europe (Mattli 1999).

ACTIVE LEVERAGE

Active leverage is animated by the fact that the substantial benefits of EU membership create incentives for states to satisfy the enormous entry requirements. One may hypothesize that for any international institution, the greater the benefits of membership, the greater the *potential* political will in applicant countries to satisfy intrusive political and economic requirements. Following this logic alone, one may conclude that the benefits of EU membership for East European states must be immense. At no time in history have sovereign states voluntarily agreed to meet such vast domestic requirements and then subjected themselves to such intrusive verification procedures to enter an international organization.

The *potential* political will to satisfy the EU's entry requirements set the stage for the effectiveness of conditionality within the EU's preaccession process. This process has mediated the costs and benefits of satisfying EU membership criteria in such a way as to make compliance attractive—and noncompliance visible and costly. In addition to the benefits and the requirements of membership, I argue that three characteristics of the preaccession process—of the way that the EU "delivers" political and economic conditionality—have made the EU's active leverage effective. They are asymmetric interdependence, enforcement, and meritocracy.[4] These characteristics amplify the incentives to comply with the EU's membership requirements, because they make the EU's threat of exclusion as well as its promises of membership more credible.[5] In the run-up to the 2004 enlargement, with certain exceptions, the right balance was struck: candidates were neither too confident (thanks to asymmetric interdependence), nor were they too disingenuous (thanks to enforcement), nor did they despair that the system was stacked against them (thanks to meritocracy).

Ultimately the preaccession process is centered on a strategy of gatekeeping. If a candidate does not comply, it can be held back from the next stage in the process. For the first eight postcommunist candidates, the main stages were beginning screening, opening negotiations after satisfying the Copenhagen Criteria, closing particular chapters in the negotiations, and completing the negotiations. A candidate could move up, thanks to accelerated reform, or slip back as a sanction for unfulfilled promises to implement reform, though toward the end of the process the decision to admit eight postcommunist states all at once in 2004 was a political one. For Bulgaria and Romania, a fifth step—a final evaluation of their administrative capabilities —was added, with the possibility of postponing accession by one year. For the Western Balkan states, several stages were added at the front-end of the process: a feasibility study for opening negotiations on an association agreement, called the Stabilization and Association Agreement (SAA); negotiating the SAA; and signing the SAA. This is not without precedent. In the early 1990s, the EU did attach conditions to signing an association agreement, then called a Europe Agreement, with the first round of postcommunist applicants, though it did not do much to enforce them.

Mechanisms that Translate EU Leverage
into Domestic Political Change

The existence of the EU's preaccession process and its deliberate use of active leverage does not explain how this form of transnational influence changes politics and policies in East Central European states. As noted in the introduction, one of the central challenges for comparative politics and international relations studies is to identify the specific mechanisms that translate international influence into changes in the behavior of domestic elites, and in broader domestic outcomes.

In my book *Europe Undivided*, I look closely at six cases: Poland, Hungary, the Czech Republic, Slovakia, Bulgaria, and Romania. I argue that the initial configuration of powerful domestic elites and institutions at the moment of regime change produced strong political competition in some states and weak political competition in others.[6] This put states on two different trajectories of political change—one moving toward liberal democracy and the other toward illiberal democracy (or worse). I argue that the EU and other international actors had little impact on the regime trajectory of either group of states until the EU began using its active leverage in about 1994.

Here I can only sketch some of the mechanisms that I found most important in shaping domestic politics once the EU's active leverage came on line. In Slovakia, Romania, and Bulgaria, EU leverage helped push democratizing states from illiberal to liberal democracy. By liberal democracy I mean a political system in which state institutions and democratically elected rulers respect juridical limits on their powers and political liberties. They uphold the rule of law, a separation of powers, and boundaries between the state and the economy. They also uphold basic liberties, such as speech, assembly, religion, and property. Important for our cases, they do not violate the limits on their powers or the political liberties of citizens in order to suppress rival political parties or groups.

In illiberal democracies where the EU requirements were at loggerheads with the sources of political power of ruling elites, progress toward the EU was slow. The EU's active leverage had little success in changing the policies of governing political parties in Slovakia, Bulgaria, or Romania (or indeed in Croatia or Serbia-Montenegro). Instead, by influencing the information and the institutional environment, EU leverage helped create what the illiberal democracies were missing at the moment of transition: a coherent and moderate opposition, and an open and pluralistic political arena. Evaluations of a country's progress within the EU's preaccession process provided a powerful alternative source of information on the political and economic performance of the government. Meanwhile, the institutional environment was shaped in three ways. First, joining the EU served as a *focal point for cooperation* for disparate groups that opposed the ruling parties. Second, EU membership created incentives for politicians and other elites to *adapt* their political agenda to be compatible with the OSCE, the Council of Europe, and other international organizations, as well as the EU. Third, political parties that promised to move the country toward EU membership had to follow through with the *implementation* of specific reforms once in office in order to move forward in the preaccession process.

These mechanisms helped open up the political arena and also narrow the parameters of domestic debate as important parties abandoned nationalist and anti-Western appeals. Altogether, they improved the quality of political competition in illiberal states. That these states were credible future members of the EU, exposed to the full force of the EU's active leverage, strengthened the hand of liberal forces against illiberal ones—not in a duel where good vanquishes evil, but in an iterated electoral game where, sooner or later, most political actors saw the benefits of moving their own political agenda toward compatibility with the state's bid for EU membership. While I focused on Bulgaria, Romania, and Slovakia in my book, today one can see adaptation and implementation happening, slowly, in the Western Balkan states, especially in Croatia and Macedonia.

For all EU candidates, three other mechanisms are important. First, straightforward *conditionality* is at play. Moving forward in the EU's preaccession process is tied to adopting laws and implementing reform (and this overlaps with the *implementation* mechanism described earlier). A critical part of this process is state building. The sine qua non of being able to implement the *acquis* and function as an EU member is high state capacity, including a state that energetically and efficiently regulates its economy. So while the EU required the withdrawal of the state from the economy through privatization and strict limits on state subsidies, it insisted that the state deliver better regulation, rule of law, and oversight in the economy (see Kopstein 2006).

Second, the process itself serves as a *credible commitment* mechanism to ongoing reform, because reversing direction becomes prohibitively costly for any future government. As candidates move forward in the process, governments are thus locked into a predictable course of economic policy making that serves as an important signal to internal and external economic actors. Third, moving toward EU membership changes the character and the strength of different groups in society. This is not just plain conditionality but transformative conditionality. The state, the economy, and the society are transformed—in positive ways but also in negative ones—as a result of taking part in a process that lasts for many years.

The Impact of EU Enlargement on Domestic Politics: The Debate

Where does my argument about EU leverage and regime change fit in the broader literature about the impact of EU enlargement on the domestic politics of East Central European states? It stands out in two ways: the first perhaps a strength and the second a weakness.

First, my argument about how the EU and other transnational actors can help push countries from one trajectory of political change to another is built on the interwoven effect of several mechanisms over a long period of time. Most enlargement studies analyze EU conditionality on government decisions *after* illiberal regimes are removed from power (see Pridham 2005; Schimmelfennig 2005). I argue that, indeed, EU conditionality has little or no direct effect on the domestic policies of illiberal elites while they hold power. However, I show how other mechanisms, besides conditionality, helped strengthen and transform opposition political parties and other groups in society during their rule, thus shaping the agendas of the political parties that would eventually win power. And, looking at the positions of political parties just before and during negotiations for EU membership over time, I show that even formerly illiberal parties have responded to EU incentives, moderating and changing their agenda to make it compatible with EU membership (see also Vachudova 2006). In a similar vein, Rachel Epstein in her chapter shows how transnational organizations are successfully able to implement their policy agendas through the building of "domestic resonance," wherein key domestic support is consolidated and potential national reactions defused (Epstein, this volume). The influence of transnational actors including the EU depends crucially on local actors, as the editors point out in the introduction to this volume. And over time, these actors may respond and adapt to transnational influence.

Second, my argument attempts to explain, in very broad strokes, the impact of transnational influence on trajectories of political change: will the country move toward liberal democracy, toward authoritarianism, or, most likely in the postcommunist world, get stuck somewhere in the middle? The drawback to this approach is that it misses the tremendous variation in how transnational influence, including EU leverage, has affected policy making in different areas in East Central Europe's liberal democratic states.

Other scholars have illuminated the differential impact of the EU and other transnational actors on the same policy area in different countries—for example, in regional policy (Brusis 2005; Hughes et al. 2004), social policy (Sissenich 2006), the environment (Andonova 2003), public administration (Dimitrova 2002), border and migration policies (Jileva 2002; Grabbe 2005), regulatory reform (Mattli and Plumper 2004), and economic policy (Epstein 2006b). Wade Jacoby's *The Enlargement of the European Union and NATO* (2004) analyzes policy transfer across six policy areas in Hungary and the Czech Republic to explain why we see considerable sectoral variation even in two states that are widely viewed as the most amenable to complying with the policy prescriptions of Western actors. In these studies rationalist mechanisms generally do the most causal heavy lifting, especially the consistency and enforcement of external rules, the density of concerned domestic actors, and the costs for them of adopting these rules. However, constructivist mechanisms such as social learning (Epstein 2006b), the transfer of ideas (Andonova 2003; Jacoby 2004), and the internalization of EU rules adopted for instrumental reasons (Grabbe 2006) are also important (on this debate, see Schimmelfennig and Sedelmeier 2005 and Sedelmeier 2006).

Somewhat separate from *whether* and *how* the EU has changed policies and regime outcomes is the question of its effect on the functioning of the polity: has it improved the quality of democracy and democratic institutions, or has it undermined them? This is a fascinating debate, and I do not have the space to do it justice here. Polities that embarked on an illiberal trajectory after 1989 suffered from violations of democratic standards, rent seeking, ethnic nationalism, and very poor state-society relations. If I am right that the prospect of EU membership helped put them on a liberal trajectory, then it follows that, on balance, it has benefited the quality of democracy. Once authoritarian rulers leave the stage and negotiations for EU membership begin, however, scholars have pointed to a variety of ways that the top-down, externally driven process of complying with EU rules and adopting the *acquis* may hollow out domestic institutions (for a survey of this debate, see Vachudova 2005).

The EU and Other International Organizations Compared

The EU, as I argued above, has had the most influence on domestic political change in postcommunist states mainly because the benefits of membership create the political will to satisfy the EU's very substantial entry requirements. Two other international organizations, the Council of Europe and NATO, had the potential for the same kind of influence. States were willing to make changes to domestic policies in order to qualify for membership. In both cases, the requirements were much less extensive—and so were the benefits. Still, NATO had considerable security guarantees to offer, while membership in the Council of Europe was viewed already in 1990 as a necessary certification for new democracies and an indispensable first step toward EU membership. It was not the small scale of the benefits on offer that dramatically diminished the potential leverage of both the Council of Europe and NATO, but the way that these organizations handled the accession of new members. While both spelled out requirements for joining, neither did much to enforce them. Moreover, these requirements were not applied consistently across candidates and across time. In contrast, the EU's enforcement of its entry requirements has been more diligent and more meritocratic across applicants. In relative terms, the EU's enforcement of its own entry criteria has been impressive—though this has not been the case in absolute terms, as candidates have been allowed much leeway, and thus still face significant regulatory and administrative challenges in implementing the *acquis* after accession—rather like existing member states (Cameron 2003).

The Council of Europe used conditionality with some success in the early 1990s, but then began admitting states such as Russia that openly violate its human and minority rights provisions. For the period that the applications of Poland, Hungary, the Czech Republic, Slovakia, Bulgaria, and Romania were under consideration in the early 1990s, the Council of Europe did have some leverage on domestic policymaking. It identified deficiencies and asked candidates to change domestic policies to improve

the situation as a condition of entry. However, it wasted much of its leverage as a result of the characteristics of its enlargement process. There was
little enforcement of council rules, and the enlargement process hardly
functioned as a meritocracy. The Council of Europe failed to apply its own
membership criteria rigorously, embracing what one study has called "democratic underachievers," with serious consequences: "It is beyond dispute
that the implicit lowering of admission criteria . . . has allowed in countries
with dubious political, legal and human rights practices. This is a state of
affairs made that much worse by an unwillingness on the part of certain
countries to live up to commitments made at the point of admission" (Croft
et al. 1999, 142, 153). The council often settled for only a commitment to
change domestic policies in the *future,* after membership was granted
(Gilbert 1996). But at the moment that a state became a member, virtually
all of the council's leverage evaporated. This led to the admission of illiberal democracies that remained illiberal, and their presence greatly lowered
the value of council membership for other postcommunist states. All together, this undermined the council's claim to be a defender of democracy,
the rule of law, and human rights.

For its part, NATO emerged as the most effective purveyor of security
for East European states after 1989. A state's prospects for NATO membership also became linked to its standing with the EU and to perceptions
about the success of its transition to liberal democracy and market capitalism. Despite these benefits, NATO's leverage on domestic policy making
has fallen short for two reasons. First, states were not invited to join NATO
because they had made the most progress in qualifying for membership—
for example, by restructuring their military. Instead, before the specific requirements were laid down, NATO governments tapped Poland, Hungary,
and the Czech Republic as the postcommunist states that should enter
NATO in the first round—because of their westerly geographic position
and because of the widespread perception that they were East Europe's
liberal democratic frontrunners. The process was a meritocracy only in the
loosest form. The Baltic states, whatever the condition of their militaries,
were disqualified from the first round of NATO expansion by Russia's dis-
pleasure. Five years later, for the second round, the pendulum had swung toward inclusiveness, and all East European states negotiating for membership
in the EU were invited to join, reflecting their general success in building
democracy—and not their particular success in meeting NATO entry

requirements. Second, the specific requirements of NATO membership pertained to a much smaller part of domestic policy making, and these limited requirements were not well enforced as a condition of accession. NATO's expansion was driven by the decision whether or not to enlarge. Once the decision was taken to enlarge both in the first and the second round, the qualifications of the candidates seemed peripheral to the outcome (see, for example, Kontra and Špurný 1998).

East European politicians did believe that the prospect of NATO membership helped, at least on the margins, to strengthen moderate, reform-oriented political parties in domestic politics. Slovak opposition politicians and activists, for example, believed that Slovakia's pointed exclusion from NATO on account of the illiberal behavior of the Mečiar governments might have strengthened their position somewhat in the next elections (though not as much as the EU's exclusion, since joining NATO was much less popular among Slovak voters than joining the EU). Conversely, Bulgarian politicians believed that the prospect of inclusion in NATO well ahead of membership in the EU helped to shore up public support for modernizing the military and for Westernizing Bulgaria's foreign policy.[7] Nevertheless, I argue that NATO's influence has been weaker and also different in kind than the EU's active leverage.

If the same mechanisms for domestic political change are not working in NATO's relationship with aspiring member states—the incentives of membership are not coupled with extensive and well-enforced entry requirements—what other mechanisms may help bring domestic change? Rachel Epstein argues for a set of mechanisms following a constructivist logic that would allow NATO to have an important impact because, for some domestic actors, NATO's norms and values are very appealing. (For a similar argument about the "soft-power" of the Council of Europe, see Checkel 2000.) Domestic actors seeking the social affirmation of NATO comply with NATO norms even in the absence of clear conditionality; and NATO actors succeed in changing domestic policies by targeting certain domestic actors with persuasion. Studying the Polish case, Epstein demonstrates how NATO helped build a civilian consensus in favor of democratic control over the armed forces and delegitimized arguments for defense self-sufficiency. Epstein concludes that whether NATO has a similar effect on other prospective members ultimately depends on the appeal of NATO's norms and values, manifested in a country's susceptibility to persuasion and to NATO's coalition-building strategies (Epstein 2005b; 2006a).

Amplifying the Leverage of Other Transnational Actors

An assessment of the impact of all of the transnational actors—from non-governmental organizations to political party foundations—is beyond the scope of this chapter. But I want to highlight what is unique about the relationship between the EU and other transnational actors: the EU's active leverage amplifies very directly—and often by design—their influence. In some policy areas, the European Commission has simply contracted out the conditions that candidates should meet, and even the process of judging whether they have done so. And across the board in candidate and proto-candidate countries, the prospect of joining the EU has made an array of domestic actors more interested in the activities of all kinds of transnational actors promoting a Western political and economic agenda.

Thanks to the EU's outsourcing, the Council of Europe and the OSCE have become probably the most powerful external standard setters and information providers for the EU's preaccession process. Put simply, governments fulfill their obligations to the Council of Europe and the OSCE because the EU has incorporated these obligations (and implicitly the approval of these organizations) into the requirements for EU membership (Papagianni 2002). The centerpiece of the Regular Reports is a general evaluation of how the candidate is meeting those Copenhagen Requirements that are above and beyond the norms, rules, and regulations in force among existing EU member states as expressed in the *acquis*. For the protection of ethnic minority rights, the European Commission has depended chiefly on the evaluations of the OSCE High Commissioner on National Minorities, and also the Council of Europe. Although there has been no formal role for either the High Commissioner or the Council of Europe in the enlargement process, their assessments have in many cases formed the core of the commission's own assessments.

In this way, the EU has boosted the influence of both international organizations, granting legitimacy to the standards that they set and creating material sanctions for the violation of those standards (see also Kelley 2004). The economic requirements of the Copenhagen criteria also include an overall assessment of whether the candidate has a functioning market economy. On the fitness of the economy, the commission has listened to the views of the World Bank, the IMF, and the Economic Commission for Europe of the United Nations, boosting their influence in a similar way. The most striking recent case of outsourcing has been the EU's insistence that Serbia, Croatia, and Bosnia-Herzegovina cooperate fully with the International Criminal Tribunal for the former Yugoslavia (ICTY) in order to satisfy the Copenhagen Criteria of robust democratic institutions and the protection of ethnic minority rights. The EU has been periodically uneasy with the ICTY's assessments of whether or not a state is cooperating fully, but it has realized that if it does not act in step with the ICTY then it will undermine and probably destroy its ability to function.

A more diffuse way that the EU's active leverage has boosted the influence of a wide array of transnational actors is by creating incentives for local elites to learn from them. The prospect of joining the EU creates incentives for political parties to change their political and economic agendas, and to translate those changes into how they govern when in power. Politicians who have chosen to *adapt* their rhetoric and policies to be compatible with European integration have needed to learn a great deal about the content of a pro-Western agenda, especially those that have recently abandoned nationalist, antimarket, or antidemocratic practices (see Vachudova 2005). But strategic learning has extended far beyond politicians. The opportunities associated with moving toward the EU for economic actors and civic groups have also created demand for the conferences, workshops, and programs offered by Western NGOs and foundations.

There is a tendency (to which I subscribe) to celebrate the overarching successes of transnational influence in East Central Europe, and to expect or hope that these can eventually be replicated in the Western Balkans. The impact of transnational actors on the rest of the post-Soviet space, however, is a very different area of research. Not only are these states far from Brussels and subject to much greater influence from Moscow, but Moscow has now openly abandoned the democratic project and turned to opposing more and more forcefully pro-Western regimes in the post-Soviet space. Alongside an unfavorable geographic and geopolitical position, the prospect of democracy in these states must contend with the evidently much less auspicious legacy of Soviet communism. The failure of liberal democracy in the region may be the result of elites adopting the wrong strategies; but, as Valerie Bunce (2003) has argued, it may also be the result of elites facing the wrong conditions and therefore the wrong menu of choices.

Meanwhile, these states have been subject to a very different mix of transnational Western influence. Some Western interests, connected to oil, appeasing Russia, and fighting the war against terror, run directly counter to promoting liberal democracy. These dovetail with Western disinterest, especially the EU's feeling of "enlargement fatigue" and its reluctance to open the way for using active leverage by giving more states, such as Ukraine, Georgia, or Moldova, the perspective of EU membership.

The EU's European Neighborhood Policy, designed explicitly to harness some of the leverage of the preaccession process by offering a stake in the internal market in exchange for democratic improvements and economic reforms, is emblematic of this problem. On the one hand, key EU member states, along with the United States, are hesitant to upset regimes that provide oil, to further alienate Russia, and to destabilize regimes that are authoritarian but cooperative (in some cases, this means non-Islamic). On the other hand, the incentives that the EU is offering in exchange for democratic reforms are too modest and too vague to be credible. The aftermath of the recent "civic revolutions" in Ukraine and Georgia highlights this much more complex transnational terrain: the Western pro-democracy groups poured in at election time, but the EU and arguably also the United States have not offered much material support to the "reformers" that took office.

Despite all of the challenges I described earlier, studying the impact of transnational actors on states with an EU membership perspective turns out to be easy: the EU has treated all of its candidates roughly the same, the United States has been a cheerleader for enlargement, and Western transnational actors have generally worked toward the same big goals when trying to influence domestic policies and regime outcomes in these countries. Beyond the line in the sand that separates these states from the rest of the post-Soviet space, the arrows no longer all point in the same direction, and the impact of transnational actors becomes much more murky. In this it resembles more closely other world regions, such as Latin America, the Middle East, and Africa. The fact that liberal democracy, economic reform, and the influence of myriad transnational actors were bundled together—and that this bundle produced good outcomes—may make political change in East Central Europe (and the Western Balkans) unique.

3

TRANSNATIONAL AGENDAS ON HUMAN TRAFFICKING IN THE BALKANS

Nicole Lindstrom

Human trafficking has become a global obsession of the international community in the past decade (Krastev 2005).[1] Numerous transnational actors are involved in combating trafficking, including the UN, the International Organization on Migration (IOM), the EU, the United States, and many international nongovernmental organizations. The Balkan countries are a focal point of transnational antitrafficking efforts, since traffickers have capitalized on the region's porous borders, rampant corruption, and high unemployment (Friman and Reich 2007). An expanding network of local nongovernmental, state, and transnational actors are directly involved in every stage of the antitrafficking policy-making process in the Balkans. One might argue, in fact, that antitrafficking policies would not exist without transnational actors. That is, transnational actors have made human trafficking a top policy priority, developed laws and policies to combat it, and overseen their implementation.

A seemingly high degree of consensus has emerged among relevant transnational actors that trafficking of persons through use of force or coercion should be prevented and suppressed. This overarching norm is inscribed in the 2000 UN Convention on Transnational Crime and its accompanying protocol on trafficking in persons. We might expect a high degree of communicative consistency in this policy area. Yet a closer inspection of antitrafficking efforts exposes as much conflict as consensus on the nature of the problem, as well as the most appropriate policies to combat it. A clear "victim" is identified—trafficked persons—around which the transnational policy community can mobilize. Indeed, issues that involve bodily harm to individuals are, according to Keck and Sikkink (1998), policy areas where transnational advocacy networks are most consensual and influential. Yet the causal chain of responsibility is much murkier. If one identifies traffickers as the main culprits, then a policy response aimed at capturing and prosecuting individual offenders is the preferred policy response. If one focuses on the demand side of trafficking, from sex industry customers to business owners who rely on low cost labor, a policy response that targets the source of the demand is warranted. If one focuses on the larger economic inequalities that create a constant supply and demand for trafficking, one might shift focus from individual to structural level policy responses. Focusing on economic rationales for trafficking could have the concomitant effect, however, of weakening the consensus around trafficked persons being considered victims of coercion, strictly defined.

These competing conceptions of the trafficking issue highlight the often ambiguous and contested nature of external conditions. According to rationalist logic, transnational actors put forth material rewards or threats of sanctions to encourage domestic governments to comply with particular conditions (see Vachudova, this volume). According to constructivist logic, transnational actors seek to promote certain norms or ideas in order to influence the actions and beliefs of policy makers. Yet neither approach devotes much attention to *how* a particular condition or norm arises in the first place. Returning to the questions outlined in the introductory chapter, in addition to analyzing *how much* influence transnational actors have at the domestic level, we must also consider the process through which transnational actors set a particular agenda—taking into account consensus as well as conflict among different constellations of actors.

Through an analysis of the construction of antitrafficking policies in the Balkans, it becomes clear that different *ideas* about the nature of the trafficking problem shape the different kinds of policy responses transnational actors pursue. These constructions of the problem can be categorized into four, and often overlapping, ideal types: migration, law enforcement, human rights, and economic. Recognizing that ideas do not "float freely" (Risse-Kappen 1994), however, one must also consider political and material interests behind the formulation and implementation of different antitrafficking agendas in the Balkans. By combining rationalist and constructivist insights, this chapter seeks to explain why migration and law-enforcement approaches have tended to prevail over, and be at the expense of, human rights or economic approaches in the region.

A Constructivist Approach to Transnational Policy Agenda Setting

International relations scholars offer varying explanations for how transnational actors set policy agendas. Realists argue that transnational policy agendas are determined by the structural conditions of the international system, with powerful actors such as the United States acting alone or through international organizations to set priorities and dictate policy strategies (Abbott and Snidal 1988; Ikenberry 2001). Proponents of an organizational approach argue that international organizations are agents in their own right, with bureaucracies acting independently from states to shape the way problems are interpreted and to design and implement policies accordingly (Barnett and Finnemore 2004). Constructivist approaches seek to understand how ideas can exert an independent effect on policy formation and policy outcomes (Blyth 1997; Checkel 1998; Price 1998). Peter Hall describes the role of ideas in policy making succinctly: "Policymakers customarily work within a framework of ideas and standards that specifies not only the goals of policy and the kind of instruments that can be used to attain them, but also the very nature of the problems they are meant to be addressing" (Hall 1993, 279).

These three scenarios point to the importance of identifying how actors frame a policy problem they seek to address. The concept of framing was first utilized by social movement theorists to explain protest mobilization, but it has since gained currency in international relations and policy studies to understand other forms of collective action. According to Benford and Snow (2000, 615), framing consists of actors negotiating "a shared understanding of some problematic condition or situation they define as in need of change, make attributions regarding who or what is to blame, articulate an alternative set of arrangements, and urge others to act in concert to affect change." What makes collective action frames significant are not so much their innovative ideational features. Rather, framing is a process through which actors articulate or tie together information and existing ideas in order to spur particular forms of collective action. Framing trafficking as an issue of transnational organized crime, for instance, entails showing the ways in which the trafficking of persons resembles the trade in other illegal commodities—which, in turn, would justify a law enforcement approach to combating the problem. Applying the concept of framing to transnational agenda setting more generally, two questions arise. First, how do frames facilitate (or constrain) certain concrete transnational policy strategies and policy outcomes? Second, why might one frame and related policy strategy prevail over another?

Peter Hall's conceptualization of policy paradigms offers one useful analytical framework to address the question of how and when ideas have a significant effect on policy outcomes. Like the concept of framing, Hall suggests that specific policy actions are contingent on how one defines and conceptualizes a problem. Hall's framework thus follows a fundamental ontological tenet of constructivism: that ideas or collective understandings can constitute interests and preferences. This constructivist turn marks a departure from rationalist approaches, which take interests and preferences as given in explaining particular outcomes. Policy paradigms, according to Hall, also set the goals, priorities, and content of policy. That is, policy paradigms facilitate action among policy makers by specifying how to solve a defined policy problem through a specific course of action. Policy paradigms or frames also help policy makers legitimize a particular policy strategy to other relevant actors as well as to the general public.[2] In other words, how transnational actors package or frame an issue provides a means to convince each other, as well as key decision makers and the general public, that certain actions constitute a plausible and acceptable policy solution. The focus of this analysis, however, is on the first-order concepts—that is, explicit policy paradigms—rather than on the broader underlying elite or mass perceptions in which policy paradigms are construed.[3]

If we accept that ideas are a crucial factor in the adoption and implementation of particular policies, then there is the question of why one policy paradigm might prevail over another. Hall outlines two sets of factors. First, a policy paradigm can predominate based on the positional advantages of its main proponents within a given institutional framework, access to material resources, or on exogenous events that can affect the power of one set of actors to impose its paradigm over others (Hall 1993, 280). Second, when faced with conflicting information and expert opinions on a particular problem, actors within a policy community will compete for authority to define the problem and chart the best course of action. Yet subsequent policy experimentation and policy failures can result in undermining the authority of the prevailing policy paradigm and its advocates. These failures can, in turn, create windows of opportunity for advocates of competing paradigms to push forth a new policy agenda. Consideration of these factors suggests, for one, that ideas and interests cannot so easily be analytically disentangled. Whether and how one idea prevails over another can be influenced by policy struggles in which political interests, material resources, and power loom large (Campbell 1998, 379). Consideration of conflict and power struggles is thus a legitimate, and indeed necessary, component of ideational analyses of policy making. Moreover, Hall incorporates a temporal dimension to our understanding of ideas. Given that policy framing is an ongoing and dynamic process, ideas can change from the agenda-setting to the implementation stages in the trajectory of any policy path.

Developing Antitrafficking Policy in the Balkans: Four Approaches

The 2000 UN Convention Against Transnational Crime and the accompanying "Protocol to Prevent, Suppress and Punish Trafficking in Persons, Especially Women and Children" was a critical juncture in the development of antitrafficking policies. The UN protocol defines trafficking as "the recruitment, transportation, transfer, harboring, or receipt of persons, by means of threat or use of force or other forms of coercion, of abduction, of fraud, of deception, of the abuse of power or a position of vulnerability or the giving and receiving of payments or benefits to achieve the consent of a person having control over another person, for the purpose of exploitation" (United Nations 2000). The protocol goes on to define "exploitation" as including, at a minimum, the "exploitation of the prostitution of others or other forms of sexual exploitation, forced labor of services, slavery or practices similar to slavery, servitude or the removal of organs" (United Nations 2000). While the definition includes numerous types of exploitation, trafficking for sexual exploitation has dominated the transnational trafficking agenda.

The protocol aimed to provide a common definition of trafficking that would serve as a general baseline from which transnational actors could develop and implement a common set of standards to prevent trafficking, protect victims, and prosecute offenders. Thus the protocol is the single most authoritative attempt to underpin trafficking policies with normative consistency. We might expect that the extensive transnational coordination that led to the passage and implementation of the protocol achieved some international consensus on the nature of the trafficking problem. Yet in practice we can observe significant differences among these transnational actors in how they frame and address the issue of trafficking. As I have argued elsewhere, these approaches can be categorized into four interrelated approaches: the migration approach; the law-enforcement approach; the human rights approach; and the economic approach (Lindstrom 2004, 2007).

MIGRATION APPROACH

The migration approach is based on the understanding of trafficking as a problem of unregulated or irregular migration. According to this approach, trafficked persons are victims of networks of traffickers who seek to facilitate and profit from the illegal crossing of borders. The subsequent policy response has been to intensify border and immigration control to thwart traffickers and to repatriate trafficked persons to their home countries.

LAW ENFORCEMENT APPROACH

The law enforcement approach rests on a definition of trafficking in persons as a crime under international law that must be prevented, prosecuted, and punished. Trafficking is portrayed as similar to other forms of organized crime, a problem best addressed through transnational and national law enforcement strategies. Efforts to apprehend traffickers focus on intensifying border control and raiding industries, like brothels, where trafficked persons work. Prosecuting traffickers requires the cooperation of their victims, who are offered temporary residence permits and other forms of social assistance in exchange for their legal testimony against traffickers.

HUMAN RIGHTS APPROACH

This approach frames trafficking in persons as a violation of individual human rights. Emphasizing the coercive nature of the human trafficking trade is central to a human rights approach. Some advocates of this approach deem all forms of trafficking as exploitative—utilizing terms such as "slavery" to mobilize action around the issue (Doezema 2000). Other advocates of a human rights approach seek to broaden the definition of trafficking as an issue of social justice and economic human rights (GAATW 2001, 81).

ECONOMIC APPROACH

An economic approach to trafficking focuses attention on the broader socioeconomic conditions underlying human trafficking. According to such an understanding, trafficking is a function of poverty and structural inequalities. Illegal migration is viewed as one of the few available means for people to escape economic hardship at home. The steady supply of illegal migrants fulfills the economic demand for cheap and easily exploitable labor. The appropriate policy solution following such an understanding of the problem is to address conditions of poverty in source countries through economic development and provide legal and social assistance to migrants in destination countries.

Diffusing Antitrafficking Policies: The Role of Transnational Actors

These four frames have shaped various policies to combat human trafficking in the Balkans. Returning to the question raised in the theoretical discussion, how and why did one policy paradigm prevail over others? Namely, why have proponents of the migration and law enforcement approaches seemingly managed to shape antitrafficking policy in the Balkans more successfully than advocates of more human rights or economic approaches? Examining in depth the different political positions, material resources, and power of advocates of each approach is beyond the scope of this chapter. However, we can draw some insights from a brief examination of the role of different policy actors—including the United States, the EU, international organizations, and INGOs—in the diffusion of antitrafficking policies in the Balkans. Returning to Hall, we must also consider positional advantages and material resources of different actors to understand how antitrafficking policy agendas have formed and diffused.

THE EUROPEAN UNION

The EU is a key actor in developing and diffusing policies to combat trafficking. Given that EU membership is a top priority of all governments in the region and that the EU is the largest aid donor to the Western Balkans, the EU can exert a great deal of direct and indirect leverage over setting the policy agenda as well as ensuring that individual governments comply (see Vachudova, this volume). Security is a key priority of the European Commission and EU member states in the Balkans. The Stabilization and Association Process (SAP) for the Western Balkans, launched in 2000, mirrored the association agreements negotiated with the eight Central and East European states, but with the notable addition of "stabilization." Antitrafficking can be considered an important element of the security agenda of the EU in the region. While the development of trafficking policy in the EU over the past decade has incorporated each of the four frames, migration control and law enforcement have superseded human rights and economic approaches in EU antitrafficking efforts.

Human trafficking first became explicitly integrated in EU law with the passage of the 1997 Amsterdam Treaty, which contains explicit reference to trafficking in human beings and offenses against children (Article 29). Leading up to Amsterdam, the European Commission set the agenda on trafficking in its 2006 communication, which portrayed trafficking as an issue involving immigration and policing, social and employment issues, and cooperation with third countries. The commission stressed that the multifaceted nature of the problem required a coordinated approach incorporating a variety of actors (Berman 2003). A 1996 European Parliament resolution cited the "vulnerability, poverty and marginalization of women in their countries of origin, the high profits and low risks experienced by traffickers, and the demand for women for prostitution and other forms of sexual exploitation" as key causes of trafficking (European Parliament 1996). In addition to these legislative initiatives, the commission also initiated a series of programs, entitled STOP and DAPHNE,[4] which coordinated antitrafficking efforts with international organizations and third countries and provided financial assistance to local NGOs.

In the 1990s the EU agenda on trafficking framed the problem as one involving migration, human rights, and economic concerns and fashioned coordinated policy responses in turn involving a wide range of actors. This began to change in the 2000s. At the 1999 extraordinary meeting of the European Council in Tampere, where EU set out to create "an area of freedom, security, and justice," trafficking was designated as "one of the specific areas of crime," along with drug trafficking and terrorism, that Europol would be given authority to address (European Council 1999). Human trafficking is now located within the intergovernmental third pillar of the EU, Police and Judicial Cooperation in Criminal Matters. With jurisdiction over illegal immigration, visa, and asylum, and judicial cooperation under the first pillar, Brussels can shape policies to apprehend and prosecute offenders consistent with a law enforcement approach. A 2002 European Council Framework on Combating Trafficking in Human Beings put forth a coordinated approach to prosecute offenders, as well as "taking measures against third countries that refuse to cooperate with the EU in preventing and combating these phenomena" (European Council 2002; see also Obokata 2003). Concerning migration controls, a 2004 council directive instructs member states to grant temporary residence permits to third-country nationals who are victims of trafficking and who agree to cooperate with authorities.

The SAP is the main mechanism through which the EU can transfer its policy agenda on trafficking to the Western Balkans. To meet SAP conditions, all applicant states must not only harmonize their legislation with the *acquis* but also meet special conditions such as cooperating with the International Criminal Tribunal for the Former Yugoslavia in The Hague, securing refugee return, and participating in regional cooperative initiatives. To combat trafficking in the Western Balkans, the EU has used conditionality to ensure that states conform to all stated rules on trafficking, as well as cooperate with regional initiatives such as the Stability Pact to create and implement national action plans (see Lindstrom 2007). The high priority the EU has placed on combating illegal trade and migration in the Balkans is reflected in the proportion of EU assistance committed toward meeting third pillar conditions on police and judicial cooperation. Among the 4.6 billion euros in aid to the Western Balkans through the Community Assistance for Reconstruction, Development, and Stabilisation (CARDS) program from 2001 to 2006, over 20 percent is allocated to Justice and Home Affairs (JHA) priorities (European Commission 2003). In Albania, over 50 percent of all CARDS funding is committed toward border control and law enforcement initiatives. Such funding allocations suggest that securing borders and combating transnational crime are key priorities in the foreign policy of the EU toward the Western Balkans.

THE UNITED STATES

In a 2006 editorial in the *New York Times* Nicholas Kristof, typically an ardent critic of U.S. foreign policy, claims that combating human trafficking is one area where George Bush is making a historic contribution. "Just as one of Jimmy Carter's great legacies was putting human rights squarely on the international agenda," Kristof writes, "Mr. Bush is doing the same for slave labor" (Kristof 2006). U.S. initiatives to combat trafficking predated the first Bush administration. The United States Trafficking Victims of Protection Act (TVPA) of 2000, drafted in line with the UN protocol, set the U.S. foreign policy agenda to combat human trafficking.[5] This legislation was backed, in Kristof's words, by an "unlikely coalition of evangelical Republicans and feminist Democrats." For evangelical Christians the trafficking issue was linked, according to Chapkis (2003), to anxieties over sexuality and illegal immigration, while feminists framed the issue as protecting women's rights. Tensions between the two very different groups of advocates surfaced when the Bush administration required that NGOs declare their opposition to prostitution to be eligible for U.S. funds, with feminists arguing that antitrafficking legislation was being hijacked by a Christian fundamentalist policy agenda.

The implementation of the act is overseen by the State Department's Office to Monitor and Combat Trafficking in Persons. Annual Trafficking in Persons Reports (or TIPs) are the office's primary policy instrument, which monitor governments' compliance with minimum standards to prosecute traffickers, protect victims, and prevent trafficking. Countries are categorized into three "tiers." The United States can withhold aid or impose sanctions on countries in Tier 1 whose governments are deemed to have not "fully complied with the minimum standards and are not making significant efforts to do so" (Mattar 2003, 164). Thus U.S. policy on trafficking relies on a combination of monitoring and shaming, as well as rewards and sanctions, to ensure governments' compliance with the U.S. antitrafficking policy objectives.

Concerning the standards set out in the TVPA, policies to combat trafficking advanced by the United States correspond most closely with the law enforcement paradigm. For one, the reports monitoring government compliance ignore government practices, such as summary deportation and incarceration of trafficked persons, diverging from a strict human rights approach to trafficking. Critics argue that victim protection, as evoked in the title of the act, has been superseded by efforts to force states to detain and prosecute traffickers (Human Rights Watch 2003). Second, the State Department explicitly places economic approaches outside its policy mandate. As the introduction to the 2005 report states: "The report does not focus on other government efforts that contribute indirectly to reducing trafficking, such as education programs, support for economic development, or programs aimed at enhancing gender equality, though these are worthwhile endeavors" (U.S. Department of State 2005c).

With respect to the Balkans, the United States has formed and funded regional law enforcement initiatives to combat trafficking, particularly through the Southeast European Cooperative Initiative (SECI) based in Bucharest. Established by the United States in 1996 to foster regional cooperation in the Balkans, SECI's mandate is now to support transborder policing of organized crime, terrorism, and illegal trade networks. In September 2002, SECI led the largest regional law enforcement action to date, coined "Operation Mirage." With the cooperation of the U.S. Department of Justice, the NATO-led Stabilization Force in Bosnia (SFOR), and local law enforcement agencies, the operation resulted in over 20,000 police raids throughout the region in bars, nightclubs, and border points. Two hundred and ninety-three traffickers were apprehended, many of whom were subsequently tried in Bosnia, Kosovo, Serbia, and Montenegro (U.S. Department of State 2003). Among the more than 2,000 women the operation found without resident permits during the raids, 237 were identified as victims of trafficking, while the rest were arrested, deported, and in several cases prosecuted (Limanowksa 2005). In terms of sustained anti-trafficking efforts, the U.S. monitors compliance of Balkan states through its TIP reports. Serbia and Montenegro have been designated as Tier 2 countries since the start of TIPs and thus threatened with the withholding of U.S. aid for failing to make sufficient progress in complying with anti-trafficking policies.

INTERNATIONAL ORGANIZATIONS AND NONGOVERNMENTAL ORGANIZATIONS

Numerous IOs and INGOs are involved in developing, diffusing, and implementing antitrafficking initiatives in the Balkans. Often working in close cooperation with the EU and the United States, many of these actors are involved in shaping the policy agendas of these two powerful actors and assist in carrying out the prescribed policies. For instance, the IOM is tasked with assisting and repatriating trafficked persons, and thus is both an advocate and facilitator of the migration approach. The OSCE coordinates antitrafficking efforts among its member states through the secretariat and its field offices, claiming to promote the human rights of trafficked persons. The Coalition Against Trafficking in Women (CATW), the Movement for the Abolition of Pornography and Prostitution (MAPP), and the European Women's Lobby actively lobby relevant state, regional, and global bodies to advance a human rights agenda that opposes all prostitution as a form of sexual exploitation. Members of CATW routinely testified in U.S. congressional hearings to support sanctions against antitrafficking NGOs that support legalizing prostitution.

IOs and INGOs also play an important role as critics of prevailing policies. The Global Alliance Against Trafficking in Women (GAATW) seeks to disentangle trafficking from prostitution, for instance, arguing that such a focus criminalizes sex workers and migrants. GAATW and other INGOs and local NGOs have sought to reframe trafficking in women as primarily an issue of economic human rights. Divisions within antitrafficking INGOs over how to frame and address trafficking tend to filter down to local NGOs. For instance, the first Serbian NGO to be formed to exclusively fight trafficking, ASTRA, became a key actor in coordinating regional antitrafficking efforts, both in terms of cooperating with relevant governments and IOs and linking local NGOs throughout the region. Yet conflicts among ASTRA's leaders arose concerning the criminalization of prostitution, cooperation with the IOM on repatriating victims of trafficking, and over whether ASTRA should expand its mandate to include other forms of labor exploitation. Those activists linked most closely to the CATW position linking prostitution to trafficking supported laws criminalizing prostitution in Serbia. They were also committed to maintaining ASTRA's close relationship with IOM and the Serbian government in facilitating the return of trafficked persons to their countries of origin. A dissident faction within ASTRA, however, advocated the decriminalization of prostitution and expanding ASTRA's mission to include advocating on behalf of all migrants, not solely victims of trafficking for sexual exploitation. This splinter group ultimately formed its own NGO, the Anti-Trafficking Center, which aligns itself most closely with the GAATW position.[6]

Rethinking Approaches to Antitrafficking in the Balkans

While the four interrelated policy paradigms have shaped policy strategies to combat trafficking, migration and law enforcement approaches have taken precedence over more human rights and economic ones. Drawing on Hall, the following section examines potential policy failures or unintended consequences of certain policy actions, which might be leading to the reevaluation of dominant policy paradigms. In other words, these unintended effects have often resulted in a feedback effect in which the frames are reconsidered. This opens windows of opportunity for advocates of other policy paradigms to put forth alternative frames and strategies. The following section briefly discusses three critiques of existing antitrafficking policies and how they are being reconsidered.

MEASURING TRAFFICKING

Estimating the scope of trafficking is difficult given its clandestine nature. Estimates of over two million women trafficked each year are frequently cited in trafficking accounts, while the European Commission reported in 2001 that an estimated 120,000 women are trafficked into Western Europe each year (Laczko and Gramegna 2003, 181). Yet these regularly quoted figures often lack supporting data (Kelly 2005). Recognizing the need for more accurate assessment of trafficking patterns, in 2003 the IOM led efforts to create a Regional Clearing Point (RCP) under the auspices of the Stability Pact. From 2000 to 2004, according to the 2005 RCP report, a total of 6,256 trafficked persons were assisted in the Balkans (Surtees 2005, 30). Explaining how trafficked persons were identified and assisted, the report states that "victims were voluntarily returned to their countries of origin through assistance programs or identified in their countries of origin upon extradition and subsequently assisted. In addition, victims were identified through police operations and investigations and subsequently referred for assistance" (Surtees 2005, 32). The 2005 report also documents different forms of trafficking. While the largest percentage of persons are trafficked for purposes of "sexual exploitation" (74 percent), the report also documents trafficking in labor, begging, and children for adoption.

The RCP authors argue that the reports dramatically underestimate the scope of the trafficking trade. Indeed, the RCP report varied significantly from estimates published by IOM headquarters in Geneva in 2001, which claimed that 100,000 women are trafficked each year *through* the Balkans to the EU and further destinations and another 70,000 women trafficked annually *into* the Balkan region (IOM 2001, 3). The RCP authors concede their data-gathering methods cannot account for the large number of women trafficked undetected through the Balkans to the EU and other markets (Surtees 2005, 12). IOM officials also attribute low figures to victims being misidentified by law enforcement as illegal migrants who are immediately deported. In 2005 the RCP authors announced a new data-gathering clearinghouse, the Nexus Institute to Combat Human Trafficking, based in Vienna, which will expand its data gathering beyond the territorial boundaries of the Balkans and incorporate a wider range of data sources.

Governments, meanwhile, argue that the RCP and assistance agencies like the IOM and local NGOs have numerous incentives to exaggerate the scope of trafficking, as their funding and reason for existence depends on identifying human trafficking as a problem of crisis proportions (see Cooley and Ron 2002; Kelly 2005). Law enforcement and government agencies are thus more inclined to accept the declining numbers as an objective assessment of the increasing effectiveness of antitrafficking efforts. Other critics accept the IOM's claim that the RCP reports dramatically underestimate the scope of the trade, but are more inclined to attribute blame to the IOM's migration approach to trafficking. For instance, Barbara Limanowska, a prominent independent expert who works closely with UN and OSCE agencies overseeing human rights in the Balkans, argues that the declining numbers of persons who seek assistance in IOM shelters is not attributable to a decreasing demand for assistance or to the difficulties of locating them. Rather, Limanowska argues that trafficked women have become increasingly aware that IOM assistance is conditional on voluntary repatriation—and in recent years conditional on testifying against traffickers in prosecution cases—and in many cases they *choose* not to seek IOM assistance (Jones 2005). The perspective of trafficked women on the possible shortcomings of migration and law enforcement strategies is rarely considered, however, in formulating antitrafficking policies (see Agustin 2005).

LAW ENFORCEMENT STRATEGIES AND VICTIM PROTECTION

Efforts to prevent, suppress, and prosecute traffickers have resulted in increased transborder cooperation among law enforcement agencies as well as high-profile operations such as Mirage. The law enforcement approach has resulted in numerous traffickers being apprehended, convicted, and prosecuted. Yet critics argue that the law enforcement approach has failed to significantly reduce the trade. Traffickers exhibit great flexibility and ingenuity in eluding police by quickly changing transportation routes and moving the trade further underground. Enhanced border control also makes illegal migration more profitable for the traffickers. Critics argue that the law enforcement approach has also resulted in a revictimization of trafficked persons. For one, they suggest that operations like Mirage result in more women being apprehended and charged on illegal migration or prostitution charges than identifying and assisting trafficked women and their traffickers. Moreover, aggressive policing has the unintended consequence of moving much of the prostitution trade to private apartments, often on the outskirts of cities and towns, where women are further isolated and vulnerable to violent abuse.[7]

Finally, because the law enforcement approach rests on convicting and prosecuting individual traffickers, prosecutors must rely largely on the willingness of victims to testify against their traffickers (Bruch 2004). Since designated victims of trafficking are granted immunity from illegal migration or prostitution charges, refusing to testify can make them more vulnerable to threats of immediate deportation or prosecution. Moreover, victim assistance programs, including emergency and short-term shelters, are increasingly being managed and funded by national governments. Thus assistance can be made conditional on the women cooperating with the prosecution. If a person does agree to testify, governments are legally required to provide witness protection. Yet in many cases the very same government and law enforcement agencies tasked with providing protection have themselves been implicated in being complicit with the trafficking trade. In sum, critics of the law enforcement approach argue that when the principal concern of this approach is to stop criminals, the interests of their victims become of secondary concern, often leading to their further exploitation.

RETRAFFICKING

Retrafficking and internal trafficking have also received increased attention. The 2005 RCP report documents that anywhere from 3 percent to 50 percent of women repatriated from destination countries to their home countries from 2003 to 2005 were retrafficked within a year. The IOM attributes the high rates of retrafficking to the predatory strategies of recruiters, who target highly vulnerable repatriated persons. Recruiters, unlike traffickers, are often embedded in local communities and are thus less vulnerable to being apprehended at border crossings or brothel raids. The IOM acknowledges that serious gaps exist in the repatriation and reintegration process, where women are returned home to face poverty, shame, and often abuse without adequate social support (Surtees 2005, 14). Critics of IOM argue, however, that the high rates of retrafficking raise fundamental questions about the long-term effectiveness of its migration approach to antitrafficking that makes repatriation and preventing illegal migration its central aim.

Local and international NGOs have created assistance and referral networks that assist women who have been repatriated to their home countries. While employment and social assistance programs can provide some short-term assistance to repatriated women, advocates of an economic approach to antitrafficking argue that the ongoing cycle of trafficking illuminates the underlying structural or economic nature of the problem. The UN protocol left "coercion" or the "abuse of power or a position of vulnerability" undefined. While "threats" or "use of force" leave less room for interpretation, persons who return to work abroad—seemingly lacking other options at home—raise difficult issues of how to define consent and coercion (Abramson 2004). Critics suggest that as the EU fortifies its borders and funds increased law enforcement initiatives in the Balkans, traffickers continue to profit on the limitless supply of persons trapped in the trafficking cycle. The problem of retrafficking points to the necessity of more comprehensive policy approaches that tackle economic development, with antitrafficking actors working more closely with national, regional, and global development-oriented organizations. The recognition that persons will continue to migrate to seek more lucrative work abroad, regardless of the high risk, suggests that easing migration restrictions will protect the human rights of the most vulnerable and, at the same time, make trafficking less lucrative for the traffickers who capitalize on restrictive migration policies.

WE CAN DRAW several conclusions from this analysis. First, antitrafficking policy has become an obsession of the international community, with a wide range of transnational actors coordinating efforts to develop, diffuse, and implement antitrafficking policy. However, there are significant differences in how transnational actors frame and address the trafficking issue. Such conflicts suggest that instead of holding norms or conditions constant in assessing *how much* influence transnational actors have on domestic change, we should also turn our attention to *how* such transnational agendas are constructed in the first place. Second, what frame prevails over another depends, in part, on the positional advantages and material resources of its main proponents. As the two most influential actors in the Balkans, the EU and the United States exert disproportionate influence in promoting migration and law enforcement approaches to antitrafficking efforts—often at the expense of more human rights or economic approaches—by promoting these agendas with material incentives and threats of sanctions. Such a finding points to the importance of combining constructivist insights on the need for competing ideas or norms with rationalist concerns with the role of material incentives in order to analyze how agendas are set and disseminated. Finally, perceived failures of antitrafficking policies to date are gradually undermining the authority and legitimacy of prevailing policy paradigms. Migration and law enforcement approaches can have the unintended effect of exacerbating the vulnerability and exploitation of trafficked persons, while making little headway in thwarting traffickers who profit on a steady supply of persons caught in the trafficking trade.

This feedback effect shows the significance of considering the evolution of policy paradigms and conditions over time.

Identifying failures of prevailing paradigms can also inform a number of concrete policy solutions. For instance, creating mechanisms in which trafficked persons can be given a direct voice in policy making can help overcome policy failures. Many antitrafficking advocates, whether local NGOs, governments, or transnational actors, are motivated to keep "victims" victims, given that often their funding and moral legitimacy depends on it. Recognizing the agency of trafficked persons, however constrained, can lead to more informed policy solutions. Second, the increasing awareness of retrafficking highlights the limitations of policing, whether of borders or sex work, and turns our attention toward the underlying economic and social causes of trafficking. Easing strict visa regimes or granting extended or even permanent resident status to trafficked persons are two immediate solutions to reduce the profitability of trafficking for traffickers and to protect trafficked persons. The EU might also rethink the EU accession model for the Balkans, which tend to stress legal harmonization and security above, and often at the expense of, more development-oriented priorities. A more development-oriented approach to trafficking would not only address supply factors that contribute to trafficking but also facilitate the long-term goal of maintaining stability in the region.

4

MINORITY TRADITIONS AND POSTCOMMUNIST POLITICS

HOW DO IGOs MATTER?

Wade Jacoby

When have IGOs been able to promote institutional and policy changes in postcommunist states? In the past few years, a framework is emerging to tackle this question. Though a number of recent books explore a rich variety of causal mechanisms, one can distill from them a widespread interest in the twin factors of external IO leverage and the attractiveness of norms operative outside the postcommunist region but in some way attractive to policy makers there (see De Nevers 2003; Ekiert and Hanson 2003; Goldsmith 2005; Grabbe 2004, 2006; Henderson 2003; Hughes, Sasse, and Gordon 2004; Jacoby 2000, 2004; Kelley 2004b; Linden 2002; McDermott 2002; Mendelson and Glenn 2002; Ottaway and Carothers 2000; Pridham 2005; Quandt 2002; Schimmelfennig and Sedelmeier 2005; Stone 2002; Vachudova 2005; Zielonka and Pravda 2001).

As this growing literature amply demonstrates, outsiders have had major effects on postcommunist reforms.[1] Such externally influenced reforms have occasionally been constitutional (e.g., electoral formulas or constitutional court designs), but more often they have prompted statutory changes that sought to promote either better economic performance (e.g., privatization programs, fiscal controls, or tax laws) or better democracies (e.g., minority protection laws, rule of law programs, or better civilian control of the military).

A central question in political science is whether norms or material incentives best move governments from rejecting to embracing IGO suggestions. This chapter offers a scope condition relevant to both sides of this debate. Its central proposition is that what I call "minority traditions" within the postcommunist states can facilitate the normative appeals or material leverage of IGOs. These minority traditions, already present in the domestic postcommunist context, mean the changes are both less dramatic but also perhaps more effective and enduring than ones due exclusively to the arguments or leverage of IGOs (see Jacoby 1999, 2004; Janos 2001). Thus, while the chapter deals with IGOs as agenda setters and also treats national responses, its central contribution to this volume is to address the linkage between IGOs and national actors.

If my central proposition is right, it is clearly important. We presently lack a literature that can both explain external influences on institutions and connect these influences to broader debates in international relations and comparative politics. A focus on external influences is a growth area for good conceptual work only if it addresses the union of foreign and domestic influences. Setting up external influences as an alternative explanation to domestic considerations is less promising for two reasons. First, empirically, external influences can almost never have any real purchase unless they are joined together with domestic influences (Campbell 1993; Crawford and Lijphart 1995; Henderson 1998; O'Dwyer 2006a). Second, conceptually, if we cast external influences as an exotic alternative form of policy change, we might produce ad hoc theories with no clear relationship to the broader literature, especially in comparative politics (see James and Lodge 2003).

International relations does have a heuristic in the diffusion concept that nominally includes both external and internal variables. In diffusion processes, the "prior adoption of a trait or practice in a population alters the probability of adoption for remaining non-adopters" (Strang 1991). In general, this literature is far better at rejecting the null hypotheses—

that the sources of institutional change are indigenous to each location—than it is in actually explaining how that change occurs or whether it leads to better outcomes. In particular, the approach gets much of its power from two assumptions: that institutions remain much the same as they spread from place to place and that the key dependent variable is the elite decision to adopt (or not) a particular innovation. The first assumption blends out diversity and adaptation; the second blends out politics. These features are bred in the bone—they are so deep in the diffusion approach that it makes little sense to adapt it for the problem at hand.

To be sure, the diffusion approach is good at what it does. It demonstrates that the institutional choices of political units often affect the choices of their neighbors and peers. An excellent recent example is Simmons and Elkins, who have tracked the spread of liberal economic policies over the past thirty years. The authors note that their aim is to model the "major policy shifts" of a "wide range of countries around the world" (2004, 176). To do so, they use binary measures of dependent variables in the areas of current account, capital controls, and exchange rate mechanisms. But to have this broad coverage, the approach generally flies at far too high an altitude to help us see clearly how external influences work on the ground. Though they take significant steps beyond most diffusion literature in showing causal pathways—emphasizing in particular the way that policy diffusion alters payoffs for nonadopters—they end with a call for research that helps us see "how and why this takes place" (Simmons and Elkins 2004, 187).[2]

A necessary complement to diffusion studies is a coalitional approach to external influence.[3] In this approach, outside actors—here, I focus on IGOs—strive to influence the choices of existing domestic actors with whom they can be seen to form a kind of informal coalition. In order to persuade or induce postcommunist reformers (PCRs) to undertake the reforms outsiders favor, outsiders must often seek to bolster minority traditions. Minority traditions are domestic movements, parties, or subsets of state officials who have pursued, but never achieved, some specific institutional solution to an important political problem. For example, U.S. advocates of a public single-payer health care system and advocates of a privatized social security system both remain, as of this writing, minority traditions in the United States. Outsiders may be able to provide material or intellectual resources that allow such minorities to finally get their way. As will be clear, it matters greatly whether such minority traditions already occupy powerful positions inside the state, such as the Finance Ministry, or are buried deep in civil society.[4]

The coalition approach thus emphasizes how outsiders could help minorities gain power (Börzel and Risse 2003; Jacoby 2000; Risse et. al. 1999; Vachudova 2005). But Westerners concerned with the staying power of reforms also must worry that PCRs may backslide after receiving initial inducements to modify their institutions or policies (Moravcsik 2000). Rather than merely subsidizing specific reforms, they may also try to strengthen like-minded reformers and thus increase the chance that the reforms will endure over time. The coalitional approach thus emphasizes that outsiders may lengthen PCRs' time horizons such that PCRs are willing to trade off short-term benefits against longer-term benefits that may flow from better policies. Alternatively, by providing a larger audience for PCR policies, connections to outsiders may underscore the normative value of reforms or threaten to shame PCRs who violate norms they had previously signed on to (see Schimmelfennig 2001). In short, the coalitional approach is intuitive, explicitly political, and avoids the either-or approach to external influence noted above.

In this chapter, I illustrate the coalitional approach and the importance of minority traditions by looking at IGO efforts to influence PCRs. The first case looks at IGO strategies, the second at state vulnerability, and the third at government preferences. I then subject the coalitional approach to three skeptical criticisms before concluding with five dilemmas that underscore just how demanding externally induced change is likely to remain.

Vetoes and Vehicles: IGO External Influences

My central concern is the extent to which reform projects promoted by outsiders are accepted (or not) by domestic interest groups or clusters of state actors. Broadly, two outcomes are possible. First, domestic interests can play the role of veto players that block (or at least hinder) externally induced transformation plans. One would perhaps expect this outcome since if domestic interests truly favored the proposed change, it would likely have already occurred. Second, and much to the contrary, domestic interests could be vehicles for the promotion of externally induced changes. Rather than block externally advocated reforms, domestic interests might actually sponsor them, which might, in turn, be enormously helpful in cases where initial designs required adjustment to new settings. In the postcommunist setting, we should expect actors to be vehicles more often than in normal times because the institutions that emerged from the communist period clearly did not reflect long-settled social preferences.

I illustrate these two broad outcomes through the use of three brief case studies, each of which reveals a mix of veto and vehicle: ethnic minority rights, macroeconomic reforms, and civilian control of the military. These cases represent a broad range of domestic and foreign policies while covering democratic rights, political economy, and security policy. The first two cases draw on research by Judith Kelley and Randall Stone, while the third case draws on my own research.

ETHNIC MINORITY RIGHTS

Different IGOs have different potential inducements to PCRs. Some can only offer acclamation; others can offer membership. The coalition approach explains ethnic minority rights reforms by looking at linkages between IGOs and parties in government and opposition in postcommunist states.

Several IGOs have attempted to influence PCRs' treatment of ethnic minority rights. As we will see is also true for macroeconomic policy, IGOs confronted politicians whose short-term incentives pushed them toward populist policies that could damage the country in the long run. In these cases, the main damage was reputational. Kelley's data on the universe of legislation on ethnic minorities from 1990 to 1999 in Latvia, Estonia, Slovakia, and Romania (sixty-four cases in total) suggests that membership conditionality played a crucial role. In particular, as Central and East European states began seeking EU membership, the EU gained significant leverage. While the Council of Europe and the OSCE both used fairly light membership criteria, the EU was much more demanding and effective. Thus, even though the EU had remarkably thin precedents for intervening in minority rights issues, its high credibility allowed it to be effective (indeed, it often borrowed substantive suggestions from both the Council of Europe and OSCE—see also Sasse 2007; Schwellnuss 2005; Orenstein and Ozkaleli 2005).

IGO strategies further mattered insofar as the EU's "tiered admission process" increased its credibility vis-à-vis PCRs (Kelley 2004b; see also

Vachudova 2005). Where the Council of Europe had no such gradual process and took Slovakia on as a member on the basis of an easily broken promise to improve its language laws, it was burned. Romania, on the other hand, long seemed so far from membership that the EU struggled to credibly assert that improvements in minority rights might make a positive difference in the country's aspirations for membership. IGOs that allowed postcommunist states relatively easy terms for membership—for example, the OSCE and the Council of Europe—found that often only normative levers remained available to them. On the other hand, since the effectiveness of conditions is linked to the attractiveness of membership in a given IGO, the normative dimension can hardly be dismissed as unimportant.

Kelley found that in Latvia, nationalist forces sustained discriminatory practices much less in policy areas where the IGOs used membership conditionality (e.g., citizenship laws) than in areas where the IGOs used normative pressure alone (e.g., education laws) or no conditionality at all (e.g., electoral laws). In Estonia, the EU membership incentives were similarly effective, particularly on the issues of citizenship laws and laws regarding stateless children. In Slovakia, even against determined nationalist leadership under Mečiar, the EU was able to prevail in two of the five key cases (the Treaty with Hungary and a draconian penal code), though it failed in the other three (laws on elections, school certificates, and minority languages). Finally, in Romania, aside from the treaty with Hungary, all three IGOs had little positive effect on Romanian policies because at the time of the research, early membership was not a credible offer.

Kelley concludes that IGO pressure—in both normative and material modes—was "surprisingly effective" (Kelly 2004b, 174). To be effective, it often had to overcome domestic actors as potential veto players. She concludes that domestic resistance succeeds better against normative pressures than against material ones. To simplify, domestic opposition to minority protection rules favored by the IGOs can be high or low. The IGOs can use normative pressure alone or normative pressure plus conditionality. Where normative pressure alone meets high domestic opposition, her model predicts that no change occurs. Where normative pressure meets low opposition, she expects that longer durations of pressure increase the probability of IGO success. Where IGO conditionality meets low domestic opposition, the model predicts that change will occur. Finally, where conditionality meets high domestic opposition, the model is indeterminate.

Overall, the basic model suggests that Central and East European states prefer to be admitted to IGOs without paying the costs of compliance, but prefer admission with the costs to no admission at all. Put differently, conditionality is a side payment to potential veto players who would otherwise prefer the status quo.

Kelley emphasizes the potential role of domestic actors as veto players, including interest groups and nationalist politicians. Her central image is of an IGO using material pressure against a recalcitrant domestic government, especially one led by authoritarian nationalists. At one level, this image is compelling—after all, if the domestic government already wanted to pursue the policy, then it would already have done so (or slight normative pressure would have brought it around). No doubt, cases in which IGOs overcome stiff domestic resistance are important ones.

At the same time, Kelley's model has little use for domestic actors as vehicles. She does show that in 75 percent of cases where ethnic minorities were part of the government, the ultimate outcomes were compatible with the aims of IGOs (as opposed to 21 percent of the cases where no ethnic minorities representation was available). Here ethnic minorities did function as "minority traditions" in the terminology of this chapter. But these cases were relatively rare within her sample, which was dominated by government configurations that excluded ethnic minorities and, indeed, whose rules against such minorities were the very object of IGO concern. Yet in other cases, Kelley's data show IGOs acting as mere "facilitating mechanisms" for domestic negotiations that produce better minority protection rules. Kelley's focus on leverage leads her to disavow these cases as ones of true IGO influence; but the coalitional approach I use here suggests that these are cases where IGO influence is not just particularly useful but also likely to lead to outcomes with less backsliding than cases where only IGO leverage could possibly move otherwise recalcitrant domestic actors toward compliance.

This reframing and partial reinterpretation of Kelley's account is consistent with important cautions about the EU role arising from more recent research on minority protection. Gwendolyn Sasse, for example, has argued that, in addition to EU norms on minority protection being controversial and largely uncodified among older EU members (and therefore presumably on less solid ground than the official *acquis communautaire*), the final effect of the norms is very much an open question. For one thing, there remains an important difference between the simple legal adoption of minority protections and the behavioral changes they are presumably meant to inspire (Schimmelfennig and Sedelmeier 2005). For another thing, there is some evidence of a nationalist backlash against ethnic minority parties, who, in concert with moderates, had often worked to enshrine IGO norms in national law (Sasse 2007). Such contention is, of course, entirely consistent with the notion that outside assistance often works by helping empower groups that would otherwise lose domestic struggles for influence. By this reading, the nationalist resentment recently evident in Latvia, Slovakia, Romania, and Bulgaria is, at least in part, a reasonably straightforward response to an outsider-insider coalition that has succeeded in changing so many laws with high salience in domestic politics.

MACROECONOMIC POLICIES

The coalition approach explains postcommunist macroeconomic reforms by looking at linkages between IGO officials and those in the postcommunist national governments, especially the Ministry of Finance. Where Kelley's data allow us to vary IGOs, Stone (2002) focuses primarily on the IMF and, by holding the IGO constant, can focus even more on variation in state vulnerability to IGO pressure or responsiveness to IGO arguments.[5]

Like Kelley, Stone begins with a commonly held perception of a postcommunist problem. Stone sees *inflation control* as the key task for PCRs, who often have short-term incentives to stimulate the economy or subsidize sectors even if, in so doing, they damage the country's long-term fiscal health. Normally, the fear of inflation and currency collapse could sustain PCRs' focus on macroeconomic reforms. But if those feedback mechanisms do not work properly in a given country, the IMF sometimes can serve as a support or even a proxy for indigenous mechanisms. Stone shows that the IMF was able to act credibly against Poland and Bulgaria, but not against Russia and Ukraine, which had much more latitude since the Clinton administration often pushed the IMF to soften its conditions. Thus, the IMF's own credibility problem stems from the proclivity of member states like the United States to intervene and means that the degree to which the IMF can lend credibility to domestic actors in reforming countries varies widely from case to case. Of course, these domestic actors are what this chapter refers to as minority traditions.

In Poland and Bulgaria, the IMF did lend credibility because it functioned as the glue for fractious and weak governments. Though a number of the central Polish reform ideas came from Polish reformers themselves, others came from the IMF, as of course did critical tranches of aid, especially in 1991, 1993, and 1994 (Appel 2004; Bockman and Eyal 2002; Greskovits 1998). But in addition to aid, Stone (2002, 115) emphasizes that the "IMF bolstered the position of the [Polish] reformers" and helped them stay the reform course in the face of substantial domestic opposition. Epstein (2005, 2006) adds further evidence that the IMF developed deep linkages inside the Polish Ministry of Finance (MoF), including some that operated even when no formal IMF program was in place. The Bulgarian case was broadly similar, but not until much later in the 1990s could the IMF use subsidies to bolster Bulgarian reformers and create another external-internal partnership. If the IMF functioned as glue between coalition parties or between the MoF and the rest of the cabinet, then these actors also functioned as vehicles for the IGO. Here again, the minority tradition was necessary but not sufficient. The IGO offered the equivalent of a side payment to the defenders of the status quo in order to move policy in the favored direction.

In Russia, external assistance was much less effective. After a four-month experiment with shock therapy, successive governments embarked on a ruinous six-year bout of fiscal irresponsibility punctuated by the collapse of the ruble in 1998. The ruble's collapse swept away the government and lowered Russian purchasing power by 46 percent between 1998 and 2000 (Stone 2002, 116). The IMF constantly faced Russian backsliding on prior commitments and struggled within constraints of U.S. policy to credibly insist that Russia meet its commitments. For several years, U.S. policies blunted IMF efforts to enforce agreements and meant that subsidies were swallowed up without making an appreciable long-term difference.

The Ukrainian case was worse. Successive Ukrainian governments' go-slow approach really meant economic misery for the Ukrainian people. As in Russia, external subsidies—for a time, Ukraine was the third largest recipient of U.S. aid—were easily pocketed without any real obligation to change Ukraine's economic policies. The IMF explicitly tried to strengthen the hand of what, for it, was the most promising segment of the Ukrainian state, the MoF. For years, the MoF struggled in vain to develop checks against the runaway spending of other ministries. But until the MoF made a partial breakthrough in 1998, the IMF found no minority tradition with which it could connect.

In terms of coalitions, the IMF, to get its way, usually had to act in concert —to tip the balance—with internal forces with which it was in close contact (in Poland and Bulgaria, successfully; in Russia, unsuccessfully). The fund was sometimes able to stretch politicians' time horizons, making them more aware of and responsive to the long-term interest in anti-inflationary policies, rather than exclusively the short-term pull of electoral constituencies (Stone 2002, 234). Where the minority tradition was so weak that the IMF tried to substitute for domestic forces (Ukraine), the IGO had no success.

The minority rights and macroeconomic stabilization cases show evidence that the coalition approach is a difficult but potentially fruitful route for external assistance. The minority rights case demonstrates the importance of variation in IGO strategies, while the macroeconomic reforms case shows that states are differentially vulnerable to IGO pressures, and these vulnerabilities are, at least in part, a reflection of enduring features like size and importance to U.S. foreign policy. The third case demonstrates how government preferences can vary in important ways, even when IGO strategies and state vulnerabilities remain constant.

CIVIL-MILITARY RELATIONS

If IGO strategies and the structural vulnerabilities of states can help explain variation in PCR choices, what role do government preferences play in explaining those choices? IGOs have a delicate task in identifying, boosting, and sustaining minority traditions. Even where IGO leverage and state vulnerability are present, the task is clearly quite difficult. One major dilemma for IGOs is that even when IGO officials mean their suggestions to be politically neutral, they often have a partisan valence in a specific national context. I illustrate this point through the case of civilian control of the military, which NATO officials meant as a neutral act but which had strong partisan effects.

The Hungarian case is particularly instructive. Changing Hungarian government preferences first insulated the military from civilian rule, then drove battles that drew the military deeply into political discussions and led some politicians to intrude far too deeply into matters often reserved for the military in NATO member states, then finally carved out a reasonable sphere for military influence that seems to have brought some stability. Since neither NATO policies nor the structural vulnerabilities of Hungary changed appreciably over this period, I attribute the principal causal weight to government preferences, which clearly did change. NATO's standards did make a difference, just not immediately. To be more precise, NATO had to be patient and first build up and then build on a minority tradition of civilian defense expertise that was quite weak in 1989.

Starting from a position of having almost no civilians trained in defense matters—and therefore in a position to exercise "democratic control"—NATO and individual NATO member states began the slow process of training Hungarian government officials on Western-style ministerial and command structures. Progress was very slow, and for several years, no critical mass of knowledgeable civilians was available. By about 1996, however, the first indicators of progress became visible. For example, what we might term an "accountability faction" inside the previously deferential Parliamentary Defense Committee began demanding weekly presentations from the military. This faction was also pushing for transparency in the defense budget, as the members tried to use defense issues to raise their own profile.

At the same time the country lacked knowledgeable civilians to give orders, its politicized army was in no mood to take them. Like almost all postcommunist armies, the Hungarian Defense Forces (HDF) lacked the well-established patterns of interaction that characterize civilian control in most NATO militaries. While NATO armies vary in their civilian control practices, NATO made clear that certain features of civilian control were essential. Jeffrey Simon, who helped design many of the bilateral U.S. assistance programs in the region, has argued that civilian control requires four necessary conditions: (1) a clear division of authority in the constitution or public law between the president and the government (prime minister and defense minister); (2) parliamentary oversight of the military through control of the defense budget; (3) peacetime government oversight of general staffs and military commanders through civilian defense ministries; and (4) restoration of military prestige, trustworthiness, and accountability for the armed forces to be effective (Simon 1996, 26–28).

All four of these steps turned out to be a challenge in the Hungarian case, though the third step—civilian control of the HDF general staff—was most visible. To be fair, the starting point was difficult. The Hungarian military had not won a war since 1487, and Hungary had seen foreign troops stationed on its territory since 1526. Like all communist-era militaries, Hungary's was overendowed with personnel (especially officers) and underendowed with modern equipment. Hungary also bordered on all three of the disintegrating multinational states (the USSR, Yugoslavia, and Czechoslovakia).[6]

In the last days of Hungarian communism, the Communist Party made a fateful decision in advance of the elections of spring 1990. Expecting to win the presidency, the party divided the armed forces between an administrative arm under Ministry of Defense (MoD) control and an operational arm under the direct command of the president (Pecze 1998, 15). While the new MoD—responsible to the government—received only 125 staff members from the old unified MoD, the new army command received the remaining 1,100 staff (Gutierrez 2002, 96). As it turned out, this division of the armed forces would long allow the HDF to resist civilian encroachments into its operational autonomy, and it prevented the establishment of a unified chain of command under MoD control (Simon 2003). Partisan politics hatched the split; technocratic steps alone could not undo it.

Unlike the EU, NATO had no formal *acquis* with which to demand changes—only the vaguer principles noted above—and far fewer officials and far less money to promote such changes.[7] NATO was thus dependent upon the goodwill of like-minded Hungarian officials if it was to have any success. As noted, the first problem lay in finding or training adequate numbers of civilians informed about military affairs. The first postcommunist Hungarian government managed to round up some token civilians, but almost none had military expertise, and the military perceived many of them as party political hacks. When the Social Democratic Party won the 1994 elections, it installed recently retired generals as civilians in the MoD and insulated the HDF even further from civilian intervention. Under the subsequent Orbán government (1998–2002), this "generals in suits" issue remained. Of the top five civilian MoD officials, only one had no professional military background. Three of these were former generals, and one was a former colonel (Dunay 2002).

The second, and larger, problem was that the slowly growing civilian expertise was never politically neutral. Just as U.S. defense experts often have partisan affiliations, so too did the newly minted ones in Hungary. And it was not at all clear to NATO officials encouraging reforms which party faction (with associated allies inside the HDF) might be the proper vehicle for building solid civil-military relations. In the Social Democratic period from 1994 to 1998, the military used its dominance of the MoD to assert its autonomy vis-à-vis the prime minister. In the Fidesz period from

1998 to 2002, the government tried to assert its control over the army by using party loyalists to circumvent the leadership vacuum at the MoD.

The central problem, to recall, was the duplication of command structures that had grown up since 1989. These parallel structures—one located in the MoD and one in the HDF's general staff—sometimes took on comic proportions. In one case, two separate Hungarian military delegations (one MoD and one HDF) with the same objective visited Sweden at the same time unbeknownst to each other (Barany 1998, 17). In the meantime, several partial efforts to clarify the chain of command had failed, and the split contributed to several crises in Hungarian civil-military relations.[8] The split thus remained, and a siege mentality prevailed on the part of many top officers.

Though Western officials frequently expressed their concern over the Hungarian arrangements, only domestic forces could effect a change (for details, see Jacoby 2004, chap. 4). After the 1998 election, the Fidesz government finally succeeded in subordinating the HDF to the MoD, though it took months of tense stand-off in which most of the principals on both sides either were fired or resigned. A deal was reached to eliminate the parallel organizations in 2001, and this deal was then codified in the 2002 defense reform overseen by the new Social Democratic government.

No telling of this case should so foreground IGO choices that the crucial domestic ones recede. Domestic party competition was crucial. But unlike the macroeconomic reform case, there was no one faction that functioned as a stable minority tradition that shared the same aims as the IGO. Rather, the domestic competition eroded the military's veto position and opened up different factions of the military to different models of engagement with civilians. Once this dynamic took shape, NATO expectations about healthy civilian control institutions seem to have been a star toward which the major parties steered, if slowly and on their own time. NATO programs to build up civilian expertise also played a role, but not in the politically neutral way that NATO officials imagined. Instead, each side used its own civilians (and its own factions in the officer corps) to negotiate the specific contours of the rather vague NATO thresholds. And unlike the ethnic minority case, the relevant IGO did not have a list of discrete policy acts that, if passed, would satisfy its demands. Rather, NATO confronted Hungary with much vaguer thresholds that probably again allowed both major party factions to see the IGO demands as potentially compatible with their own ambitions.

The Coalition Approach in Light of Dynamism,
Domestic Politics, and Divergence

The cases just discussed suggest the utility of the coalitional approach to external influence, which insists on linking IGO policies to specific actors at the domestic level. Those domestic actors—labeled minority traditions —were increasingly available across the three cases considered.[9] In this coalitional approach, IGO actions are at least *potentially* crucial, but they are rarely the *exclusive* causal force. On the other hand, three other common rhetorical tropes overstate the either-or nature of external and domestic politics. These rhetorical tropes often function as prima facie cases that external influences are simply not worth imputing with much causal weight. I label the three tropes dynamism, domestic politics, and divergence.

First, some scholars have noted the undeniable fact of IGO inconsistency. In the cases noted above, this would be most true of the EU, and some have argued that EU inconsistency makes a "myth" of the "Europeanization" thesis that pressures emanating from the EU are having profound effects on individual member states (Hughes, Sasse, and Gordon 2004, 3, 19, 25, 29). Yet neither the EU's indecisiveness nor its many policy zigzags falsify the Europeanization argument or the conditionality arguments associated with much of the Europeanization literature. Kelley notes many instances where the EU changed its policies, yet does not find this undercut its ability to affect CEE policies. Stone also has plenty of room for intra-IGO disputes, delays, and reversals in his discussion of internal IMF debates without rejecting the conditionality hypothesis. IGOs may not need to play their hands perfectly in order to get results.

Second, some scholars imply that if domestic politics are demonstrably important—and they almost always are—this too undermines the hypothesis that IGOs matter in shaping PCR choices (O'Dwyer 2006a). But why should external influences only count where domestic politics does not? Indeed, the opposite is more plausible: that external influences matter precisely where they best connect with domestic processes, not where they act independently (see also Carothers 2004, 15; Phillips 2000, 180).

Third, some authors imply that arguments about IGO influence must also predict convergence, so that evidence of cross-national diversity would mean disconfirmation of the hypothesis about IGO influence (Hughes, Sasse, and Gordon 2004, 140, 168–69). Yet the best recent work on Europeanization in CEE explicitly disavows the claim that the process must lead to identical outcomes (Schimmelfennig and Sedelmeier 2005). For example, Dimitrova (2005) argues that Europeanization is stronger in Central and East Europe than in the old EU-15, but still finds plenty of variation in the administrative structures of postcommunist states. Similarly, Schwellnuss (2005, 69–70) finds Europeanization of nondiscrimination policy to be "decisive" even if "mediated" by various national factors.

In short, all three rhetorical frames—dynamism, domestic politics, and divergence—stretch the external-internal dichotomy beyond reason. If we expect external influence to consist only of clear external IGO commands, clear domestic responses unanticipated by domestic precursors (including minority traditions), and resulting in convergent cross-national outcomes, we will always conclude that external influences do not exist. Here the diffusion literature makes a major contribution by showing so clearly that policies and practices often do spread.

Further clues about the potential utility of a coalitional approach come from the literature on democracy promotion. Though primarily focused on the programs of the U.S. government, some of the findings speak to the issues raised earlier on IGO influence. Thomas Carothers's path-breaking work shows why the overtly coalitional approach to external change so seldom occurs: it is difficult for even a single state to pull off. Carothers has chronicled, instead, a Western attachment to checklists that inform their democracy promotion programs. These checklists generally do not require significant complementary action in the target country. For Carothers, such checklists embody an "overattachment to forms and underattachment to principles" (2004, 154). According to Carothers, real reform demands "powerful tools that aid providers are only beginning to develop, especially activities that help bring pressure on the legal system from the citizenry and *support whatever pockets of reform may exist*" (2004, 129, emphasis added).

Carothers's work on U.S. and EU efforts to oust Serbian strongman Slobodan Milošević also strongly emphasizes the strengthening of minority traditions that lies at the heart of the coalitional approach. As he notes, the core Western objective was to "defeat Milošević in credible national elections and simultaneously build core institutions and processes for a long-term process of democratization" (Carothers 2004, 54). Doing this clearly required inside partners. Carothers notes that the Western democracy promotion programs in Serbia had several advantages: both the U.S.

and EU programs were large and sustained. They also were decentralized, sending aid directly to Serbian civil society. Finally, aid reinforced diplomatic and military efforts and was well coordinated between U.S. and European donors (Carothers 2004, 57-59). Carothers concludes that specific Serbian traditions of rule of law, civil society, and pluralism will make this pattern hard to replicate elsewhere. As he put it, Western accomplishments "generally entailed strengthening features of Yugoslav political life that already existed" (Carothers 2004, 56).

One could readily add that the current difficult state of Serbian democracy is a further caution against promising too much for externally driven reforms. Again, my point is less that external influence always works—it clearly does not—than that when it works, it is particularly hard to see precisely because it is so bound up with domestic politics.

Five Not So Easy Pieces

The coalitional approach presumes that external IGO actors rarely make substantial and sustained contributions without a partnership with domestic actors. This conclusion therefore sketches the possibilities and dangers of the coalitional approach. The evidence from all three policy areas—minority protection, macroeconomic stabilization, and civilian control of the military—is positive about coalitions. Kelley found strong external effects, stressing both EU signals not only to incumbent governments in Estonia and Latvia but also to the opposition forces that ended up being the major carriers of the reforms in Slovakia and Romania.

This is not an isolated finding. Vachudova (2005) emphasizes even more strongly the informal partnership the EU and opposition parties in Bulgaria, Romania, and Slovakia. In many cases (not all), these were strong enough to overcome domestic veto players. Stone obviously emphasizes IMF connections to the state, and he also has rich descriptions of the links between IMF conditions and the programs of various opposition parties or parts of the state struggling to influence the policy agenda. These act as vehicles for the IGO agenda, though they clearly have interests of their own. The civilian control case showed that NATO had to wait much longer for results than did the EU and the IMF, and that it was even more dependent upon complementary programs from its member states. But over time, external influences reshaped both the institutional structures and the key actors involved in civilian control.

At the same time, however, other research on postcommunist transitions has shown that some of the worst outcomes were also the result of coalitional approaches. Phillips (2000) argued that Western pressure and attempts to co-opt particular movements could sometimes make PCRs defensive and harden their positions against reforms desired by the West. Wedel (2001) goes further and argues that some Western-PCR coalitions were vehicles for plundering public assets, especially in Russia.

How should we understand these very different findings about the coalitional approach? One possibility is to look more closely at the policy process in order to appreciate just how challenging the coalition approach is. Here it seems that every promising generalization about external assistance runs up against an equally plausible generalization that limits it. I conclude with five examples, each with direct relevance to the coalitional approach, where contradictory advice poses as robust generalization.

BE FLEXIBLE (BUT BE FIRM)

How can transnational outsiders know which practices to insist upon on and which can be relaxed? It seems they can know only by focusing on the principles that underlie particular institutions, rather than the institutional design itself. Once the underlying principles are identified, then—assuming reformers really want to codify those principles in institutions—one can be flexible about which forms best promote it in the setting in question. Using this functional equivalent approach to institutional change, external actors assert their principles without fetishizing their own institutions. Development practices are often fetishized as well (Easterly 2006). Many strategies tried in postcommunism were developed in the third world and made assumptions inappropriate to Central and East Europe or Russia. Here, too, the underlying principles of the reform strategy are more important than the actual aid mechanism. The more external actors are involved in trying to reform the same policy, the more that coordination problems will make the "firm on principles, flexible on practices" formula hard to achieve. Still, the EU, OSCE, and the Council of Europe were all involved in promoting better protections for ethnic minorities in Central and East Europe without undercutting each other. The council took the lead in articulating standards, and the EU picked up that language and made the sustained effort to enforce change.

Moreover, when external actors try to promote institutional and policy reform, they face another dilemma: institutions do not have clear boundaries and yet all good projects do. Institutional reformers have to decide where to stop. This boundary problem is related to the issue of the functional principles of institutions versus specific institutional practices. Initially, many external reformers see a fairly narrow institutional fix as a promising solution, and the more they learn about the place they want to change, the less they tend to make such claims. But the way out of this dilemma is not to suggest that institutions do not really matter—for example, "the culture there is hopeless"—but to recognize that they do depend on a variety of noninstitutional factors (Woodruff 2000). Absent a serious focus on such supportive factors, externally driven projects (even if nominally accepted by domestic elites) may be just an institutional version of a New Year's resolution: easily made in a moment of focus but quickly eroded in the routines of daily life.

ADAPT TO LOCAL CONDITIONS (BUT CHANGE AND IMPROVE LOCAL CONDITIONS)

The first idea that brings many people to study development is "if it works here, it ought to work there." The second idea—which often follows hard on the first—is "good ideas from the outside must be adapted to local conditions." Yet often reformers want new institutions *precisely because they do not fit* the culture or standard operating procedures of some particular place. Indeed, the presumptive aim is to *change* some aspect of local culture.

The coalitional approach advises reformers to be specific about which cultural practices or procedures are ripe for change. Then, rather than attributing problems to abstract ills like "inefficiency" or "lack of consultation," reformers might aim institutional redesign against specific constituencies that provoke inefficiency or backroom deals. For example, perhaps the underprovision of personal security or sound corporate governance in Russia is less an institutional omission—gaps to be plugged by putting the right institutions in place—than situations sustained, if not engineered, by those who provide personal security or use corporations to launder money or plunder public assets.[10] Taking on concrete political opponents always sounds harder than taking on abstract ills. Concrete opponents fight back, after all. But since they do, perhaps it is better to go in with eyes open.

PLAN FOR SUSTAINABILITY (BUT DON'T RE-CREATE TRADITIONAL STRUCTURES)

Donors want their efforts to endure after they leave. Planning for sustainability is another purported magic bullet that, upon closer inspection, draws most of its magic from the appallingly poor planning that characterizes many development programs. Given this low baseline, some imagine that planning for sustainability is a huge step forward, rather than a single important precondition for success. If, as noted above, reformers always ought to ask, "who benefits from institutional dysfunction?" then they also have to ask who could benefit from institutional function. Who could carry these programs after the external actors leave?

The coalitional approach requires buy-in from domestic actors—and not just passive acceptance but also a positive contribution. Yet the obvious danger is that the new institutions or the funds that accompany them reward only those partners. Outsiders should thus try to steer toward the provision of public goods that benefit a broader constituency rather than club goods that benefit a narrower one. In the best case, the domestic partners are then paid in electoral benefits or enhanced legitimacy—two kinds of currency that might boost competition to provide more public goods.[11]

BE DETERMINED (BUT DON'T RAISE THE BARGAINING POWER OF VETO PLAYERS)

In many cases, external help makes no difference because it gives such a modest or brief impulse for change. So it helps if prospective external change agents are determined and ready to make a sustained commitment. Yet the coalitional approach should also incorporate elementary bargaining theory, which says that even when two parties want the same thing, the one who wants it most will end up paying most of the costs (usually through side payments to the less enthusiastic). In some cases, deep-pocketed donors may accept this distribution of costs. But most effective strategies to truly engage locals (and to smoke out real opposition) should ask for some local buy-in. The key is to help donors avoid having to make huge side payments for things that local people do not really oppose (or may even support).

The perception that outsiders are determined can signal some locals to bid up their price for removing obstacles. Yet it may not be possible or wise for donors to disguise how much they are interested in a particular reform. So what to do? Here the coalitional approach dovetails with older lessons that donors are increasingly trying to put into practice. One big step can lie in funding and supporting demand-driven programs. That was one of the real strengths of the Marshall Plan: the United States told the Europeans to work out what they wanted before it could be funded. Yet recent scholarship underscores the powerful incentives behind donor-driven grant making, and donors ignore those findings at their peril (Henderson 2003). Second, whenever possible, local cofinancing also seems a crucial tool. Even if the amounts seem trivial to the donors, such copayments should oblige domestic actors to share in any artificial inflation in the costs of domestic cooperation and give them incentives to attend to the sources of that inflation.

MAKE REFORMS INCREMENTAL (BUT DON'T MISS A WINDOW OF OPPORTUNITY)

Politics is more art than science, and knowing when to move can be as important as knowing what to do. It is possible to make a strong case for incremental reforms, especially where the EU is concerned, since it had a large bureaucracy of its own (to manage incrementalism) and because post-communist states wanted membership. Few external actors have these resources. Incremental reforms can reassure domestic skeptics and undercut opponents who claim that the sky will fall if a certain reform is implemented. In some cases, slow reforms create a larger circle of winners who, in turn, are a constituency for even more reforms. Fast reforms can do this as well, but with substantial democracy costs if small change teams of economic technocrats are deliberately isolated from politics in order to drive purportedly necessary reforms.[12] Even when changes will have beneficial long-run results, there is a strong tendency to blame outsiders for the short-term costs of these reforms. In postcommunist settings, this often leads to conspiracy theories that outsiders are driving them to ruin and hovering around to buy their national treasures on the cheap.

One way out of this dilemma may be for external actors to err on the side of incremental reforms but leave domestic actors free to occasionally, as their political sensibilities deem fit, accelerate the reforms. The coalitional approach suggests that external actors should function like cruise control on a car: they strive to make sure that the state does not lose focus and stop moving forward but leave open the possibility that the state's leaders may occasionally surge ahead by hitting the gas on their own. The key is that it should be clear to voters that it is their own elites (and not their foreign advisers and partners) who are responsible for the surges, especially when, in policy terms, those surges may mean substantial economic costs to some.

The multifaceted findings of the scholars of transnational politics combined with the maddening complexity faced by policy makers adds up to a lively intellectual agenda that stretches far beyond the postcommunist area. This chapter has offered the minority tradition concept as a heuristic to explain informal, coalition-style linkages between IGO officials and subsets of PCRs and so to understand postcommunist reforms. Such linkages represent a scope condition that is consistent with both logic of appropriateness and logic of consequence causal mechanisms. When posed in this way, questions of external influence should enjoy significant staying power in the discipline *because they can be linked to existing theories of comparative politics,* rather than functioning as static snapshots of transitory best practices or as a shallow alternative explanations to domestic politics. Indeed, as the evidence cited shows, anywhere external influence has lasting effects, it is deeply implicated in domestic politics.

5

TWO-TRACK DIFFUSION

AND CENTRAL BANK

EMBEDDEDNESS

THE POLITICS OF EURO
ADOPTION IN HUNGARY
AND THE CZECH REPUBLIC

Juliet Johnson

Why did central bankers in the postcommunist European Union accession states initially press strongly for a rapid adoption of the euro, despite the questions and costs involved? Why did their efforts fail in the Czech Republic and Hungary? Most important, what can these events teach us about the nature of the EU convergence process in Europe's postcommunist states?

Postcommunist Europe's dramatic moves toward greater convergence with European Union norms and forms—especially from the mid-1990s onward—generated contentious scholarly debate over the underlying impetus for this change. Did the material incentives and implicit coercion inherent in the EU accession process prod East Central European leaders in their reform efforts, or did they instead adopt new institutions because of the deeper effects of persuasion and socialization, "a process by which states internalize norms originating elsewhere in the international system"

(Alderson 2001)? In short, as Schimmelfennig and Sedelmeier (2005) put it, was East Central Europe's rapid institutional transformation due primarily to the influence of "external incentives" or "social learning"?

While neither approach explains the entirety of postcommunist Europeanization, most scholars have emphasized one over the other. In response, Checkel (2001) has called for building intellectual bridges between the two positions, and others have injected nuance into the debate by arguing that the approaches' relative explanatory powers may vary by issue-area (e.g., Epstein 2005), country (e.g., Dyson 2000), or time period (e.g., Jacoby 2005). Moreover, while determining the relative influence of incentives and socialization proved difficult before 2004, the EU accession of eight postcommunist states in May of that year provided a fresh opportunity to evaluate and refine these arguments. Once EU accession was assured and then achieved, would East Central European states continue to reaffirm and deepen the convergence process in the absence of the EU's ability to withhold membership, or would further convergence slow and stall?

I use central banking to make two broad arguments in relation to this debate. First, differently situated domestic actors may support EU-style institutional convergence in the *same* issue-area for *different* reasons; while external incentives may primarily motivate one group, another may fully accept and internalize the underlying EU norms. In particular, while small groups of domestic insiders working in a specific issue-area (and/or organization) may have experienced intensive training, exposure to, and socialization with their relevant EU counterparts, the broader government and public may have accepted and supported change in that issue-area for shallower, more incentive-based reasons. Second, the most problematic consequences of such a two-track diffusion process appear only after EU accession becomes assured, when the socialized insiders may find that they no longer enjoy the wider support to which they have grown accustomed.

Central banking provides a clear example of such a two-track diffusion process and its results. Postcommunist central banks have changed radically since 1989, making institutional transformations from command-economy cash cows into independent guardians of price stability. Yet international factors, not domestic demand, fueled this transformation process. The collapse of the Soviet bloc provided the initial opening for change; the training and technical assistance efforts of the transnational central banking community spurred ideological and organizational development within the central banks; while the attraction, assistance, and detailed requirements of European Union membership provided a blueprint for further transformation. The postcommunist central bankers now share the transnational central banking community's belief that protecting price stability and central bank independence is the key to economic development in democratic states.

However, this recent, externally driven transformation process meant that these central banks had converged ideologically and institutionally with EU norms without the need to develop significant political support or economic credibility among domestic actors. East Central European politicians and publics accepted independent central banks as an EU requirement and as a symbol of economic modernization and sovereignty, not because they believed deeply in the institution and its core goals. As a result, in the post-accession period the central bankers have found themselves politically embattled and undermined because other domestic actors often did not share their policy priorities and did not always see the central banks as credible and trustworthy actors.

This friction and its consequences revealed itself in the central bankers' curious battle to adopt the euro as quickly as possible after EU accession. While rapid euro adoption made sense for the smaller accession states (especially those like Estonia with its euro-based currency board), it carried significant risks for the bigger, more economically complex states of the Czech Republic, Hungary, and Poland. Entering the European Monetary Union (EMU) would significantly reduce the power of their national central banks and cause major economic upheaval if the adoption turned out to be premature. Moreover, both the European Central Bank (ECB) and the IMF had actively discouraged the largest new entrants from planning an early move to the euro. Proposing to leap into monetary union in the face of such obstacles seemed to fly in the face of central bankers' noted conservative impulses.

I argue that the central bankers' stance was motivated by domestic political considerations resulting from the two-track diffusion process. The central bankers wanted to adopt the euro quickly in order to tie the hands of their own increasingly unsupportive governments, forcing the governments to first cut their fiscal deficits enough to meet the Maastricht criteria, and then to cede control over monetary policy to the more powerful ECB. The postcommunist central bankers took this position out of weakness, not strength, viewing the external constraint of euro adoption as the only way to ensure conservative fiscal and monetary policies in their own countries.

I develop these arguments through case studies of central banking in Hungary and the Czech Republic. They provide an apt comparison, as both countries' central banks failed to persuade their governments to adopt the fiscal restraint necessary for rapid euro adoption and both subsequently had their independence undermined as a result. Moreover, these similar results cannot be blamed on a general atmosphere of Euroskepticism, as the Czech Republic has exhibited significantly greater political Euroskepticism than has Hungary (Greskovits 2005; Klaus 2004). The article is based on over thirty interviews carried out in the Czech and Hungarian national banks; primary documents and speeches regarding euro adoption from the EU, the Czech National Bank, and the National Bank of Hungary; and local press reports. It is part of a larger research project analyzing the transnational central banking community's training and technical assistance programs in the postcommunist world.[1]

The transformation of postcommunist central banks did not initially create central banks firmly embedded in their domestic environments. One important consequence of this weakness was that the central bankers' push for early euro adoption, an ill-advised effort which exacerbated existing conflicts between the central banks and their governments, ultimately undermined the central banks' domestic authority and credibility. For new EU members, this relatively weak central bank embeddedness poses significant challenges for sustainable economic convergence with the EU and, in particular, for their long-term participation in the monetary union.

The Transformation of Postcommunist Central Banks

Rapid institutional change takes place in a three-stage process. The first stage, *choice*, concerns the initial decision to undertake institutional reforms. The second stage, *transformation*, concerns the process of change itself. The third stage, *embedding*, concerns the sustainability of change. Each stage gives rise to a different research question: Why was the initial decision made? How was the transformation conducted? To what extent does the surrounding environment accept, reinforce, and deepen the changes that have taken place? Although this chapter is concerned primarily with the third stage, embedding, many of the problems evident in this stage have their roots in postcommunist central bank transformation.

As I have argued elsewhere (Johnson 2002), a transnational policy community of central bankers, possessing a shared ideology and significant material resources, actively guided the transformation of postcommunist central banks. This network encompassed the central banks in the advanced industrial democracies (engaging both current and former central bankers), the Bank for International Settlements (BIS, the "central bankers' bank"), and the departments responsible for working with central banks within the international financial institutions (e.g., the IMF's Monetary and Exchange Affairs Department). By the early 1990s, these bankers had effectively coalesced into an epistemic community capable of delivering massive, coordinated assistance to postcommunist central banks.[2] Scholars widely identify European central bankers in particular as comprising an effective epistemic community, citing their successful promotion of central bank independence and price stability in the creation and maintenance of European monetary institutions (Andrews 2003; Dyson et al. 1995; Kaelberer 2003; Marcussen 2000; Verdun 1998).

Central bankers typically describe themselves as an often-misunderstood and underappreciated club of similarly minded and educated individuals working in a unique institution. Two key principles—price stability and political independence—ideologically unite this central banking community (Blinder 1998). At the domestic level, central bankers generally believe that a narrow focus on price stability as an operational goal for monetary policy keeps inflation in check and promotes economic development. Furthermore, they believe that only politically independent central bankers can credibly commit to achieving price stability in a democracy.[3] More broadly, central bankers generally believe that states should remain open to international financial markets; that the most common causes of international financial crises are poor domestic monetary, regulatory, or supervisory policies in individual states; and thus that central banks must protect their independence and coordinate their efforts in order to preserve international financial stability (Evans 1997; Goodman 1989; Helleiner 1994).

The transnational central banking community not only controls extensive financial resources, but also has wide-ranging professional legitimacy based on its specialized macroeconomic expertise. Moreover, its members possess both political legitimacy (as government institutions) and political autonomy (as independent central banks). This unity and power allowed the community to move quickly into the postcommunist region. The community directed its assistance efforts in the 1990s toward instilling its ideological principles in postcommunist central bankers and equipping them with the technical and organizational tools needed to turn these principles into reality. Initial preparations for this campaign began at a series of high-profile meetings and conferences after 1989, with the IMF and the BIS taking lead roles. The transnational central banking community presented postcommunist central bankers with a widely accepted institutional model that not only neatly defined the problems and solutions to their economic woes, but also provided powerful individual incentives for central bankers to adopt it. This alternative model promised postcommunist central bankers political independence, control over their budgets, better salaries, and higher status. It treated them as knowledgeable professionals and offered them international travel, training, and ultimately membership in an influential, cohesive transnational community. As a result, most postcommunist central bankers embraced the integration efforts.

By the mid-1990s, the EU accession process had begun to strengthen and reinforce these initial transformation efforts in the East Central European countries, as the requirements to join the European Union provided an impetus and guide for further institutional development. In the area of monetary policy, the major accession requirements reflected the preferences of the transnational central banking community, including central bank independence, adopting price stability as the main objective of the central bank, a prohibition on central bank financing of the government, and liberalizing capital movements.[4] While these countries had already made most of the required changes by the time accession became a realistic medium-term goal, the accession process provided additional financial and technical assistance for fulfilling the requirements and played a key role in maintaining government commitment to central bank independence during a period when it might otherwise have been severely threatened.

The Challenge of Embeddedness

As Kathleen Thelen (1999) has observed, institutional transformation must be distinguished from institutional reproduction; merely creating an institution does not necessarily mean that it will have the ability to maintain and further develop itself in the future.[5] This process of embedding is particularly important and tricky when international forces have played the primary role in generating domestic institutions. Jacoby cogently points out that this kind of institutional transfer creates significant challenges of "adaptation and legitimation," and argues that "for effective institutional change to persist and perform, it must be 'pulled in' by social actors rather than decreed by policymakers alone" (2001, 15). Postcommunist central banks have quickly converged toward a Western-style model of central banking, but through an externally driven process and under significantly different domestic economic and political conditions than in advanced industrial democracies. While their rapid transformation required massive external intervention, embedding then demanded that these central banks develop a broad base of domestic support.

This imperative highlights an important imprecision in much of the scholarly literature on diffusion. When social scientists talk about the diffusion of ideas, policies, and institutions, they typically evoke an image of their adoption by entire states. For example, "states" become democratic (Kopstein and Reilly 2000), adopt liberal economic ideas (Simmons and Elkins 2004), and so forth. However, this image often distorts the reality of the diffusion process. In practice, diffusion may affect only one institution, one set of policy makers, or one region of a country. Helleiner recognizes this in the broader realm of economic globalization, pointing out, for example, that the development of financial centers reconfigures specific geographical areas, not entire states. As such, "economic globalization . . . must be located in specific spatial contexts in order to understand its significance" (Helleiner 1997, 92). In postcommunist central banking, ideational diffusion has occurred through two different and initially complementary processes: an intensive socialization process within the central banks themselves, paralleled by a shallower, more incentive-driven acceptance process in their broader domestic environments.

For the postcommunist central bankers, I argue that a wormhole metaphor more accurately captures the socialization process. Integrating postcommunist central bankers into the transnational network created what geographer Eric Sheppard calls a spatial wormhole, which opens "when two relatively isolated places become closely connected" (2002, 323). While Sheppard uses the wormhole metaphor to capture the "non-Euclidean" way in which the global economy has expanded over the past few centuries, I employ a more narrow use of the term. In this context, the wormhole refers to an arena of intense transnational communication among a small number of similar actors and institutions physically located in multiple countries. The wormhole effect encourages constant transnational interaction and ideological reinforcement among the individual nodes in the central banking network, but does not engage domestic actors outside of these central banks. The postcommunist central bankers became deeply socialized through this transnational integration process, accepting the causal beliefs and norms of the transnational central banking community (Johnson 2002). As a result, they grew to have more in common with central bankers abroad than with other political and economic actors in their own states.

In contrast, external incentives rather than socialization encouraged other postcommunist domestic actors to support the creation of independent central banks. Postcommunist publics, governments, and commercial banks exhibited little initial demand for conservative, independent central banks. Unlike in many countries, independent central banks in postcommunist states were not created as a response to inflation.[6] Rather, postcommunist governments granted central banks significant statutory autonomy in emulation of the advanced industrial democracies, with the prodding of established central bankers and the international financial institutions. Independent central banks symbolized sovereignty and Westernness, and legislating them into existence did not imply widespread acceptance (or even understanding) of the tradeoffs involved in conservative monetary policy. In addition, the financial sectors of these countries did not necessarily welcome independent central banks either, as the central banks took an active role in financial sector transformation that placed continuing constraints and pressures on commercial banks. These newly independent central banks thus began the postcommunist period with shallow domestic support and maintained this support primarily because of EU accession requirements. Therefore, once accession seemed assured and central bank policies became more controversial, the central bankers quickly became isolated.

In short, the transnationally driven transformation of postcommunist central banks led to their ideological and institutional convergence with central banks in the advanced industrial democracies, but under difficult domestic political and economic conditions. The two-track diffusion process meant that the newly socialized central banks often enjoyed little serious domestic support, and that whatever support they did manage to build could easily be undermined by perceived policy failures beyond their control. The completion of the accession process for eight postcommunist states in May 2004 opened a new chapter in central bank-government relations in East Central Europe. An examination of the central bankers' failed push for early euro adoption in Hungary and the Czech Republic illustrates the post-accession problems created by these deep divisions between these two central banks and their governments.

The Curious Battle for the euro

According to the terms of EU accession, the new member states were committed to entering monetary union once they had fulfilled the Maastricht criteria and received the official blessing of the current EMU members. The Maastricht criteria involve four primary requirements, widely interpreted to mean inflation rates of no more than 1.5 percent (and long-term interest rates of no more than 2 percent) above the average of the three member states with the lowest inflation rates; a public debt less than 60 percent of GDP; a budget deficit below 3 percent of GDP; and participation in ERM II for at least two years within an exchange rate band of up to +/- 15 percent (but likely narrower in practice). Therefore, according to these criteria and EU practices the earliest possible date that a new entrant could have considered adopting the euro would have been January 2007, assuming entry into the European Exchange Rate Mechanism II (ERM II) almost immediately upon EU accession. There were no guarantees, however, as to when these states would fulfill the Maastricht criteria or even whether they would do so—Sweden has stayed out of EMU so far by continually failing to meet the criteria. From the late 1990s it had become clear that the fiscal criteria would be the most challenging ones for the largest new accession states to meet.

CENTRAL BANKERS PUSH FOR THE EURO

By 2001, as near-term EU accession became realistic, Hungarian and Czech central bankers were advocating adopting the euro as quickly as possible, emphasizing the benefits and downplaying the risks. Hungary introduced its inflation-targeting regime in 2001 and in August of that year National Bank of Hungary (NBH) governor Zsigmond Járai declared that Hungary should introduce the euro as of January 2006. The following August the NBH and the government set a joint goal to fulfill the Maastricht criteria by 2005 in their Pre-Accession Economic Program, allowing for euro adoption in 2007 (Csajbók and Csermely 2004). Well-publicized research by NBH analysts in 2002 found that Hungary and the Eurozone consti-tuted an optimal currency area, and that Eurozone membership promised lower transaction costs, increased foreign trade, and lower real interest rates (Csajbók and Csermely 2002). Moreover, it warned that remaining out of the zone exposed Hungary to disruptive capital flows, and that a commitment to early entry would increase the credibility of Hungary's macroeconomic policy program. In early May 2003 Járai stated that Hun-gary ought to enter ERM II in 2005 in order to maintain the possibility of adopting the euro in 2007, opining that "early euro adoption would have overwhelming benefits for economic growth and monetary stability" (*Dow Jones International News* 2003a).

The Czech National Bank (CNB) also suggested 2007 as the Czech Republic's target entry date, most notably in the CNB's draft Euro Acces-sion Strategy of December 2002. This draft strategy, which the CNB debated for several months before presenting it to the government, stated that "the first possible year for joining the eurozone is 2007.... The evaluation of the positive effects and possible risks speaks in support of the Czech Republic's fast entry into the eurozone" (Czech National Bank 2002). Published CNB research and prominent statements on its Web site suggested that euro adoption would not cause significant inflation, would strengthen macro-economic stability, and would encourage real convergence. Vice-governor Oldřich Dědek in particular often published articles pressing for a fast-track strategy of euro adoption (Dědek 1998, 2002, 2004), stating that "while the benefits are obvious, the costs are in some ways both vague and embedded in an environment that is either archaic or hypothetical . . . the Czech Republic should adopt the Euro as its currency as soon after accession to the EU as possible" (2004, 45).[7] Governor Zdeněk Tůma sent a warning as well, arguing that financial markets would react unfavorably if the Czech Repub-lic lagged behind its neighbors in adopting the euro (Reuters 2003d).

The central banks of the Czech Republic and Hungary were not alone in their push to adopt the euro in 2007; central bankers in the other soon-to-be member states held the same opinion. Polish central bank governor Leszek Balcerowicz, for example, regularly stated that Poland should attempt to join in 2007 (see Pawlak 2004). Yet the central bankers' rush to adopt the euro in the largest East Central European states seemed curious in at least three ways.

First, joining the Eurozone would mean sacrificing the central banks' power to conduct monetary policy. The central banks would be reduced to mere appendages of the ECB, committed to helping carry out ECB policies designed for the EU as a whole and not necessarily suited to economic conditions in the transition economies. Moreover, unlike the West European central bankers who created, staffed, and directed the ECB, the postcommunist central bankers would be joining the already existing monetary union as relatively uninfluential junior partners. It is unusual to see central bankers eager to abdicate their hard-won independence, as this independence represents a primary part of their identities and the source of their institutional power (Grabel 2000; Maxfield 1997; McNamara 2002). It also contradicts the expectations of realist theories, which emphasize the primacy of national sovereignty and independence in state decision making (Sandholtz 1993). Indeed, this was precisely the problem that former NBH governor György Surányi had warned of earlier, stating that "the Hungarian central bank would be forced to relinquish its monetary policy independence upon joining the monetary union. It would be irrational to give up the maneuvering opportunity (MTI News Agency Budapest 1999). The accession state central bank governors generally acknowledged this loss of independence as a negative aspect of monetary union, but said that they would make the sacrifice because of EMU's promised economic benefits (Pringle and Carver 2004).

However, the central bankers also appeared to be downplaying the economic risks involved in an early adoption of the euro. One critical report by the *Economist Intelligence Unit* denigrated Hungarian central bankers as "Euro Freaks," while George Soros, who profited so handsomely from the ERM's unsustainability in 1992, warned his native country not to fix its currency in ERM II too early and leave itself vulnerable to speculators (Arai 2004; Economist Intelligence Unit 2003). Many outside experts believed the risks to be high because the large East Central European states had both significant investment needs and productivity and price levels well below the EU average (Dumke and Sherman 2000; Égert et al. 2003;

Krenzler and Senior Nello 1999). Moving to fulfill the Maastricht criteria too quickly through a rapid reduction of budget deficits and public debt could retard economic growth, while the risks involved in premature euro adoption were potentially greater. Those often mentioned included misalignment from entering the Eurozone with an overvalued exchange rate, interest rate shocks leading to a credit crunch, and the likely inflationary impact of Eurozone entry in the wake of high productivity growth in the traded-goods sector (the Balassa-Samuelson effect) (Dumke and Sherman 2000; Kenen and Meade 2004; Vintrová 2004; Watson 2004). Others doubted whether the enlarged Eurozone would meet the conditions of an optimum currency area (De Grauwe 2003; Frenkel and Nickel 2005; Klaus 2004; Mahlberg and Kronberger 2003).[8] In particular, many experts concurred that maintaining exchange rate flexibility for at least a few years after accession could be beneficial for new entrants as they adjusted to the new economic patterns brought on by EU membership. Moreover, allowing more time for financial market deepening, coordinating payments systems, working with EU statistical and accounting systems, and other elements of financial system development would improve the transmission mechanisms for monetary policy and thus allow the postcommunist central banks to more effectively implement the ECB's monetary policies. As central bankers typically eschew unnecessary risk (Blinder 1998), these problems —especially considering the euro's own instability at the time—should have dampened the central bankers' strong enthusiasm.

Finally, although scholars regularly point out instances in which would-be member states have made EU-required institutional changes only reluctantly and/or minimally (Jacoby 1999; Schimmelfennig et al. 2005; Sissenich 2005), in this case the postcommunist central bankers pressed to adopt the euro more quickly than even the EU itself thought desirable. The ECB (backed by the IMF) was dead-set against the large East Central European countries moving toward early euro adoption. ECB president Jean-Claude Trichet stated repeatedly that the new member countries should not rush to adopt the euro, and said that they must fulfill the Maastricht criteria "not only nominally, but in a sustainable manner" (Pattanaik 2004). The postcommunist central bankers had strongly suggested that the EU relax certain elements of the Maastricht criteria in order to ease the way for faster entry. In particular, they requested that the EU be more flexible on the interpretation of the Maastricht inflation-level rules, on the requirement to stay in ERM II for two years, and on the width of the ERM II exchange-rate band (BBC 2004; Dawson 2004; Reuters 2004a). On the permissible inflation rate, for example, the central bankers argued that the EU should require them to meet only the Eurozone average rather than that of the three best performers, and they should take the Balassa-Samuelson effect into account (Gaspari 2004; Rosati 2002). Yet the ECB not only refused to relax these criteria but also planned to interpret them in very strict terms. Numerous other ECB officials consistently sent clear, public messages not to rush, including ECB Vice President Lucas Papademos; ECB Executive Board members Tommaso Padoa-Schioppa, Gertrude Tumpel-Gugerell, and Otmar Issing; and ECB Governing Council members Klaus Liebscher (Austrian National Bank governor) and Vitor Constancio (Banco de Portugal governor). Constancio chided the East Europeans for their haste, stating that "they expect great benefits but they tend to disregard some of the possible costs" (Pattanaik 2004).

Given the potential risks of early euro adoption, why were sitting postcommunist central bankers so universally supportive of rapid entry? Their own statements made it clear that they felt helpless in the face of rising government spending, and decided that only an early commitment to fulfill the Maastricht criteria and join the Eurozone could effectively restrain government spending and protect price stability in their countries. As one Hungarian central banker put it, "Eurozone convergence provides a unique opportunity for accession countries to abandon macroeconomic stabilization policies that suffer from weak credibility" (Csermely 2004). The Maastricht criteria could restrain the governments now, while after euro adoption the ECB and EU would be more effective fiscal watchdogs than the embattled postcommunist central banks. As a Czech economist pointed out, "It is one thing for a national prime minister to call his nation's central bank governor and ask him to cooperate, and quite another for him to call the ECB's governor, who has much wider responsibilities and is shielded from any one member state's policy" (Schneider 2003). In short, the central bankers wanted to use this external constraint to tie the hands of their own governments in the absence of domestic support for the central banks and a lack of consensus on the primacy of price stability. Their actions echoed earlier efforts by Italian leaders to use EMU as a *vincolo esterno* (external tie) to overcome their domestic political divisions over economic policy (Dyson and Featherstone 1996, 1999). Featherstone has aptly observed that "the instrumental use of EMU as a *vincolo esterno* ... is a more likely strategy in states that have not fully 'internalized' the norms and values associated with the 'sound money, sound finances' paradigm of the EMU. A strategic lever is a welcome tool in the relative absence of a shift in norms and beliefs" (2001, 17). In Italy, however, central bankers and leading politicians worked together to apply the *vincolo esterno,* and did so in a context of relatively greater domestic support for independent central banks as institutions. In contrast, central bankers in the Czech Republic and Hungary were more isolated and thus implored their governments to move quickly toward meeting the Maastricht requirements in ever-more urgent terms.

The CNB clearly hoped that a push for early euro adoption would encourage the government to adopt greater fiscal restraint. CNB board member Jan Frait argued that the EU accession process itself had been responsible for the economic success of the East Central European states, because it had provided economic benchmarks and put external pressure on the politicians to achieve them (Frait 2003). The EU information on the CNB Web site made it clear that the country had reached compliance with all but one of the Maastricht criteria, and that "its main challenge for the future is to reduce its public finance deficit." Furthermore, the CNB stated bluntly in its 2002 draft euro accession strategy that "the current outlook in the fiscal policy area is not fully consistent with [the CNB's strategy to adopt the euro in 2007]. Accordingly, the aforementioned economic and political measures [reducing public budget deficits and increasing the flexibility of the labor market] must be implemented in such a way as not to rule out the possibility of joining the eurozone sometime around 2007." This same document observed that "Membership of the eurozone should have positive impacts on domestic economic policy, since the key elements of the system are a requirement for balanced public budgets in the medium term and a requirement to undertake structural reforms supporting sustainable economic growth." Top CNB officials from Governor Zdeněk Tůma on down regularly chided the government for not adopting more radical fiscal reforms, stating that it threatened the Czech Republic's ability to adopt the euro in 2007 (Interfax 2003; Reuters 2003).

The NBH had even more fundamental differences with its government, especially after the April 2002 elections ushered in a new ruling coalition led by Prime Minister Péter Medgyessy and the Hungarian Socialist Party (MSZP). The MSZP quickly increased government spending once in power, threatening to further inflate Hungary's already problematic budget deficit and public debt. Hungarian central bankers repeatedly slammed the government for overspending and attempted to use imminent entry into the Eurozone as a club with which to threaten politicians. Importantly, although the NBH primarily employed the rhetoric of euro adoption to attempt to persuade the government to change course, its concerns with fiscal policy went far deeper. The central bankers believed that the MSZP's policies would lead to rising, unsustainable deficits that would eventually spark a severe economic crisis in Hungary. Invoking the authority of Europe by pushing the government to fulfill the Maastricht criteria and join the Eurozone as soon as possible seemed to be its most promising bargaining strategy. For example, NBH governor Járai said on numerous occasions that higher budget deficits and debt would threaten Hungary's planned early euro adoption. He pressed for budget reform, criticized plans to reduce income taxes, and encouraged the government to stick to its spending commitments (Interfax 2003a; Reuters 2003d, 2003e, 2003f). Similarly, NBH vice governor György Szapáry explicitly stated that East Central European states needed target dates for euro entry in order to set "a fixed point for necessary fiscal policy adjustments and an anchor for wages" (Peto 2003).

Even more tellingly, although the postcommunist central bankers had demanded that the EU relax the Maastricht requirements on inflation and ERM II, they all strongly opposed the EU allowing more flexibility in the fiscal criteria for both Maastricht and the Stability and Growth Pact (which committed Eurozone members to maintain the low deficits and debt required for Eurozone entry). Most dramatically, in an August 2003 interview with the *Financial Times* the governors of the Czech, Hungarian, and Polish central banks all heavily criticized the move by France and Germany (whose deficits had risen above the 3 percent limit) to ease the pact's rules. The NBH's Járai stated that "this lack of discipline . . . sets a very bad example for us," while the CNB's Tůma observed that "we must have sustainable public finances. The EU club cannot afford to forget that . . . some rules must be respected" (Krosta and Major 2003). Without the external constraint of EU requirements, the central bankers feared that their governments would ignore their calls for fiscal rectitude.

THE EARLY ADOPTION EFFORTS FAIL

Unfortunately for the central bankers, their efforts to restrain government spending by pressing for early euro adoption met with strong resistance. Their governments did not take the central bankers' initial proposed adoption dates of 2006–2007 seriously, and not only failed to reduce their budget deficits and public debts in the wake of central bank pressure but actually increased them. Hungary's fiscal deficit had widened from 4.2 percent of GDP in 2000 to 9.2 percent by 2002 and in late 2003 was still at 5.9 percent, well above the 3 percent Maastricht limit. Public debt in Hungary was at 55.7 percent of GDP in 2000 and had crept up near 60 percent by late 2003. While the Czech Republic's public debt remained safely below the 60 percent limit, its deficit went from 4.2 percent of GDP in 2000 to 6.7 percent in 2002, and had climbed to 7.0 percent by late 2003. This led to continuing revision of the euro adoption dates, increasing tensions between the central banks and the governments, and ultimately a loss of credibility and influence for the central banks.

The NBH's attempt to use the Maastricht criteria as a weapon in its ongoing battle over fiscal policy failed, as the government ultimately preferred to promote Hungary's economic competitiveness rather than adopt the more conservative policies favored by the NBH. To make matters worse, the MSZP viewed NBH governor Járai as a political opponent, since he had been appointed by the previous Fidesz government and had once served as its finance minister. As a result, the MSZP saw Járai's critiques of fiscal policy as politically rather than professionally motivated and took them even less seriously than they might have otherwise. Large deviations from the fiscal and inflationary commitments expressed in Hungary's Pre-Accession Economic Program eventually led to speculative attacks on the forint in January 2003, followed by a downward readjustment of the exchange rate band in June and a depreciation of the currency. In May, Járai suggested that imprudent fiscal policy might force a delay in euro adoption until 2009 or 2010, which the government strongly denied (Népszabadság 2003). In July 2003 Hungary revised its planned euro adoption date to January 2008, a date jointly announced by Prime Minister Péter Medgyessy, Finance Minister Csaba László, and NBH Governor Járai (*Dow Jones International News* 2003b). As a part of this announcement, the government committed to reduce the budget deficit target from

4.8 percent in 2003 to 3.8 percent in 2004. This seemed to signify a relaxation of earlier tensions between the central bank and the government, and some agreement on policy goals. However, within weeks the central bank had again begun accusing the government of not taking its commitment seriously, and in September Járai stated publicly that while adopting the euro in 2008 remained a feasible goal, a "fundamental change in economic policies is needed" (Interfax 2003a). The central bank suffered another blow when the deteriorating economic situation led to the January 2004 firing of Finance Minister László, a supporter of euro adoption in 2008.

Prime Minister Medgyessy then asked the new finance minister, Tibor Draskovics, to "review" the feasibility of the January 2008 date. The central bank continued to express hope that Draskovics would recommend retaining the 2008 target (see MTI News 2004a, 2004b; Peto 2004a). However, at the review's end in May the government and finance ministry set 2010 as the new target for joining the Eurozone, with the central bank reluctantly "supporting" the decision (Condon 2004; Reuters 2004a). Almost immediately afterward the central bank began criticizing the finance ministry and the government again, saying that the euro convergence program they proposed was too slow even to meet the new target date (Economist Intelligence Unit 2004; Interfax 2004a; Packer 2004; *WMRC Daily Analysis* 2004). While leading Hungarian business associations had previously called for Járai's resignation and for changing the country's legislation to make competitiveness instead of price stability the central bank's primary goal (Magyar Nemzet 2002), by July 2004 the government and the finance ministry had also become united in their criticism of the central bank's monetary policies (Interfax 2003c; Peto 2002). One MSZP leader opined that "the central bank should take the general state of the economy more seriously into consideration when making its decisions," while Draskovics blasted the central bank for focusing on "how weak we are and how it will not succeed" (*Dow Jones International News* 2004b; Peto 2004b).

In August 2004 Medgyessy resigned and was replaced by Socialist Ferenc Gyurcsány, kicking off another wave of public warnings and recriminations among Járai, Draskovics, and the new leadership. Attempting to bring the NBH to heel, in December 2004 the Hungarian parliament amended the Central Bank Act to expand the size of the NBH's monetary council from nine to thirteen members. Although Járai deemed the amendment "uncultured, against the constitution, and against Europe," four new council members personally selected by Prime Minister Gyurcsány began their terms in March 2005 (Aris 2005; Blahó 2004). The campaign to force the government to support the NBH's preferred monetary and fiscal policies had failed, with the NBH's domestic support reaching perhaps a new low in its wake. By late 2005 the fiscal situation in Hungary had deteriorated so significantly that international ratings agency Fitch downgraded Hungary's sovereign credit rating and the EU threatened to impose sanctions.

Remarkably, the situation for the CNB was even worse. After the CNB presented the government with its draft plan recommending euro adoption in 2007, months of discussion followed during which the CNB regularly criticized the government for badly missing its fiscal deficit targets and not taking the Maastricht criteria seriously (Reuters 2003b). President Václav Klaus, a longtime opponent of the central bank, hit back by criticizing the CNB's inflation targeting as "fiction" and stating that it would be "unwise" to adopt the euro (*CTK Business News* 2003b; Interfax 2003d). In September 2003 the CNB and government finally agreed on a revised euro adoption strategy, one which represented a significant loss for the central bank (Czech National Bank 2003). The document stated bluntly that joining the Eurozone in 2007 would not be possible because "the current outlook ... does not indicate that the public budget deficit criterion will be fulfilled by [June 2006]," and it revised the expected entry date to 2009–2010 at the earliest. It is perhaps telling that CNB governor Tůma failed to appear at a subsequent cabinet meeting in which the new plan was to be discussed (*CTK Business News* 2003a). Commenting on the revisions, CNB board member Jan Frait (2003) said that "the key reason behind the decision of the Czech government not to struggle for the earliest adoption of the Euro was the desire to have a few years more for using fiscal measures to promote growth and convergence. The opinion of the CNB is nevertheless different. We understand deep structural reforms in public finances as a way of promoting growth and convergence."

Prime Minister Vladimír Špidla confirmed these differences the following February, arguing that 2009–2010 was a more realistic entry date considering the domestic political difficulties involved in meeting the Maastricht criteria (*AFX International Focus* 2004).[9] Tensions between the CNB and the government grew throughout 2004, egged on by President Václav Klaus and his opposition Civic Democratic Party (ODS). Klaus, who as president had the power to appoint CNB board members, revised the board's membership when the terms of vice governor Dědek and members Pavel Štěpánek and Pavel Racocha ended in February 2005, adding three close allies and fellow Euroskeptics to the board. In declaring his intentions, Klaus stated that "a change is necessary and I am convinced that quite a big one is needed. I would like to see more pragmatic and mature people among the CNB management" (meaning board members who preferred to wait on euro adoption) (Interfax 2004c). He made this announcement in the wake of public opinion polls showing an increasing polarization over whether to adopt the euro at all, with 56 percent in favor and 35 percent against (as opposed to 52 percent and 23 percent in 2001, with many more undecideds) (Interfax 2004b). Like the NBH, the CNB suffered a loss of influence and credibility during its failed battle for early euro adoption, dealing a further blow to its already low levels of domestic support.

Toward the euro, Ready—or Not?

Weak domestic support for their desired policies encouraged Czech and Hungarian central bankers to press for euro adoption faster than their governments and the EU preferred, and faster perhaps than was economically advisable. Without consistently effective tools to address inflation and with price stability threatened by increasing budget deficits, they turned to the Maastricht criteria and the euro to attempt to restrain their governments' fiscal policies. The two-track diffusion process fueled this policy conflict between the central banks and their governments. The transnational central banking community had effectively worked to socialize the postcommunist central bankers, opening wormholes of intensive interaction between them and central bankers in the advanced industrial democracies. This process reinforced the postcommunist central bankers' identities as independent promoters of price stability without requiring (or generating) sustainable domestic support for their institutions. This pattern has a range of implications, both for the euro's future and for our understanding of convergence and diffusion processes more generally.

The East Central European central bankers expect the euro and ECB to tie their governments' hands for them, enforcing macroeconomic discipline in a way that they themselves cannot. However, the central banks' domestic support and credibility will have been compromised in the process, raising questions about the long-term sustainability of macroeconomic convergence in the EU. Most importantly, although independent central banks can increase the credibility of monetary policy, macroeconomic stability ultimately requires coordination and cooperation between monetary and fiscal authorities. Both must agree on the general direction and goals of economic policy. When this cooperation is lacking, it can lead to higher interest rates, fluctuating monetary and fiscal policies, and declining investor confidence (OECD 2004). Critics often question central bank independence as counterproductive and undemocratic on these grounds, arguing that independent central banks undermine the economic policy decisions of elected officials in the service of narrow technocratic goals (Berman and McNamara 1999; Levy 1995; Stiglitz 1998). Independent central banks in postcommunist states often face even greater challenges in this regard because of their internationally spurred transformations (Johnson 2006).

In the EU, already under fire for its own alleged democratic deficit, such coordination problems become multiplied by the number of Eurozone states. Current Eurozone members have already successfully challenged the ECB's tight monetary policies and the fiscal restrictions of the Stability and Growth Pact. Reacting to this development, Slovenian central bank governor Mitja Gaspari (2004) observed with concern that "a system where there is one monetary policy and 25 completely independent fiscal policies is not viable." When postcommunist countries with little respect for their independent central banks and with less-developed transition economies join the Eurozone, then the ECB, the Stability and Growth Pact, and the economic philosophy on which they are based will face their severest challenges to date. Defying expectations, public opinion in both current and prospective Eurozone members has already turned further against the euro over time. Although 51 percent of Eurobarometer respondents in the Eurozone states in 2005 still felt that adopting the euro had been advantageous overall, this represented a fall of 8 percent from three years earlier (EOS Gallup Europe 2005a, 2005b). Moreover, a stunning 93 percent of respondents believed that adopting the euro had led to price increases in their countries, a major public fear in the prospective Eurozone states. In the ten new EU member states, 46 percent expected negative consequences from euro adoption as opposed to only 38 percent expecting positive consequences, a significant decrease from the previous year's survey (EOS Gallup Europe 2005a, 2005b). European economic convergence and monetary union are not necessarily irreversible; things fall apart.

More broadly, diffusion processes within a single issue-area may occur with different speeds and intensities among domestic actors. While external incentives may motivate some and indicate a shallow commitment to change, others may become heavily invested in new institutions and mind-sets through socialization. Such two-track diffusion is more likely to occur when an epistemic community plays a central role in the socialization process, because under these conditions a small group or single organization can become socialized without the active encouragement or participation of other domestic actors. If the external incentives generating domestic tolerance and support for such transformed institutions change (as after EU accession), the socialized entity may find itself unexpectedly embattled. Public struggles are most likely to result in arenas such as economic policy making, where central banks' newly granted statutory independence and international support empowers them to challenge recalcitrant politicians.

Two-track diffusion will not necessarily lead to open conflict. If external incentives remain strong, socialized and strategic actors will continue to cooperate. Alternately, socialized actors and institutions can demonstrate their worth to their broader domestic audiences through policy efficacy and persuasion, gradually embedding themselves in their societies by building domestic constituencies. Finally, socialized entities without strong domestic constituencies or independent power bases may simply become increasingly marginalized once the external incentives to support them vanish. In each instance, however, two-track diffusion allows the transformative transnational socialization of groups and organizations to occur regardless of the domestic political, social, and economic conditions needed to sustain them over the long term. The unprecedented role that international forces have played in nearly every aspect of postcommunist transformation should encourage us to continue to examine the specific implications of this process more closely. Although discussions of globalization, foreign aid, and policy convergence often tend to either laud or malign these international influences in sweeping terms, reality does not conveniently lend itself to such rhetorical judgments. Rather, the effects are typically mixed, somewhat unpredictable, and context-specific—no less important or consequential, but much more complicated to unravel.

6

TRANSNATIONAL
ACTORS AND BANK
PRIVATIZATION

Rachel A. Epstein

The transition to democracy and capitalism in Central and East Europe should have made postcommunist countries more like their West European counterparts. And in some respects it has. But in other respects, the newest members of the EU have embraced the market more vigorously than states traditionally have been willing to do, resulting in historically unprecedented levels of foreign ownership of Central and East European financial institutions.[1] This chapter argues that transnational actors were key to producing the high levels of foreign ownership, specifically in banks, that had materialized by 2004 in much of Central and East Europe.

There were compelling arguments on both sides of the debate about how to privatize the state-owned banks that had resulted from breaking up socialist-era monobanks into two-tiered banking systems. On the one hand, protectionists could point to the longer-term developmental advantages of maintaining state or at least domestic private ownership (Gerschenkron

1962). On the other, there was a strong case to be made for breaking up existing political and business networks, for maximizing state revenue, and for quickly initiating an efficient method of allocating resources. Neither argument prevailed strictly on merit in any country. Rather, I argue that where international institutions, particularly the IMF and the World Bank, exercised the greatest power, domestic reformers tended to favor privatization with foreign capital. Relative openness to foreign advisers allowed international institutions to frame the debate in favor of privatization and foreign investment in ways that altered what postcommunist states sought to maximize—in this case rapid modernization and efficient resource allocation over national security and developmental concerns.

A possible alternative explanation for postcommunist openness to foreign investment would be that the combination of starting conditions and globalization left Central and East European states little choice but to attract foreign capital as a means of rescuing what were admittedly fragile banking sectors in many cases. Low levels of domestic capital accumulation, know-how, professionalism, and technology, together with the need to increase state revenue through privatization, might have conspired to limit the options available to economic reformers. Moreover, there were strong efficiency arguments to be made in favor of foreign participation. External creditors held out the promise of putting an end to political lending, increasing transparency and ensuring that resources accrued to those best equipped to achieve returns.

I reject the globalization alternative explanation, however, for two reasons. First, if states in fact had no choice in the matter, then one would expect to find little variation in outcomes. Indeed, although the major trend has been toward financial sector internationalization, postcommunist Europe nevertheless does manifest significant variation in the degree of foreign ownership in banking. Second, I find that such variation is more closely linked to states' evolving relationships to international institutions than to those same states' exposure to international markets.

Although Central and East European levels of foreign ownership in banking are markedly high (usually over 70 percent) relative to the OECD average, with some exceptions, outcomes across the region reflect only a partial embrace of the foreign investment logic. To be sure, selected states in postcommunist Europe, including Croatia and Estonia, with 87 percent and 97 percent foreign ownership, respectively, have almost completely privatized their banking sectors with foreign capital (Naaborg et al. 2003, 26). But the more usual pattern has been for states to maintain at least some domestic or even state control over banking through authoritative allocation to the private sector or through the failure to privatize at all. In addition, postcommunist states have exercised control by limiting the share that any single foreign entity can own, thereby balancing control among multiple interests and thus limiting the recipient country's vulnerability to any single state. Thus, although transnational actors have contributed to a banking ownership outcome that is strikingly more internationalized than one finds in western Europe, it is not the case that international financial institutions or the EU have had unmitigated influence.

Piecemeal efforts to prevent total foreign domination notwithstanding, Central and East European states have nevertheless demonstrated a striking willingness to use the market as a means of resolving the political conflicts inherent in distributing state assets after the fall of communism. Whereas protracted state ownership or privileging domestic buyers were viable options (both of which Slovenia, exceptionally for the region, exploited) most states put their long-term strategic concerns aside.[2] By opting for international bidding instead, Central and East European states have traded national autonomy for greater efficiency. The central question this chapter addresses is why postcommunist states did this and what role transnational actors, most often in the form of international institutions, played in the process.

I will provide a brief review of financial liberalization in comparative perspective, paying particular attention to the ways in which states have traditionally used banking sectors to build competitiveness. I will establish how anomalous the postcommunist trajectory has been and further motivates the question of what favored liberalization in the 1990s and early 2000s—domestic conditions, globalization, or the ability of international institutions to forge transnational coalitions in favor of foreign investment.

Foreign Ownership in Comparative Perspective

Despite OECD and EU regulations that ostensibly allow open market access to banking sectors among member countries, in reality most industrialized states have maintained high levels of domestic ownership. Where data are available, the usual rate of foreign ownership among the wealthiest countries is well below 20 percent and more often below 10 percent, with only a few exceptions limited to those states that were either financial centers or that for other reasons had bucked international trends. Although it is true that by 1990 most OECD countries had desisted from "state banking"—i.e., the state's involvement in direct credit allocation (Verdier 2000)—they were nevertheless reluctant to embrace full market liberalization. In the late 1990s and well into the 2000s, industrialized states continued to use whatever informal means were necessary to prevent foreign takeovers. In a spectacular example of such interference, Italian central bank chairman Antonio Fazio was caught on tape in the summer of 2005 conspiring with local bank managers to foil a Dutch bid to buy an Italian bank. Although Fazio came under fire and the Dutch offer ultimately prevailed, both the indignant international response to Fazio's conduct and the success of the foreign takeover were virtually unprecedented in the European experience (see *Economist* 1999).[3]

OECD trends away from state banking by the 1990s might have suggested that changes in the global economy had taken place that would also bode poorly for state intervention in postcommunist credit markets. Post–World War II economic development success stories, however, particularly from Asia, led some scholars to ask in the early 1990s why Central and East European transition states were not keener to pursue industrial policies with the assistance of state financial capacity (Albert 1993; Amsden et al. 1994; Bryant and Mokrzycki 1993; Chang and Nolan 1995). Traditionally, states had four kinds of tools at their disposal. They could pursue financial repression, direct credit through state-owned banks, provide loan guarantees on foreign borrowing, or simply reach a *modus vivendi* with private banks—assuming they were domestically owned.[4] Where it was made, the choice for central bank independence and price stability ruled out financial repression, but commercial banks remained a potential conduit of influence.

Given that never in the history of economic development had states become competitive through the market alone (Amsden et al 1994; Landesmann and Abel 1995) and that states had often been able to improve on the efficiency of markets through state credit allocation (Haggard and Lee 1993), it was not clear at the outset of transition how Central and East European states should manage their strategic assets. South Korea, Taiwan, and Japan had all flourished economically in the postwar period in large measure because those perspicacious states were able to pick winners and use domestically controlled credit to cultivate vibrant export sectors. On the other hand, similar strategies in the Philippines not only failed to produce economic gains but created rent-seeking classes that became a drain on growth. Although one study hypothesized that the Asian Tigers could not have served as a reference point for democratizers in Central and East Europe because of their semiauthoritarian character through much of their high growth years (Amsden et al. 1994), economic liberalization is hardly a guarantee of political pluralism. After all, sweeping liberalization was unleashed under Chile's Pinochet, while it was democratic forces in Brazil that ultimately curbed an economic liberalization plan there (Haggard and Lee 1993).[5]

More important than the fact of whether state-directed credit allocation is inimical to democratic governance was the ideological commitment to the idea that the two were incompatible. Bretton Woods's assessments of Asian Tiger economic strength reinforced the belief that state intervention was not the source of success by highlighting how important "getting the prices right" had been as opposed to focusing on the institutional arrangements that very likely facilitated high levels of growth (World Bank 1993). Where they existed in Central and East Europe, oppositionists to communist regimes had a generally negative view of state power. In the transition, forms of monetarism and neoliberalism—to the extent that the latter term referred to market-led policies—held particular appeal (Bockman and Eyal 2002; Shields 2003). International institutions' own misgivings in the early 1990s about market intervention bolstered arguments in favor of internationally competitive privatization.

Comparative Openness to External Advice: Poland, Hungary, and Romania

External actors supported rapid privatization of state assets in Central and East Europe as an essential component of the transition to a market economy. To be sure, there was also powerful domestic impetus for privatization in some states (including especially in the Czech Republic), even if others showed much less appetite for it (as in Romania). But the peculiar influence of international institutions was nevertheless on display in the participation of foreign capital—particularly in strategic sectors. Across the postcommunist region, foreign ownership was controversial. As in other cases explored in this volume, however, international institutions, with the help of their domestic interlocutors, were often able to overcome opposition to the loss of national control by shifting the terms of debate in favor of liberal economic principles.

The power of transnational actors depends on their ability to mobilize politically positioned domestic reformers in favor of a shared set of policy prescriptions. The mobilizing capacity of transnational actors in turn hinges on the degree of uncertainty of domestic reformers, their desire for social recognition from external advisers or multilateral institutions, and the perceived international credibility of the policies under consideration (Epstein 2008). I operationalize uncertainty and the desire for social recognition by assessing the degree of political turnover in the transition and the robustness of political competition thereafter (Vachudova 2005). The perceived credibility of the policy in question—privatization of strategic assets with foreign capital—was problematic for transnational actors in all three countries examined here. Although international institutions were consistent in their recommendations that the state limit its involvement in the economy by pulling back on ownership, and although the same institutions could point to the lack of state ownership of banks in most OECD economies, the issue of foreign ownership was trickier.

Because of the low level of foreign ownership in banking sectors across the OECD and because of many OECD member states' evident discomfort with foreign ownership in their financial sectors, Central and East European skeptics of internationally competitive bidding questioned the consequences of high levels of ownership for themselves. Previous research has shown that where transnational actors are normatively consistent in what they prescribe, there is much less room for domestic reformers to take issue with the credibility of particular policies (Epstein 2005, 2006). In the banking case, however, the discrepancy between Western states' practices and what international institutions were asking East Europeans to do was a constant source of friction. Normative inconsistency explains in part the circumscribed power of transnational actors in shaping banking outcomes.

Along the other two dimensions that explain postcommunist openness to external advising, however, there was some variation across Poland,

Hungary, and Romania. From the outset of transition in Poland, there had been competing views about when and how to privatize state-owned enterprises. Linked to privatization debates were disagreements about what role the state should play in the economy. Because a key conduit of economic influence has traditionally been control over domestic credit allocation, a particularly sensitive issue was the privatization of state-owned commercial banks, fifteen of which resulted from transforming the socialist monobank into a two-tiered banking system in 1989 and 1990 (nine were regional, six were specialist). Despite controversies over how to handle the state's assets, by the early 2000s, nearly 70 percent of the Polish banking assets were foreign owned. After more than a decade, however, Poland's enthusiasm for strict efficiency wavered, leading to multiple delays in the privatization of the state savings bank, Powszechna Kasa Oszczędnošci Bank Polski (PKO BP). In a reversal of earlier policy, the government, led by the postcommunist SLD and Prime Minister Marek Belka, resolved to keep Poland's biggest bank (in terms of assets) in Polish hands. An IPO in November 2004 limited foreign access to the close to 40-percent stake that went on the market while the state maintained its controlling share (*Warsaw Voice* 2004).

The preference for Polish ownership had many manifestations through the transition (Reed 2000). In the mid-1990s, the Democratic Left Alliance-Polish Peasant Party (SLD-PSL) coalition had made a serious bid to exercise state influence over the course of bank privatization—specifically to ensure a greater share of domestic control. That effort failed, however. I argue that the cultivation of a transnational coalition, spearheaded by the international financial institutions and the European Bank for Reconstruction and Development (EBRD), shifted the domestic balance of power in favor of foreign capital during the 1990s. Having institutionalized a free-market logic early in the transition, the barriers to reversing it in the banking sector proved prohibitive.

Ironically, although Hungary appeared even more explicitly determined than Poland to maintain a powerful share in domestic banking, by the early 2000s it had proven even less able to do so. By 2003, 88.8 percent of Hungary's banking assets were foreign owned compared to Poland's 68.7 percent (Barth et al. 2006). In most respects, the outcomes in Poland and Hungary are comparable, although Poland, by retaining a state share in the country's largest bank, proved marginally more able to resist international pressure than Hungary. Equivalent outcomes are what my theoretical framework would lead one to expect, starting with the fact that Hungary, like Poland, was relatively open to international institutions' influence due to strong measures on uncertainty and a desire for international social recognition.

It is also true, however, with respect to bank restructuring as well as other features of the transition, that Hungary and Poland differed in important respects. Vis-à-vis banking, Hungary was slower than Poland to implement an apolitical and effective system of regulation, the country experienced foreign participation in the sector sooner and on a larger scale in the first years of transition, and had a more protracted and costly bank bail out than Poland (Hjartarson 2004). Moreover, whereas Hungarian political parties were basically united in believing that a strong domestic presence in the banking sector was essential (Hjartarson 2004, 17), at least a few liberal reformers in Poland who held decisive positions in the MoF and the central bank were ready to argue that not just any domestic ownership would be better than foreign.[6] Variation along these dimensions between Hungary and Poland notwithstanding, they had comparably internationalized banking sectors by the early 2000s. Consistent outcomes highlight the salience of certain similarities between the two countries in making them susceptible to external influence—namely the noviceness of actors and Poland and Hungary's drive to be identified as within the Western fold.

Before the 1996 elections in which the Democratic Convention of Romania came to power, Romania was a most different case from Poland and Hungary. Although political competition and ultimately EU accession would increase Romania's desire for international social recognition in ways that would encourage the country to behave more like Poland and Hungary, by 2003 the share of foreign ownership in Romanian banking was only 43.5 percent. In keeping with what my theoretical framework would predict, Romania was both slower to allow foreign investment and more determined to maintain domestic ownership in the pr   ~f privatization, despite the fact that the country faced basically the
structures as Poland and Hungary. The initial continuity
class through the transition, combined with Romania's ir
international opinion, effectively limited the salience o'
icy prescriptions as reference points until late 1996.

Transnational Coalitions in Poland

Measures on noviceness in the banking sector were high in Poland at the outset of transition, making the country relatively open to the influence of transnational actors. Leaders from Solidarity replaced the communist regime as a consequence of the roundtable negotiations and the first partially free elections in June 1989. It was also a period of enormous uncertainty and fluidity when anything seemed possible—a time of "extraordinary politics" (Balcerowicz 1995). As elsewhere in the region, the introduction of price liberalization and credit markets rendered those working within the newly formed state-owned commercial bank neophytes, as previously they had performed essentially administrative functions in connection with the centrally planned economy.

Uncertainty, coupled with the first wave of reformers' desire for international recognition, allowed international institutions and Solidarity reformers to set a liberalizing trajectory together beginning in 1989. Although the Bretton Woods institutions began advising Poland on financial reform somewhat earlier (1986), the opportunity for dramatic change obviously widened with the roundtable negotiations and the first partially free elections in 1989. One of the first foreign interventions with regard to banking reform occurred in late 1989 at a conference on the outskirts of Warsaw.[7] Jeffrey Sachs, the Harvard economist who would also figure prominently in Poland's macroeconomic stabilization plan by providing his imprimatur (Kuroń 1991; Myant 1993), made a number of sweeping remarks about the imperative of modernizing and privatizing Poland's banks. He suggested that the Polish government enlist the assistance of the international financial institutions (IFIs) to initiate a training program between Western and Polish banks. Such an intellectual and technical exchange, Sachs argued, would provide Polish banks with much-needed Western know-how while generating investor interest among Western banks in their Polish counterparts. Although Sachs may not have been the first to imagine pairing banks as a means of transferring knowledge and possibly capital from West to East, it was his impetus that established a liberalizing frame and set things in motion (see Kahneman and Tversky 2000, 209–223; Lukes 1974; Riker 1996; Schoppa 1993, 1997, 1999).

In response to Sachs's ideas, the Polish deputy minister of finance in charge of banking reform contacted an International Finance Corporation

(IFC) official later the same day to discuss the feasibility of putting Sachs' ideas into action.[8] The IFC, including this particular representative, had been active since 1987 building independently financed business networks in Poland. Both men had attended Sachs's lecture. Sachs's speech and their meeting marked the beginning of an ideationally based strategic coalition among Polish and foreign actors that ultimately launched the "Twinning Arrangements" in the spring of 1991. In terms of encouraging investment between Western banks and their assigned Polish partners, the Twinning Arrangements were only modestly successful. Only one bank, Allied Irish, invested in its "twin" in Poznań, Wielki Bank Polski S.A. (WBP) (Wallace and Mayhew 2001, 21–22), while none of the other partnerships material-ized directly into business ventures. However, both the Italians and Dutch who had participated in the program did invest elsewhere in Poland's bank-ing sector at later dates—and on a large scale.[9]

Another indication that Poland's first postcommunist regime was mov-ing toward an internationalizing strategy in the commercial banking sector with the assistance of international institutions was the design and imple-mentation of the bank bailout plan of the same period, beginning in 1991. Familiar with the IFI's priorities and orientation, Polish MoF officials de-vised a bank restructuring and recapitalization scheme that they hoped would win IMF approval.[10] Based on that plan, the IMF agreed to reallo-cate a substantial portion of the unused złoty stabilization fund (originally worth $1 billion) to the proposed bank bailout program. The IMF added one informal condition to the reallocation of the stabilization fund to bank recapitalization: that the MoF make a good faith effort to privatize a number of Poland's state-owned commercial banks by the close of 1996.[11] Because the Polish politicians in power at this time were market enthusiasts from Solidarity who were already bound to the IFIs by a shared understanding of the value of markets, they welcomed this conditionality.[12]

Poland opened its banking market to foreign participation in still an-other way in the first phase of transition. Believing that the presence of foreign competitors would accelerate Polish bank reform, the Polish gov-ernment went to some lengths to encourage greenfield investment in the financial sector. Early, liberal licensing allowed foreign firms to set up and enjoy three years of generous tax relief as well as flexible arrangements with the Polish government concerning foreign currency holdings and capital mobility (National Bank of Poland 2001, 51). By 1993, however, incentives for foreigners were eliminated, and licensing, especially for new domestic banks, was tightened up in an effort to bring greater stability to the banking system. Nevertheless, the number of foreign banks operating in Poland continued to increase. Internationalizing the banking market, not only by allowing foreign investment in state assets but also by opening the Polish market to foreign participation, was broadly consistent with what foreign advisers and international institutions had urged postcommunist states to do (Bonin et al. 1998).

The desire for social recognition, together with the uncertainty of actors, further facilitated international institutions' influence over Polish bank restructuring in the early 1990s. I operationalize this variable by measuring the presence or absence of political competition, which in Poland was strong from the outset of transition. The opposition to the communist regime took power in 1989 and 1990 but was followed by the return of the communist successors to power in 1993. Further rotations in political groupings took place in 1997, 2001, and 2005. Although political competition facilitates the flow of information as other scholars have noted (Grzymała-Busse 2002; Vachudova 2005), equally important is the way in which the existence of political competition changes a series of relationships. Competition heightens the salience of external actors because domestic political parties can use them as reference points against which to assess a country's status. Equally, political competition permits international institutions to pick sides and potentially change the balance of domestic forces.

There is evidence that in the first phase of transition, the Solidarity-led government sought social recognition from international institutions. Political competition actually extended back into the communist era in Poland, when Solidarity served as an alternative source of authority and legitimacy to the state-socialist regime. Thus Western ideals and institutions had long served as a competing vision of how to organize power relations. The Twinning Arrangements, in which Western banks were paired with Polish ones, was legitimate in Poland, not for the proven quality of the idea, but because of its origins. There was initial disagreement, for example, about whether the program was worthwhile. While the Poles were enthusiastic, the World Bank was reluctant to support the experiment precisely because of its novelty.[13] While the World Bank's pessimism might be explained by the risks associated with bearing the costs of the venture, the first round of potential Western partners that the IFC solicited rejected the idea out-right.[14] This controversy points to the fact that an untested program can nevertheless appear attractive to those with few prior assumptions about how to restructure a sector, in this case Polish banking officials, especially if they seek social recognition from the institutions offering the assistance.

Political parties' mimicking of one another also provides evidence for the argument that where international reference points of comparison are relevant, policy spectrums narrow. The SLD-PSL coalition that won the parliamentary elections in late 1993 initially viewed the diminishing scope for state intervention in the economy with concern. Although some re-search has shown that the Polish public did not put the postcommunist parties back into power primarily because of pocketbook issues (Ekiert and Kubik 1999; Powers and Cox 1997), the SLD and PSL did distinguish themselves during the campaign by publicly urging slower-paced privati-zation as well as by displaying a greater suspicion of international institu-tions.[15] Their skepticism was reversed during the course of their term in office, however, as they discovered how dependent their political reputa-tions were on international approval of their policies. The importance of that approval explains why, after proposing a sweeping state-led bank con-solidation program, the coalition ultimately shifted back to a rapid priva-tization course in keeping with international institutions' wishes.

In the first four years of transition, international institutions had forged a transnational coalition in favor of privatizing Poland's banks quickly—regardless of whether it would mean a significant, even dominant, role for foreign capital. That coalition was comprised of international institutional representatives, Western and Polish bankers who had participated in the Twinning Arrangements, and Solidarity-affiliated liberals who by 1994 were once again part of the opposition. International institutions had cul-tivated a pro-privatization coalition by exploiting the uncertainty of the transition and the desire for social recognition among the first wave of Western-oriented reformers. The IFC and World Bank had established the primacy of Western know-how and capital with their training program, while the IMF had used the MoF request for bank bailout funds to extract a commitment for rapid bank privatization. Because of low levels of domes-tic capital accumulation in postcommunist countries, rapid privatization privileged foreign investors. The EBRD had consolidated the coalition fur-ther by investing in Polish banks in an effort to push privatization forward.

The normative inconsistency in what the international institutions were recommending was an ongoing source of friction, however, and ultimately led the SLD-PSL coalition to formulate a bank consolidation plan to upend rapid financial privatization with foreign capital.

Appointed in early 1994, the SLD-affiliated minister of finance, Grzegorz Kołodko, wanted to commercialize a limited number of the state-owned banks, consolidate them into two groups (around Bank Handlowy and Pekao SA), and postpone their privatization for two reasons. He wanted to both maximize the state's revenues from the sales and to facilitate the banks' purchase by Polish interests. Moreover, Kołodko had two developmental goals in mind. The first was to maintain the state's role in bank management and credit allocation. The second was to eventually create a Polish-owned internationally competitive banking conglomerate—a capacity that other industrialized countries had routinely preserved for themselves. These objectives were embodied by a bank consolidation plan that the Polish MoF, under Kołodko's direction, made public in late 1995 (*Życie Warszawy* 1995).

When the government announced the specifics of its bank consolidation plans in the fall of 1995, the IMF and the EBRD were among the first to object. For those foreign actors whose self-perceived job it was to help shepherd Poland toward the market, the most alarming aspect of the proposal was that one of the banks slated for consolidation had already been partially privatized by, among others, the EBRD. Bank Przemysłowo-Handlowy of Krakow (BPH) was in large part divided between four major shareholders, including the Polish State Treasury (46.6 percent), the EBRD (15.06 percent), ING Bank (10.1 percent), and Daiwa (4.57 percent). In addition, GE Capital, as well as other Polish banks, had expressed interest in investing in BPH not long before the consolidation announcement. The other proposed group for consolidation included Pekao SA (the lead bank), Bank Depozytowo-Kredytowy, Powszechny Bank Gospodarczy, and Polski Bank Rozwoju (*Warsaw Business Journal* 1995).

While support for the plan at home was mixed,[16] international misgivings were immediately made known to the press and to the Polish MoF.[17] Kołodko did not change course, however, until he and his deputy, Vice Minister of Finance Krzysztof Kalicki, confronted direct pressure from members of Poland's bank recapitalization fund steering committee, which included Larry Summers and David Lipton. U.S. Treasury officials in

Washington, D.C. were in this instance the final arbiters of IMF policy and were also acting on behalf of the EBRD.[18] They urged Kołodko to drop the program. Building on the criticisms Kołodko had already received at home, they argued that state-led consolidation was at odds with basic principles of a market economy, that such plans were anticompetitive, that it was not appropriate to appear to be "picking winners," and that these were protectionist policies designed to favor domestic, over foreign, investors. This was especially problematic in Poland, they argued, where it was the former communists who were pursuing policies that resembled central planning of the previous era. The U.S. Treasury warned that this would raise concerns among foreign investors more generally and that, further, the Polish government could not afford to potentially slow the privatization of state-owned enterprises in light of the government's budgetary priorities. Finally, the U.S. Treasury, contending that bank consolidation was not in the spirit of the IMF's earlier agreement to privatize all the state-owned banks by 1996, threatened to withhold the next installment of bank recapitalization funds.[19]

In 1996, Kołodko and the SLD dropped the bulk of the bank consolidation plans and shifted strategy back to privatizing the banks on a one-by-one basis, inviting foreign capital to participate (*East European Banker* 1996; *Gazeta Wyborcza* 1996b).[20] The intensity of the conflict with the IMF, EBRD, and U.S. Treasury, coupled with the criticism at home, provoked a sufficient sense of opprobrium and isolation in Kołodko and his colleagues at the Polish MoF that they implemented a series of pro-market policy changes well beyond the scope of the consolidation issue. Needing "a way out," Kołodko justified the change in policy by arguing that the government had decided to pursue privatization revenues sooner rather than later.[21] Thus, not only did the SLD drop bank consolidation and the push for domestic ownership, but they also initiated a fast-track privatization scheme for the banks that had previously been slated for consolidation and sought out foreign capital for the task. Further, they used the revenue from those privatizations to justify a tax cut. SLD deputies in the parliament supported legislation outlawing the consolidation of any bank that was not 100 percent state owned (*Gazeta Wyborcza* 1996b), and Kołodko went on to become a visiting scholar at IMF headquarters in Washington, D.C., after his tenure as Polish minister of finance ended.

Comparative Evidence from Hungary and Romania

According to the scope condition on uncertainty and the desire for social recognition, international institutions should have enjoyed access to Hungarian debates about banking reform. The political party that came to dominate in the transition the Magyar Democratic Forum (MDF) had previously been the opposition and price liberalization rendered banking bureaucrats novices. Moreover, the Hungarian drive for social recognition from Western transnational actors was high. Political pressure to return to Europe set up a competitive dynamic in which the communist successors would ultimately out-Westernize the communist-era oppositionists in terms of liberal economic policy.

The New Economic Mechanism of 1968 left banks remarkably unchanged. Even after the 1987 creation of a two-tiered banking system in Hungary, a political-administrative logic to finance endured instead of a market one (Young 1989,71–3). Indeed, at least three pieces of evidence suggest that international institutions were able to privilege foreign capital in Hungary's bank restructuring and privatization debates early on. In keeping with its international advisers' counsel, Hungary introduced a liberal regulatory framework that allowed foreign banks to begin operating within the country almost immediately (Hjartarson 2004, 18). Theoretically, this was to spur innovation within domestic banks. Hungarian politicians and international institutions alike believed that competition would force Hungarian bankers to update their skills more quickly than if Hungary had introduced protectionist measures.[22]

The second kind of evidence indicating that international institutions exercised influence over bank restructuring debates was that the first major law on the subject in 1991, the law on financial institutions, foresaw a winnowing of state ownership to less than 25 percent of state-owned banks by 1997 (MTI EcoNews 1991). Further, the law stipulated that if Hungary failed to go below the 25 percent threshold, the state nevertheless would abdicate voting rights beyond 25 percent (Piroska 2005). By 1992, Hungary had established a bank privatization committee expressly for the purpose of removing the state from credit allocation functions—despite continuing Hungarian uncertainty over how and to whom to privatize the banks and regardless of industry's dependence on domestic credit.

Finally, the catalysts for a sudden shift in policy in favor of privatization were apparently two *Financial Times* articles in May 1993 that, based on

IMF and World Bank sources, painted a bleak picture of Hungary's banking sector (Denton 1993a, 1993b). Noting high levels of bad loans and insufficient provisioning, the articles' use of the term "insolvency" put Hungarian policy makers on the defensive. Within five months, the MDF government would launch a bank recapitalization plan with the World Bank's help and chart the privatization of two of Hungary's largest commercial banks, Budapest Bank and the Hungarian Foreign Trade Bank (MKB) (MTI News 1993a, 1993b). A few months later, in April 1994, the Bayerische Landesbank Girozentrale (BLB) and the EBRD agreed to buy 25.01 and 16.7 percent stakes in MKB, respectively. The state would cut its holdings from 49 percent to 25 percent, with the remaining shares being widely dispersed (*Finance East Europe* 1994).

It is also important to note, however, that despite the MDF's sensitivity to the international business press and the Bretton Woods institutions, there was a wide-ranging debate in Hungary about how to manage bank restructuring. Foreign advisers hardly dictated the terms of privatization. Conservative MDF members were committed to encouraging small business participation in bank privatization and to preventing socialist operatives from winning exclusive access to state assets. Members of the liberal opposition (SzDSz) were more enthusiastic about limiting the state's role and allowing markets greater jurisdiction—and it was their sentiments that had the most explicit support of the IFIs. Moreover, the laws on foreign access expressed contradictory preferences—at once prohibiting limits on foreign participation *and* declaring a central role for state ownership in the transition process (Piroska 2005, 113–19). Even as the first freely elected government attempted to strike deals with foreigners keen to buy Hungarian banks, those deals ultimately foundered in the first three years over precisely those tricky issues of long-term strategic control (Hjartarson 2004, 17). Indeed, by the end of the MDF's first term, the government and population alike were growing anxious about what conservatives viewed as excessive foreign investment. By the second half of 1993, measures were in place to encourage domestic purchase of state assets, although notably not in the banking sector (Hanley et al. 2002, 153–57).

Romania had a strong measure on the noviceness of bankers at the outset of transition, but the continuity in the political leaders from the communist period through the first seven years of transition limited the impact of transnational actors. Romanian bankers were novices in the sense of having had little exposure to a market-based logic for lending. As in other state-socialist countries, Romania's banking functions were concentrated in the monobank and were administrative in nature, conducted on the basis of fulfilling the centralized economic plan for the country. The Romanian monobank issued currency, directed credit, and handled deposits. To the extent that interest rates were ever applied, it was without regard to the scarcity of money or the presence of risk. The only area in which Romanian bankers ever operated within a liberalized environment was in foreign exchange—not an insignificant realm given the scope of Romanian borrowing on Western capital markets starting in the 1970s (Ritson 1989, 98–102). Nevertheless, when Romania liberalized prices in 1991 (with the exception of some heating, basic food, and housing prices), most bankers in the original four commercial banks and the dominant savings bank hived off from National Bank of Romania (NBR) had little to no experience in a market environment.[23]

The potential access that foreign advisers would have to Romania banking reform debates was limited by the continuity of the regime. For even if bankers were eager to upgrade their skills in accordance with Western standards, it would prove to be difficult for them, foreign assistance notwithstanding, to mobilize the political class in favor of privatization (*Banker* 1993). Romania's hesitation, not unlike Poland and Hungary, stemmed from the sentiment that "banks [were] considered to be among the most important, strategic assets of the state" (Tsantis 1997, 201). The principle difference between Romania on the one hand and Poland and Hungary on the other would be the desirability of anticipatory EU accession reforms and the meaning of Bretton Woods conditionality. Whereas both Poland and Hungary were leery of breaking ranks with the IMF and the World Bank, Romanian politicians during the first years of transition would enter into agreements about which they were very ambivalent and to which they had less than a clear commitment.[24]

There was no shortage of international institutional engagement with Romania, as the many conditionality agreements between the country and the IMF and World Bank attest to (Cernat 2006). After little liberalization in the early 1990s, the IMF predicated its 1994 stand-by agreement with Romania on the drafting of a law on bank privatization. Subsequent agreements linked to banking reform included the IMF's 1995 stand-by agreement with Romania that called for commercial bank restructuring and the privatization of the Romanian Bank for Development. The World Bank's

1996 Financial and Enterprise Structural Adjustment Loan also called for the privatization of the Romanian Bank for Development in addition to a tightening of conditions under which the NBR would provide banks with refinancing credits (Tsantis 1997, 173, 200). Despite these commitments, under the conditions that prevailed until the 1996 elections, Romania avoided significant banking sector reform, engaged in ad hoc refinancing, and held on to the Romanian Bank for Development as well as other majority state-owned banks. IFI conditionality failed to elicit compliance because the Romanian governing class was neither seeking IFI advice as a way of gaining confidence in its policies nor social recognition.

Despite the lack of noviceness among governing elites, their lack of desire for social recognition from transnational actors, and the seeming inability of international institutions to exercise influence, Romania did comply with some internationally sanctioned policies. The two-tiered banking system was consistent with market-based reforms throughout the region. Four foreign bank subsidiaries were already operating in Romania when transition began,[25] and the 1991 legislation on foreign investment appeared to be nondiscriminatory (*BBC Summary of World Broadcasts* 1991). Measures suggesting international openness did not result in similar levels of foreign participation in Romania's banking market compared to those of Poland and Hungary by the same date, however, because of simultaneous countermeasures. Whereas, for better or worse, Poland and Hungary actively encouraged early entry of foreign banks into their respective markets, Romania initially maintained rigorous capital and regulatory requirements that discouraged new entrants—both foreign and domestic. The Romanian preference initially was to try to consolidate the domestic banking sector (including state-owned banks) without excessive competition (*Banker* 1993). Second, although putatively nondiscriminatory, the 1991 foreign investment law did require interested parties to seek permission—which was granted to a foreign bank for the first time only in October 1994, to Holland's ING.

Like Poland and Hungary, Romania enlisted the financial and technical assistance of international financial institutions, including the IMF and the World Bank, and also sought EU membership. So while the availability of new information and incentives did not vary across countries, Romania was decidedly less receptive to external advising in the early 1990s. Banking market outcomes for much of the 1990s therefore reflected particular

Romanian priorities rather than international norms of market openness and robust competition. International institutions' failure to penetrate Romanian reasoning was reflected in the fact that the primary goal of banking through the decade was not the efficient or even profitable allocation or resources, but rather the continued financing of state-owned enterprises. Romanian authorities did not even accept the idea of bankruptcy among banks until the very end of the decade—regardless of whether the bank in distress was publicly or privately owned (Doltu 2002). Thus whereas the uncertainty of actors new to power and their desire for social recognition increases international institutions' access to domestic reform debates, the absence of those conditions in Romania insulated the country from external pressure for much of the 1990s.

By the second half of the 1990s, a key variable that influenced the power of international institutions to shape reform trajectories had changed. Romania's sensitivity to international opinion increased as political competition intensified, particularly when the Democratic Convention of Romania (CDR) finally prevailed in the elections of late 1996. As the opposition to the National Salvation Front in Romania, the CDR had premised its campaign in part on developing constructive relations with a range of international institutions, and in that spirit adopted a series of liberal economic policies. In addition to a macroeconomic austerity program and increased independence for the central bank, the CDR began privatizing the country's banks and sought out foreign capital for the task—with the assistance of the IFIs. So whereas foreign ownership of banking assets was close to just 10 percent at the beginning of CDR's tenure, it was well over 40 percent by the time the socialists took power again in 2000. In keeping with the social recognition variable, however, the socialists mimicked many of their liberal counterparts' policies in an effort to maintain international institutions' support. By the close of 2006, foreign ownership of Romanian banking assets had climbed to close to 80 percent.

IN ALL THREE CASES, transnational actors tried to affect bank privatization outcomes. The IMF, World Bank, EBRD, and foreign banks generally preferred rapid privatization of state assets in postcommunist countries. Because of low levels of domestic capital accumulation in Central and East Europe, however, rapid privatization was a de facto call for international bidding and reflected the presumption that foreign investors would play a major role. There was significant variation between Poland and Hungary on the one hand and Romania on the other concerning the timing and degree of foreign participation by 2004. Although transnational actors were present in all three cases, their power was uneven across countries and over time largely because of variation in domestic political variables.

This chapter corroborates an earlier finding that, indeed, ideas do not float freely (Risse-Kappen 1995). Where banking assets were mostly foreign owned, as in Poland and Hungary in 2004, it is clear that even in these Western-oriented countries that the international financial institutions exercised a strong degree of influence. However, the presence of transnational actors with an agenda hardly guarantees a particular outcome. Rather, those transnational actors have to have the capacity to mobilize domestic actors around their cause. Absent postcommunist reformers' own uncertainty and desire for social recognition from external advisers, it becomes less likely that transnational actors will be able to promote policy diffusion.

7

A TRANSNATIONAL
CHURCH IN
NATIONAL SETTINGS

Timothy A. Byrnes

The Roman Catholic Church is a transnational institution with global scope and reach, but with particularly deep social and political roots in Europe. There was a time when the Catholic Church was a central governing institution on the European continent. The Holy See exercised temporal rule over much of Italy, while popes crowned emperors and kings. The church's Latin was the language of official communications and documents, and European society and politics were organized and structured around the theme and concept of Christendom. All of these aspects of Catholic power have now been consigned to the past, of course, but that does not mean that the Catholic Church does not still play a role in world politics in general, or in European affairs more specifically. It most certainly does.

The Holy See, for example, holds a seat as a Permanent Observer at the United Nations, and it conducts formal diplomatic relations with many countries around the world. It participates in international conferences and processes on subjects as diverse as debt, ecology, and the role of women in the modern world, and bishops, priests, and nuns are central players in political contexts as widely diverse as El Salvador, the Philippines, Uganda, and the state of Massachusetts. In the specifically European context, the Holy See is a full member of the Organization for Security and Cooperation in Europe, and it can use its sovereign capacity to recognize (or not recognize) governments as a diplomatic tool in cases such as the breakup of Yugoslavia. Finally, I imagine that even the most hardheaded secularist would concede that names like Wyszyński, Popiełuszko, and especially Wojtyła will be cited in history as central players in a Polish political revolution that changed forever the trajectory of European politics.

Even beyond these concrete everyday matters, however, the Catholic Church under Karol Wojtyła (better known as Pope John Paul II) also offered a broader, actually quite sweeping vision for the structure of European politics following the fall of the Berlin Wall. World politics is undergoing some kind of structural shift these days, and Europe is far from exempt. Regional bodies, nonstate actors, and transnational institutions of a dizzying variety have all joined the territorial state on the stage of European politics. No one seems to have a very clear notion as to what is actually happening or where this all will lead, but the idea of Europe neatly divided into territorial states that interact with each other and only with each other from a position of equal and inviolable sovereignty is definitely being challenged. Nothing should be surprising about this, of course. What we take for granted now in terms of political structure is, after all, a relatively recent invention. But just as we might say that Brussels has a vision for the future of Europe that diverges from, say, London's, so we can also say that the Vatican has a vision for the future of Europe that is all its own.

Pope John Paul II was many things, but among them he was, very clearly, a European, a Polish European. And as such, he had very well-defined ideas about what Europe is, as a concept as well as a place, and where that Europe's appropriate borders ought to be drawn. What's more, he was also perfectly clear about the role that he thought his native Poland, and the other formerly communist countries, should play in calling all of Europe, from the Atlantic to the Urals, back to its rightful place as a unified Christian civilization.

Most people remember John Paul's triumphant first visit to Poland in 1979, for example, for the galvanizing effect it had on the Polish dissident movement, and for the way in which it symbolically revealed the weak hold that communism had on the Polish people. But far fewer remember, or frankly even noticed at the time, that the new pope also took the occasion to begin what became a lifelong emphasis on the proper meaning of European union (lowercase "u"), and the role that he and his church were destined by God to play in it. "Is it not Christ's will," he asked in Gniezno, "is it not what the Holy Spirit dispenses, that this Polish pope, this Slav pope, should at this very moment manifest the spiritual unity of Christian Europe" (Paltrow 1986, 16).

From the very beginning, John Paul was very clear that there was only one Europe, that it was founded and built upon Christianity, and that his East not only had the right to retake its place with the West in European institutions and structures, but that on a more symbolic or spiritual realm, the East had much to teach the West about what it actually meant to be authentically "European." For this reason, the Polish pope was always perplexed, for example, by the prospect of Poland "returning to Europe," as the popular saying had it in the 1990s. Given Wojtyła's worldview, Poland not only was an indispensable part of Europe, Poland had actually saved Europe, defined Europe, at the gates of Vienna through Jan Sobieski's sword in 1683, and in the Battle of the Wistula against the emergent Russian Bolsheviks in 1920. "Poland has no need to join Europe," he said in one particularly clear moment, "because it already is in Europe, at its center." Poland should become a full member of European political institutions like the European Union, he argued, "with its own values, without adapting itself uncritically and blindly to Western customs" (Kwitny 1997, 650). Poland, after all, was the "Christ of nations," sacrificed on the cross of imperial partition, only to rise again, in 1918 but also in 1989, to play its central role in European salvation (Szajkowski 1983).

Wojtyła was never a man of timid ambition or limited vision. Instead, he was a man who believed as a matter of religious doctrine that the Holy Spirit had chosen him, personally, to lead God's church through an era of great change in European society. It was his solemn and sacred duty, therefore, to be unmistakably clear about what he believed to be the proper future of European unity. The foundations of European identity, and therefore of any prospective unity, "are built on Christianity," he declared over and over again during his long reign on St. Peter's throne. "How can a common house for all of Europe be built," he asked in Poland in 1997 in a representative oration, "if it is not built with the bricks of men's consciences, baked in the fire of the Gospel, united by the bonds of fraternal social love, the fruit of the love of God?" (Pope John Paul II 1997, 27–28).[1]

Over time, John Paul II sought to turn this vision into reality, or at least save this vision from contemporary obliteration, through repeated admonishments to the peoples of the formerly communist countries of Europe to preserve their faithfulness in the face of their social and political integration with their Western neighbors. He implored his Polish compatriots to resist Western Europe's "civilization of desire and consumption" (Engelberg 1991, 3). He warned an audience in Prague that the newly freed peoples of Europe needed to "prepare immunizing defenses against certain viruses such as secularism, indifferentism, hedonistic consumerism, practical materialism, and the formal atheism that is so widely diffused today" (Bernstein and Politi 1997, 496). And very near the end of his long papacy, he begged Slovaks in a fragile voice never to forget as their "country becomes a full member of the European Union" that "great affluence can also generate great poverty," if society is not built on the "respect for human life in all its expressions" (Pope John Paul II 2003b). Summing up the theme rather eloquently in Ecclesia in Europa, John Paul II asserted that the Catholic Church of the formerly communist region "can offer Europe as it grows in unity, her attachment to the faith, her tradition inspired by religious devotion, the pastoral efforts of her bishops and priests, and certainly many other values on the basis of which Europe can become a reality endowed not only with higher economic standards but also with a profound spiritual life" (2003a). In short, John Paul II was a self-conscious leader of a transnational institution who wanted that institution to play what he saw as its rightful role in defining and shaping the structures of European politics in the very dynamic and portentous era in which he lived.

This chapter is an assessment of John Paul II's efforts to advance Christian union within contemporary Europe. But it is surely worth noting briefly the degree to which this vision also animates John Paul II's successor, Pope Benedict XVI. There are, I think, three relevant points to make in this regard. The first is that Pope Benedict, the former Cardinal Ratzinger, has adopted a pontifical style that is dramatically distinct from his predecessor's. There has been much less papal travel, much less papal fanfare, and many fewer papal statements that one could readily characterize as political. Benedict has been pope for just about two years at this writing, and it seems unlikely that he will carve out for himself the kind of grand (or even grandiose) political profile that characterized the long papacy of Pope John Paul II.

Having said that, Benedict definitely does share John Paul's conviction that Catholicism ought to play a prominent role in any future that can be described as authentically European. Benedict (Ratzinger), as a German, obviously does not manifest or embody John Paul's (Wojtyła's) Polish messianism. But Benedict is still a European pope, and it comes as no surprise therefore that he has firmly held views on what he calls "the contribution that Christianity has made and is continuing to make to building Europe" (Pope Benedict XVI 2005). In some ways, Benedict has even gone beyond his predecessor in this regard, worrying aloud that "Europe seems to be following a path that could lead to its departure from history." European identity, the German pope has said, is "comprised of a set of universal values that Christianity helped forge, thus giving Christianity not only a historical but a foundational role vis-à-vis Europe" (Pope Benedict XVI 2007). Benedict has also been outspoken in terms of the challenges currently posed to European Christianity by Islam, and in terms of his fervent desire to forge greater unity between Roman Catholicism and the Orthodox Christian churches of the East.

Third, it is notable and maybe even remarkable that the College of Cardinals chose yet another European to ascend the throne of Peter in 2005. With the demographic weight of the church shifting dramatically southward, the decision to elect Ratzinger as Benedict XVI revealed that the Catholic Church is still, at least at the level of its top leadership, a distinctly European institution with an identifiably European worldview and a clearly defined set of expectations for its role on the European continent. I will define both the transnational nature of this religious institution that these European men lead and the national contexts within Europe in which this institution actually lives much of its pastoral and political life. The purpose of this juxtaposition is to arrive at an assessment of the degree to which this transnational church can advance a coherent and consistent political program within particular national contexts.

A Transnational Church

The pope plays the leading role in setting the teachings of the church. He directs with absolute authority a Vatican bureaucracy tasked with ensuring that those teachings are promulgated and at least nominally enforced throughout the Catholic world. And he personally appoints each and every bishop in each and every Catholic diocese, and those bishops report either directly to him or to Vatican representatives who are fully beholden to him. Moreover, the pope is even deemed, according to Catholic doctrine, infallible (incapable of error) when speaking authoritatively on matters of faith and morals.[2] True, he plays a specifically territorial political role as the absolute monarch of the Vatican city-state in Rome. But as the unquestioned leader of the church's Holy See, and as the Supreme Pontiff of the universal Catholic Church, the pope is a paradigmatically transnational figure in world politics. He is, to put it another way, a nonstate actor of great repute and broad influence, and maybe even, in the words of Mikhail Gorbachev of all people, the "highest moral authority on earth" (Weigel 1999, 602).

But Catholic transnationalism is characterized by more than just the authority and universal status of the pope. Catholic transnationalism is also built on the institutional role and identity of the thousands of Catholic bishops who serve the church all around the globe. These men exercise fundamentally local authority in their individual dioceses, but that authority is only exercised legitimately because they are members of a collegial teaching authority that shares authority as a collective body over the entire church. This collegial teaching authority, or magisterium in Catholic parlance, along with each bishop's individual relationship with the bishop of Rome, renders Catholic bishops the central players in a kind of global/local dynamic that absolutely defines transnational Catholicism. These bishops can be usefully defined, I think, using Sidney Tarrow's category of "rooted cosmopolitans" (Tarrow 2005, 2). They have a transnational role and a transnational focus. But both are firmly grounded in a national foundation.

At the same time, these individual bishops are also members of specific national episcopal conferences, groups of bishops within each country who "form an association and meet together at fixed times" in order to "fulfill their office suitably and fruitfully" ("Decree on the Bishops' Pastoral Office in the Church" 1966). In practical terms, episcopal conferences are the specific vehicles for articulating and disseminating the social and theological teachings of today's Catholic Church. These conferences have the effect of nationalizing the day-to-day activities of an otherwise transnational·church, but they also provide institutionalized avenues of communication and inter-action for bishops from different, and especially neighboring, countries.

Each European country houses its own episcopal conference, of course. But interestingly enough, the church has also sought to accommodate its own governing structures to evolving political circumstances by establish-ing an entity called the Commission of the Bishops' Conferences of the European Community. This body is made up of bishops who are delegated by their individual national episcopal conferences to a supranational or-ganization that is served by an administrative secretariat based, appropri-ately enough, in Brussels.

The Catholic "people of God" also serve as an important layer of Catholic transnationalism, and, in this sense, the specifically Catholic ethos of collective identity has a particularly vibrant history in the European context. The original notion of Christendom was a Catholic notion, after all. Indeed, medieval Christendom is often cited as an indicator that European politics has not *always* been structured around individual states and there-fore does not necessarily have to be structured around individual states in the future (see Bull 2002, 255; Meyer 1989). Nelsen, Guth, and Fraser have argued, in fact, that this historically based transnational worldview renders the Catholic populations of Europe more amenable to notions of Euro-pean identity and perhaps European government than their Protestant and Orthodox neighbors are (Nelson, Guth, and Fraser 2001). The relevant point here is that like their bishops, though in very different ways, the Catholic peoples of Europe are also prepared by their shared religious tra-dition to conceive of themselves as a continental community.

These transnational characteristics of the Roman Catholic Church make it in some ways a model for what political scientists and students of inter-national relations have in mind when they speak of transnational actors on the world's political stage. That is presumably why Keohane and Nye's original volume on the subject included a chapter on Roman Catholicism (Vallier 1971). The problem for Pope John Paul II, however, and for his ambitious vision for Christian unity, was that in terms of his church's in-stitutional structures and political priorities, *trans*national never implied *non*national; the church's global scope never negated its local focus. In

Tarrow's descriptive term, the cosmopolitans never eschewed their roots. The pope, for example, could hold up his native Poland as a Catholic exemplar to the rest of Europe. He could insist that his church served as a symbol and instrument of unity across the continent. And he could personally travel across Europe calling in the post–cold war environment for renewed religious commitment, and for peace and reconciliation between Catholicism and other religious communities. But because of the multilayered and multileveled structure of the church itself, it was always the case that the actual advancement of any of these projects or hopes depended largely on parts of the church that were not fully controlled by the pope. Moreover, these nationally rooted elements of the church were often closely linked to historical traditions, political processes, and social conflicts that may not have reinforced the grand vision of European unity that was articulated by Pope John Paul II. To take one prominent example, it turned out that in the postcommunist context of the 1990s, the Catholic Church was in all sorts of ways at least as Polish as it was Roman.

Poland

As mentioned, Pope John Paul II viewed his native Poland as a necessary member of any authentically "European" community that might be built in the post–cold war era. Crucially, he also saw Poland, and its enduring Catholic identity, as a source of Christian renewal for the broader European community that could finally be built across the entire continent and not only on its western half. Poland's formal accession to the European Union proved a controversial prospect for some of the more Catholic, integralist camps in Polish politics, but the Polish pope was always in favor of it. John Paul wanted Poland to be part of "Europe," in all its manifestations. But that was because he thought that through that process, and in time, "Europe" would become more like Poland, rather than the other way around.

Just putting matters in such terms, of course, shows how sweeping, and one might even say quixotic, John Paul's vision for Europe's future actually was. But at the same time, recognizing the important role that Poland, and its enduring faithfulness to its Catholic identity, played in the Polish pope's transnational vision reminds us that this vision necessarily had to be artic-

ulated, given specific shape and form, and implemented through the context of individual national institutions and processes. To cite Tarrow one
more time, the pope's transnational vision needed to be "internalized"
through the "migration" of papal "international pressure" into "domestic
politics." (Tarrow 2005, 79). If the pope's renewed Christian European
unity relied upon Polish faithfulness, then a transnational political role for
the Roman Catholic Church relied equally clearly on a national political
role and influence for the Catholic Church *in Poland*.

There is a broader lesson here about the meaning and importance of
transnationalism as a category of political organization and behavior per se.
It may be true that states are "fading," if even just a little bit. Globalization,
regional integration, and the growing importance of nonstate actors from
al Qaeda to Google, may actually mean that we are entering the very early
stages of some kind of poststate era in world politics. It seems to me much
more likely, however, that we are instead in the process of taking greater
notice of the extent to which territorial states do not hold the stage of
world politics exclusively on their own. States are still the central fact of
international relations. But those states, and the political contexts they
define, are now engaged in complex relationships with nonstate entities of
all different kinds. What that means here is that one must pay careful attention to the multileveled relations that pertain between the Catholic
Church and European politics in the postcommunist era. The Vatican interacts with the EU, and the Vatican interacts directly with individual
member-states. But at the same time, the Vatican also interacts with Catholic
bishops inside those individual states, and those bishops themselves interact with their governments, with other political actors in domestic political
processes, and with bishops from other nations. This complexity is not a
conceptual difficulty in this case. It is, instead, a particularly clear example
of the kind of borderless political networks that the concept of "transnationalism" was originally designed to capture.

The Polish bishops, being Catholic bishops and being Polish, shared
their pope's conception of the roles that they, their church, and their nation
ought to play in articulating a new definition of European unity. Moreover,
they understood that Catholic Poland's role in these processes relied in
the very first place on Poland remaining in some way identifiably, reliably
Catholic. The Polish bishops' first political priority, therefore, after the
fall of communism, was to protect the Catholic Church's own institutional

interests by assuring its long-term ability to participate in Polish public life. And the most basic manifestation of those efforts was the Catholic hierarchy's attempt to influence the wording of the new Polish constitution.

The bishops' efforts in terms of the constitution involved four points. First, they called for a clear reference to God in the document's preamble, and for a prominent recognition of the church's role in the nation's history. Second, the bishops opposed any reference to the constitution as the "supreme" law, because, in the words of the secretary general of their episcopal conference, "the Lord God is the ultimate source of world order, and of laws that govern mankind" (Foreign Broadcast and Information Service 1994, 36). Third, they wanted the constitution to establish the Lord's "existing and unchangeable law" as the "foundation of the state's order" on issues related to "the natural forms of interaction" (37). In other (and clearer) terms, they wanted explicit constitutional provisions outlawing abortion from the moment of conception and banning gay marriage. Finally, the Polish bishops objected to any constitutional language describing a "separation" of church and state. Their argument in this case was that any declaration of separation would imply a need for separation, and that need might imply that the church under communism was a "religious association that [existed and operated] thanks to the state, that [was] ruled in line with the state's rules, and that could be dissolved because of the state's will" (38). The bishops decried any such implication of the term "separation," regardless of how indirect and implausible such an implication might seem to outsiders.

The bishops threw themselves into efforts to influence constitutional wording, but in the end they were fairly disappointed in the results. The "reference to God" issue was settled with a compromise statement, referring in equivalent terms to "those who believe in God," and "those not sharing such faith, but respecting those universal values as arising from other sources." Worse from the bishops' point of view, the constitution did refer to itself as the "supreme law" of the Republic of Poland. On the specific policies that the bishops wanted to be declared settled according to the Lord's "existing and unchangeable" law, however, the constitution did limit marriage to a "union of a man and a woman," and it did say that "the Republic of Poland shall ensure the legal protection of the life of every human being."[3] The latter formulation fell a bit short of the bishops' preferences, but it nevertheless proved sufficient in time to the task of voiding a liberalizing abortion law passed by Poland's parliament some years later.

The bishops' declaration of their own defeat in terms of the constitutional text, which led them to unsuccessfully recommend its rejection, was both overheated and shortsighted. Most of the disappointments claimed by leading bishops were actually compromises that at least paid some heed to the church's concerns. And in many ways, not least of which was the stipulation in the constitution that relations between the government and the church would be governed largely through a formal concordat between the Polish state and the Holy See, the interests of the Catholic Church were actually fairly well represented in the final draft.

The problem that the bishops had with the compromises in the constitution was the very fact that they were compromises. The church's successes under communism had been few and far between, of course. But the church nevertheless enjoyed in that period an unrivaled status as the representative of authentic national consciousness. In the heady days immediately following the fall of communism, the church was free to trade on that status and play a central role in the formation of all sorts of public policies. But by the time the constitution was being ratified in 1997, the Catholic Church had been joined in political contestation by a multitude of interest groups, political parties, and social institutions of all kinds. The vibrant civil society for which the church had substituted for so long was coming into being, and in that shifting context, the church in Poland was now only one political actor among many others. The church was still a very important institution in Polish public life. But the church was no longer the overriding social and political institution it had been in Polish civil society during communism. In a word, pluralism was taking root in Poland, and the Catholic bishops would have to learn to advance their interests, not through presumed legitimacy and exclusive negotiation with a repressive regime, but rather through navigation of the complex, uncertain, and transparent processes of modern democratic government.

The power of national context could be seen with particular clarity in terms of electoral politics and the development of the Polish party system in the postcommunist era. Immediately after communism fell, the old joke that wherever you found three Poles you were likely to find four political parties was nearly lived out in reality. The Polish population responded to the rebirth of democracy with a veritable explosion of party fragmentation. This was particularly true on the right end of the political spectrum, where the church's political allies were most likely to be found. What that meant for the church's approach to national politics was that the bishops were forced to accept that their role in public life was not likely to be articulated through the voice of a particular political party. There were so many parties in play, and any party to which the church might pledge its allegiance would only be able to garner a small percentage of the electorate in such a fragmented system. What's more, such a party, like many others, might not even exist for more than one turn in a rapidly spinning electoral cycle.

The bishops have to accommodate themselves to the fact that Poland is now a firmly consolidated democracy where political power is transferred peacefully through the ballot box, fairly regularly actually, as the electorate's preferences swing from one set of partisan forces to another. Sometimes the leadership of the church will be sympathetic to the governing parties in Warsaw, and sometimes they will not be. But in this specific political environment and partisan context, the bishops were challenged to shift their understanding of their own political influence from elite bargaining to interest mobilization among the Polish people. The Roman Catholic Church, in that sense, had to project its political influence in Poland *as a Polish church*. It had to preserve its institutional and political role in Europe, not in the abstract arena of "europeanness," but in the very concrete context of a rapidly evolving Polish party system, and also in a remarkably complex democratic governing structure. Semi-presidentialism, coalition cabinets, bicameralism, judicial review, proportional representation—none of these postcommunist institutions were likely to make a Polish bishop nostalgic for the deprivations of communism. But they certainly did make political life remarkably more complicated.

Similar dynamics face Catholic bishops in other places, of course. But in each place, certainly in each postcommunist state, the political challenges and institutional complexities are unique to that specific place. The people of the Slovak Republic, for example, like all their neighbors from the former Warsaw Pact, had to build democracy and a free economy—at the same time and under very difficult conditions. However, the Slovaks, unlike, say, the Poles or the Hungarians, also had to actually build a new Slovak state. And they had to do so among a population that included over a half million souls who had no interest whatsoever in being Slovak, in any meaningful sense of the term.

Slovakia

The deeply transnational nature of the Catholic Church makes it at least possible that shared religious identity within the church might create solidarity and cooperation that can overcome, or at least ameliorate, divergent national or ethnic identities that create political conflict. National hierarchies, and in different ways national laities, share all sorts of transnational interactions and institutional commonalities. Indeed, Pope John Paul II repeatedly emphasized these ties and repeatedly called for his church to transcend its national and ethnic divisions through greater attention to its Catholic unity. These were not surprising positions for the late pope to take, of course. A central theme of his entire papacy, after all, was the notion of a renewed and reconceived definition of European community based on Catholic teaching, and on the shared Christian heritage of the otherwise diverse European peoples.

Between Catholic Croats and Orthodox Serbs, for example, religious identity tended to reinforce national identity and thereby drive the two communities ever further from each other. But if Catholic identity is able to transcend national identity in a way that ameliorates rather than reinforces ethnic conflict, then we ought to be able to observe such a dynamic in relations between Catholic Hungarians and Catholic Slovaks. In short, we ought to be able to see Catholicism serving as a source of unity for these two European peoples.

The breakup of Czechoslovakia through the Velvet Divorce of 1992–1993 is sometimes referred to as a model for peaceful resolution of competing national claims in the postcommunist context. Regardless of what the divorce meant for Czechs and Slovaks, the split may have actually served to heighten ethnic tensions between Slovaks and *Hungarians* in the new Slovak Republic that emerged. The several hundred thousand ethnic Hungarians residing just within the southern border of Slovakia were transformed overnight from citizens of a self-consciously multiethnic Czechoslovakia, rhetorically in thrall to international socialism, to citizens of a spanking new Slovakia, whose first independent government was anxious to bolster its legal autonomy through greater emphasis on its national Slovak identity.

As a result, long-standing ethnic tensions in southern Slovakia (which, by the way, had been known as "northern Hungary" for centuries) were purposefully manipulated for political advantage by Vladimír Mečiar, a former communist functionary who dominated (and blighted) the politics of independent Slovakia throughout the 1990s. Mečiar and his allies, both within his own movement for a Democratic Slovakia and within the even more virulent Slovak National Party, repeatedly adopted rhetoric and policies clearly designed to enflame ethnic divisions within the Slovak Republic, and to set up the Hungarian minority population as a convenient scapegoat for the many political, social, and economic problems faced by the newly independent Slovak state (see Carpenter 1997).

The Catholic Church was involved in these circumstances in a number of ways. First of all, the Catholic Church has been closely linked to Slovak national identity for centuries. In historic terms, the Catholic clergy played an important role in identifying a separate Slovak nation within the old Hungarian kingdom, for example by championing and transcribing an independent and separate Slovak literary language (Brock 1979). The church also served as the social and institutional setting for the reaffirmation of Slovak nationalism between the two world wars. And Jozef Tiso, the leader of the Nazi client state of the 1940s, was himself a Catholic priest (Jelinek 1976). This church, perhaps in part because of these national credentials, suffered tremendously under communist rule in Czechoslovakia. But the church emerged from the revolution of 1989 in relatively vibrant institutional health, and its leaders once again sought to associate themselves publicly with Slovak cultural and political autonomy.

However, and importantly, unlike many other churches with similarly close ties to a national history (for example, the Catholic Church in Poland or the Romanian Orthodox Church), the Catholic Church in the Slovak Republic has within its ranks a large, unassimilated national minority population. Not only is a majority of the Hungarian population of the Slovak Republic also Catholic, but the Catholic Church also served in historical terms as an important locus of Hungarian national identity in this particular region as well. Some observers have argued, moreover, that the Catholic Church's identification with the rights of Hungarians living outside the borders of the Hungarian state has served for years as the central nationalist credential for a Catholic Church in Hungary not otherwise known for its nationalist zeal (Laszlo 1991).

Pope John Paul II made it clear that he wished these Slovak and Hungarian Catholics would use their shared Catholicism as the basis of national reconciliation between their communities. During a visit to Hungary in 1991, the pope spoke vividly of the need to protect minority rights throughout the postcommunist region, of "the need to overcome prejudices or hostilities inherited from history." He also pointedly reminded Slovaks in attendance (in the Slovak language) that he expected them to commit themselves to mutual respect and "tolerant behavior" (BBC 1991). Four years later, speaking during his first visit to an independent Slovakia, John Paul II (1995) reminded the Slovak Bishops Conference that "besides Slovaks, Catholics belonging to other national communities (in notable measure Hungarians) also live in your country," as he called on the prelates to "respect the rights and duties both of the majority community as well as those of the minority communities present in the nation." Calls such as these for his church to play a constructive role in interethnic relations were a central aspect of the pope's program for a reconstituted Christian unity on the European continent. Any real progress toward his vision, after all, would require real cooperation and real levels of mutual support among the various national elements of the Catholic community across Europe.

How successful, then, was the pope in this regard? What was the nature of the relationship between Slovak and Hungarian Catholics during his papacy? And what does that relationship tell us in more general terms about the potential for the Catholic Church to serve as an institutionalized instrument of European union? At the level of the leadership of the church, relations both within Slovakia and between Hungary and Slovakia could best be characterized as strained. Formal meetings were held, for example, between the Slovak and Hungarian Bishops Conferences, and during John Paul's frequent travels, large delegations from one conference would be welcomed by the other conference whenever the pope was visiting one site or the other. These two episcopal conferences also interacted with each other directly on the specific question of ethnic relation between Slovaks and Hungarians within the Slovak Republic. The Slovak bishops, for example, sent Hungarian-speaking seminarians to Hungary for theological instruction on the assumption that these priests-in-training would later serve in the Hungarian-majority parishes in the south of the Slovak Republic. In addition, Hungarian bishops offered to join with their Slovak colleagues in resisting a particularly restrictive, and manifestly anti-Hungarian, language law when it was proposed by Mečiar's government in 1995.

I do not have the space to evaluate these matters in detail here, but suffice it to say that relations, interepiscopal relations, as it were, were neither as cohesive as these introductory remarks might suggest them to be, nor as mutually cooperative as Pope John Paul II surely wanted them to be. The seminarian exchange program was quite limited, for example, and in fact a source of considerable friction between the two capitals; the "offer" of cooperation on the language law was more or less rebuffed by the leadership of the Slovak conference, who viewed attempts by the Hungarian bishops to advocate on behalf of Hungarian language rights as "wholly unnecessary"; and personal relations between the two groups of very proud men tend toward the chilly.[4]

Any firm conclusions about day-to-day relations between the Hungarian and Slovak Catholics who actually live, work, and worship together along the Slovak-Hungarian border would require a level of detailed knowledge that could only be gained from a kind of intensive ethnographic research that I have not conducted. Speaking more anecdotally, however, one must concede that relations between these communities are relatively peaceful, if the standard used is, say, sectarian conflict in the former Yugoslavia. There has been no violence to speak of; local conflicts get worked out, by and large, at the local level; and thousands of Hungarian and Slovak Catholics attend services each Sunday in either joint or adjoining parishes without incident. But again, just as with their bishops, relations among these two Catholic populations are strained and, importantly, defined by their ethnic divisions.

Hungarian citizens of the Slovak Republic, for example, have complained for years about the shortage of Hungarian-speaking priests sent to serve in their dioceses, just as they have bemoaned the lack of a bishop with "Hungarian blood" (whatever that is) to lead a diocese they would like to see established around their cultural and population center of Komárno. For their part, Slovak Catholics, or at least those who take the time to comment on the issue, tend to dismiss Hungarian complaints as sour grapes, and even claim that it is Hungarian language priests who discriminate against Slovak parishioners in mixed-language parishes. Whatever truth is contained in these charges and countercharges, it is clear that for at least significant segments of the two populations, substantial ethnic tension and resentment still endure within the Slovak Church.

Maybe it is that very phrase—"the Slovak Church"—which defines the matter most clearly. Slovak leaders of the Catholic Church within the

Slovak Republic, lay and episcopal, tend to remain devoted to Slovak national aspirations and to the traditional ties between those aspirations and the Roman Catholic Church. These leaders are more than willing to serve the religious needs of Hungarian Catholics within their dioceses and parishes, so long as those Hungarians do not threaten the status of the church in Slovakia as a Slovak institution. This insistence on national control of a central national institution, together with the separation between Slovak Catholicism and Hungarian Catholicism that results from it, suggests that the common Catholic identity that unites these two communities has not been able to supercede the divergent national identities that divide them. And so long as that is true, then it seems fairly obvious that the Catholic Church can act as no more than a very limited vehicle of ethnic reconciliation in the region, if even that. Neither the church's clearly transnational institutional structure, nor its self-consciously global pastoral ethos, nor even the clearly expressed wishes of its pope, can erase long-standing ethnic divisions that fly directly in the face of a vision of European Catholic unity, as defined in Rome. The words of the pope do not, on their own, create new political realities in terms of European unity. John Paul II said repeatedly that he wanted his church to be an agent of unity in post–cold war Europe. But in the very specific case of the Slovak Republic, John Paul II's church turned out to be more of an arena of ethnic conflict than it did an instrument of supranational unity.

When I first came to this understanding in the process of writing a book on the church in postcommunist Europe (Byrnes 2001), I was tempted to draw the more general, but too simplistic, conclusion that this is a case where nationalism had won out over religion. I decided, however, that such a conclusion would not acknowledge the degree to which religion actually serves as a basis for nationalism in the first place. Catholicism was not simply trumped by Slovak and Hungarian nationalism in this case. Instead, and frankly more interestingly, the religion that the two peoples share—Catholicism—was itself deeply related to and deeply implicated in the very national identities that divide the two communities so fundamentally. That kind of highly complex connectedness between transnational religion and national context is not very easily disentangled. Indeed, that kind of complex interconnectedness can also come to define, and frustrate, the unifying efforts of even the most transnational of religious actors—the Roman Catholic pope himself.

Croatia

Any concrete advancement of Pope John Paul II's vision for European union, characterized by and furthered by Catholic tradition, required more than the support and success of individual bishops living in specific national contexts, and even more than interethnic cooperation between and among Europe's many Catholic national communities. In addition to all that, advancement of the Polish pope's hopes for Europe also required that he personally overcome the historical and political contexts in which his own words and actions were understood and given meaning by specific audiences. Whether John Paul II liked it or not, the very meaning of his words as pope were powerfully shaped by the local contexts in which they were uttered, local contexts which themselves were deeply influenced by the traditional role that the Catholic Church had played in particular national settings. When the pope turned his attention to the Balkan wars of the 1990s, for example, one could say that he was, in part, trapped by his church's history in the region. His contemporary political role was, in large part, destined to be shaped by historical factors that had taken on a life of their own.

Pope John Paul II, along with most of the civilized world, looked on in horror as Yugoslavia burst into chaos and violence after the fall of the communist regime. The pope used his uniquely prominent pulpit to good use in those days, speaking out persistently and specifically in favor of respect for individual human rights as well as for the collective rights of the several national communities that were emerging from the crumbling Yugoslav Federation. In a typical statement at a General Audience in Rome in 1991, John Paul asked Croatian refugees to "know that the Pope is close to you [and] to all those who are suffering from this senseless war in your beloved land" (Pope John Paul II 1992, 62). And in the same year, he intoned from his apartment window one Sunday afternoon, that as pope, he was "begging the international organizations and all persons of good will who are in a position to stop this war, to make every possible effort to put an end to the fratricidal violence which is bathing defenseless peoples in blood" (Pope John Paul II 1992, 51).

On the formal diplomatic track, the Holy See's secretariat of state engaged in multifaceted efforts to attract greater attention to the brewing crisis in the Balkans. Vatican diplomats worked at the Organization for

Security and Cooperation in Europe in Vienna and the European Union in Brussels to try to convince European states to press harder for a peaceful solution to the conflicts in Croatia and Bosnia that were then threatening to turn genocidal. And once the pope's diplomatic representatives had lost all hope of a revived federation, or even a redesigned confederation, as solutions to the problem, the Holy See formally recognized the breakaway Republics of Croatia and Slovenia as a way of helping to clarify Belgrade's actions as "international aggression."

It would be hard to argue that the Holy See plays a central role in modern European diplomacy, and I am certainly not doing so here. For many Europeans, surely, things like Vatican embassies, or the Holy See's membership at the OSCE, are seen as either quaint nonentities or bothersome anachronisms. But in this particular case, the Holy See did actually play a fairly influential role. The pope's representatives aggressively cajoled other European states on these matters; the Holy See used its seat at the OSCE as the pulpit from which to preach its preferences; and as a matter of historical record, the Vatican did offer recognition to Croatia and Slovenia first, in hopes that any attendant publicity would nudge EU member states to follow.

At a more personal level, the pope supported these diplomatic efforts by making the crisis a central focus of his multifaceted public activities. And not surprisingly, given his peripatetic style, the traveling pope's interests turned to the prospect of visiting the former Yugoslav Republics as a "pilgrim of peace." His hope was to make well-publicized successive visits in the fall of 1994 to Zagreb (Croatia), Belgrade (Serbia), and Sarajevo (Bosnia-Herzegovina) in order to express his sorrow at the violence and his hopes for reconciliation. In the event, however, Serbian Orthodox objection to the Roman pope's presence scuttled the stop in Belgrade, security concerns kept the pope from Sarajevo, and the pilgrimage of peace to the three troubled capitals ended up as a visit to Zagreb—Catholic Zagreb. And that major change in itinerary opened the whole trip up to the charge that the pope's presence in Zagreb, at that particular moment, was a sectarian act designed to offer his pastoral support to an embattled Catholic nation, and even more problematically, his political endorsement to that nation's controversial president, Franjo Tudjman.

While in Zagreb, John Paul II did, in fact, reemphasize his support for Croat independence. And in saying that an "individual nation" within a federation is free "to leave and organize itself as an independent state," he was (surely self-consciously) endorsing the (at that time still controversial) Croat national reading of the Yugoslav constitution (Cohen 1994). But it would not be fair to characterize the pope's message in Zagreb, as some critics did at the time, as a narrowly sectarian one. At the same time that he celebrated Croat independence, the pope also reminded the Catholics of Croatia that it was their "sacred duty" to seek a "culture of peace that does not reject a healthy patriotism, but that keeps far away from the ex-asperations and exclusions of nationalism" (Cohen 1994). Reminding Croats that as pope he "had tried every means [and] knocked on every door" in order to stop "this bloody fratricidal war," John Paul implored his Catholic listeners to remember that "wounds produced by hatred will not be healed by rancor, but rather by the therapy of patience and the balm of forgive-ness" (Montalbano 1994).

In a certain sense, however, it did not really matter what the pope said in Zagreb, or how often he said it. His presence in that city, in that very specific national context, was bound to be interpreted by parties to the conflict in a more narrow way, in a word, in a specifically "Catholic" man-ner. I am not denying that he was, from his point of view, what he said he was—a "defenseless pilgrim" imploring Catholics, Orthodox, and Muslims alike to reject "bloody fratricidal war" and to recommit themselves to the "reciprocal tolerance and exemplary collaboration" that Yugoslavia had once symbolized (Montalbano 1994). But Karol Wojtyła of Krakow was not speaking in Zagreb as the leader of some kind of global peace movement, or as the executive director of some transnational NGO. He was speaking as Pope John Paul II, the unquestioned leader and spokesman of the Roman Catholic Church, the same Roman Catholic Church that had played such an important role in Croat national history, and the same Roman Catholic Church that in the eyes of many in the former Yugoslavia (whether fairly or unfairly) was deeply implicated in the nationalist excesses that had defined Croatia's history.

Characterizing the historic role of the Catholic Church in Croatia is no simple matter and therefore I will attempt no simple characterizations here. Indeed, in this case it is not necessary at all for me to offer conclu-sions on matters that are of such great contestation and controversy. The most prominent examples from the World War II era are the following: Was the Catholic Church in Croatia implicated in the brutal practices of the Ustaše regime that governed Croatia during the war? Or did the Catholic Church try to distance itself from the government and from its undeniable excesses? Was Archbishop Alojzije Stepinac an apologist for that wartime regime (and thereby at least an accessory to war crimes)? Or was he instead a courageous patriot who spoke out against the Ustaše in the name of authentic Croat patriotism (and therefore a national hero and a Catholic saint)?[5]

In the 1990s, at the time of the pope's trip to Zagreb, questions such as these, and the debates to which they refer, were matters of great political importance and prominence across the former Yugoslavia and beyond. For politicians, journalists, and the men and women of the region (not to mention, by the way, Western scholars), the very words, "Stepinac" or "Catholic" or "Ustaše" were enough to spark heated argument that transcended historical "facts" and virtually defied unbiased interpretation.

The second observation is that this highly charged context allowed the pope's words and actions to be distorted and stretched to fit all kinds of political agendas. In fact, it appeared in practice that it was virtually impossible for Pope John Paul II, the "defenseless pilgrim" of peace, to separate himself and his intentions from these highly sectarian controversies and conflicts.

Pope John Paul II visited Zagreb twice in this period (the second time to beatify Archbishop Stepinac, thereby placing him one step away from sainthood). The pope did not intend either of these trips as a "benediction for Croatian statehood and the (Croatian) government's struggles against Serbs."[6] In fact, I would be willing to stipulate that the pope's intentions were more likely the exact opposite of such a claim. I also would not accept that Pope John Paul II either shared or endorsed Tudjman's "nationalist excesses," nor that the pope in Zagreb "only repeated what . . . Tudjman had already said."[7] Indeed, these distortions of the pope's intentions are pretty much absurd, on their face, and I do not want to lend them credence by repeating them. What I do want to argue, however, is that these claims and distortions were both inevitable and significant. In short, the transnational pope's voluminous and laudable statements in favor of peace in the Balkans must be understood in terms of the very specific national setting in which they were uttered, or at least received.

Pope John Paul II was an undeniably global figure who led a church that is paradigmatically transnational in both structure and, in many ways, in ethos. But that very same church also lives much of its institutional and political life in decidedly particular local and national places. As the leader of that local church in Croatia, no less than he was the leader of the global church in Rome, Pope John Paul II could not escape the historical controversies and contemporary loyalties that clung to the church in Croatia like a tightly fitted jacket. Indeed, when I consider John Paul's provocative decision to declare at that very heated and freighted moment that Archbishop Stepinac had been called to join the church's "blessed," I must admit that I am left wondering whether the pope himself was really able to view events in the Balkans from something other than a Catholic, and therefore in this case an inevitably Croat, perspective.

THE CENTRAL QUESTION I have been considering in this chapter is whether or not the political activities of the transnational Catholic Church in postcommunist Europe amount to a cohesive, consistent, and coordinated role in setting the trajectory of European political life. Does this church act, in any meaningful sense, as a single entity, under the direction of its pope, as it faces the great challenges of European life after the revolution of 1989? Did it manifest the unity of purpose that Pope John Paul II clearly wanted it to embody as he spent twenty-seven years positioning his church as a kind of alternative locus of a European "union" built on more than shared markets and a common currency? Based on the brief review that I have been able to present here, I would have to say that the evidence on this question is mixed. Therefore, any conclusions drawn from that evidence must be relatively cautious.

In some ways, transnational Catholicism exhibits an impressive degree of unity of purpose as it seeks to preserve and defend its place in European social and political life. In part, this unity is a function of the remarkable discipline that a highly centralized authority structure imposes on the words and actions of the church's clerical leadership. There is, for example, broad agreement among bishops, regardless of their nationality, that the European "community" must be animated by religion and culture, just as there is a shared commitment to the conviction that their church should play a prominent role in defining that community in the future.

This level of institutional cohesiveness should not surprise us, of course. These bishops share much more than an evident devotion to the Catholic Church and to its teaching and traditions. They also share the experience of professional and spiritual formation within a system that marks them for life as priests and bishops of their church. That system, along with the pontiff in Rome, who is in a sense its pinnacle, is a very powerful force for unity within the church. Indeed, that system would be the envy of any transnational body seeking to articulate and advance a coherent global agenda.

However, despite these institutional dynamics, the transnational Catholic Church remains, still, deeply local and nationally rooted in terms of its outlook and conception of itself. In terms of the church's political role, the remarkable cohesiveness of the church's institutional structure is counteracted in the first place by the idiosyncratic national structures and processes within which that political role must be played. But even more significantly (and perhaps distressingly), the cohesiveness of the church's approach to political conditions in Europe is also counteracted at the moment by the national(ist?) focus that frustrated John Paul II in Slovakia, and that attached itself to his own person in Croatia.

There is, again, a broader lesson to be drawn from the relationship between global and local, or transnational and national, within Catholicism. The Roman Catholic Church is one of the world's oldest global institutions; the very term "Catholic" denotes, after all, a broad frame of reference. Nevertheless, the cases I have reviewed here have revealed the church also to be a stubbornly local institution, tightly organized by national community, and quite often deeply devoted to the narrow interests of a particular national population. The set of institutional relationships implied in these observations pretty much defines one category of transnational relations, while at the same time setting the limits of its political scope and analytical utility.

The Catholic Church's difficulty in coordinating its role in the revolutionary and portentous context of postcommunist Europe suggests that other transnational institutions—religious communities, commercial enterprises, and political entities of all kinds—are likely to find it at least as difficult to overcome the national parochialisms that lie just beneath the surface of the complex phenomenon known as globalization. There is no need to strain too hard for broader, generally applicable conclusions, however. It is surely self-serving of me to say so, but the Catholic Church is a large, almost uniquely universal institution that is deeply embedded in virtually every level of contemporary world politics, from the most systemically global to the most locally individual. Analysis of the political role of this institution ought to be able to stand on its own. But any analysis of the church's political role must be grounded in close attention to the ways in which the church is, at one and the same time, both defined by and limited by its transnational institutional structure. The Vatican's hope that a revitalized Catholic Church will sit near the heart of what Pope John Paul II called Europe's common home is being frustrated today by the combined effects of secularism in the West and uncertainty in the East. However, at an even more fundamental level, the Vatican's vision of European unity is also being blurred by the national structures and national identities that are deeply rooted in the very life of the church itself.

8

CORRUPT

EXCHANGE IN

DIVIDED SOCIETIES

THE INVISIBLE POLITICS OF

STABILITY IN MACEDONIA

Robert Hislope

> The mafia represents the best example of
> interethnic cooperation in the Balkans.
> —*A popular joke in Macedonia*

Anticorruption rhetoric is a central part of the dominant discourse that shapes global politics today.[1] The UN, the EU, the World Bank, and scores of other IGOs, as well as an array of NGOs (Transparency International, the Open Society Institute, etc.) have identified corruption as *the* major barrier to economic and political development. Since the 1990s, the international community has launched a host of initiatives and campaigns aimed at eradicating corrupt practices and promoting good governance in developing southern countries and transitioning eastern countries (Eigen 2002; World Bank 2000). Behind this new, post–cold war consensus is the premise that transparency and accountability will bolster markets and help secure private property rights, constrain rent-seeking bureaucrats, promote democracy, and contribute to political stability.

This essay questions these purported political payoffs and advances the reverse thesis; namely, in deeply divided societies, where political consensus is thin and the state is weak, corruption can provide a much-needed adhesive for political stability. Corruption in fact can be conceived as a strategic maneuver adopted by state actors when the instruments of consent and coercion are not politically viable. By promoting a policy of zero-tolerance for corruption, the international community may in fact undermine frail states by eliminating the only political mechanism that stands between politics-as-bargaining and politics-as-war.

In ethnically divided societies, corrupt exchange across ethnic lines may work to tame the destructive impulses of nationalism. Ethnic party systems are prone to a politics of centrifugal outbidding because competition occurs within ethnic blocs and is driven by flanking parties pushing a maximalist ethnic agenda. In these conditions, interethnic party relations tend to be marked by a basic lack of political consensus regarding the character of the constitutional order and the legitimacy of the state. Corruption represents a political lever or mechanism that can break this impasse and convince impassioned chauvinists to cooperate across ethnic lines. Because corruption at the commanding heights of the state involves substantial material rewards if not "control over the distribution of modernity itself" (Theobold 1990, 123), those who participate in corrupt networks have a substantial interest in maintaining the status quo (Bates 1974; Huntington 1968). By giving each group a stake in the system, interethnic corrupt exchange creates an incentive structure that promotes cooperation over conflict. Likewise, corrupt multiethnic ruling coalitions are more likely to create demobilizing regimes, as no coalition member has an interest in agitating and mobilizing its community against the other. The upshot is regime stability, an unintentional public good produced by actors pursuing private benefits. In the long term, corrupted interests may turn into vested interests, demanding a new legal framework that legitimizes ill-gotten gains but also strengthens the institutions of the state. In short, therefore, the basic proposition explored here is that corrupt exchange among ethnic party elites fosters durable multiethnic coalition government and thereby reduces the possibility of interethnic violence.

Unlike most of the former Yugoslav republics, Macedonia succeeded in maintaining interethnic peace for the first decade of its independence. This was a remarkable achievement, particularly given the severity of its internal ethnic cleavages and the numerous external challenges posed by neighboring states. A key factor that made this possible was corrupt exchange between Macedonian and Albanian party elites, which facilitated effective elite unity and enabled the regime to survive several domestic and regional crises. Over time, however, changing regional conditions contributed to the rise of new political forces in the Albanian community. Nascent Albanian elites blamed Skopje's ruling coalition for derailing progress on Albanian rights in exchange for the enrichment of politicians. They subsequently launched an insurgency in 2001 that shattered Macedonia's delicate peace and brought the country to the brink of civil war. Thus, the mechanism of corrupt exchange purchased a temporary peace in Macedonia but ultimately could not contain new political forces emerging from an unstable region.

The sections below contain the following themes: an exploration of the theoretical literature on the links between corruption and political outcomes (such as interethnic peace and regime stability); a consideration of the role played by international forces and actors that introduced and pushed the anticorruption campaign in Macedonia; and a detailed discussion of how corrupt exchange within interethnic ruling coalitions contributed, at different moments in Macedonia's transition, to both interethnic elite unity and minority rebellion.

The Transnational Politics of Anticorruption Discourse and Practices

Corruption is notoriously difficult to define. For some, it centers on the use of public office for private gain; for others, it violates public expectations and the public interest; and for still others, it represents the moral decay and perversion of the public sphere.[2] As a perennial political problem, it has inspired a variety of vivid metaphors, such as *cancer* or *rust,* and sometimes *oil, grease,* or *lubricant* (Elster 1989). This study examines the appropriateness of a different set of metaphors: can corruption provide effective *glue* or *cement* for a deeply divided society? In weak states, when politically significant actors lack basic agreement over the rightness of the constitutional order, can corruption serve as a *"hyphen* which joins, a *buckle* which fastens the otherwise separate and conflicting elements of a society into a body politic?" (Leys 1965, 219).

The dominant discourse in the global community answers with an unqualified "no" to the above questions. In the current era of globalization, corruption is framed solely in "cancerous" terms—it is said to be uniformly harmful to economic growth, the institutional effectiveness of the state, the consolidation of democracy, and the reinvigoration of civil society in transitioning and developing countries.[3] Enforcing this consensus is a vast array of international organizations, Western governments, and numerous influential INGOs, all of whom pressure developing nations and post-communist regimes to root out corrupt practices. For example, the OECD takes an absolutist position on corruption, regarding it as unacceptable no matter the "value of the advantage, its results, [or] perceptions of local custom" (OECD 1997). It is no longer enough for developing and transitioning countries to accept economic liberalism and endure the structural adjustment demands of Western creditors. On the contrary, political and economic decisions must become more transparent, and the state more accountable for its management of aid and loan packages. This global anticorruption agenda has been promoted with such a missionary zeal that some call it the new "ethical infrastructure" of capitalism (Cirtautas 2001).

The nonstate transnational actors that monitor and police the anticorruption agenda can potentially exert an enormous influence on the domestic politics of southern and eastern transitioning countries. Organizations like Transparency International, the Open Society Institute, and the International Crisis Group hire country monitors with staff and a budget, interview elites at all levels of government, investigate corruption claims, and write reports whose results influence the court of world opinion as well as the course of domestic politics. Domestic politicians themselves have numerous incentives to be compliant with such nonstate monitors, as a favorable rating on a TI scale or some other investment climate index can help enhance the country's image and thereby assist the realization of other ends, such as securing a loan from the IMF, attracting foreign investment, or gaining entry into an important IGO. However, the relationship between domestic and transnational actors can turn in antagonistic directions as well. Meddlesome INGO activists can run afoul of government interests and become the target of repression. Additionally, internationally driven anticorruption campaigns are vulnerable to being high-jacked by opposition parties and the domestic media who seek to score political points against ruling parties. Indeed, the current anticorruption milieu is capable of fostering a destructive political dialectic of scandalization, in which government and opposition get entangled in increasingly sensationalized charges of wrongdoing. In this political game, demonizing one's political adversaries becomes an electoral strategy that trumps serious anticorruption reform (Blankenburg 2002; Heidenheimer 1996; Krastev 2004).

The fact that the international anticorruption agenda can generate tensions and unanticipated outcomes in target states should come as no surprise; for the very origins of the agenda have as much to do with advancing Western interests as they do with promoting good governance in transitioning and developing countries. During the cold war, developing nations were forced to choose sides in the bipolar rivalry but then were subject to little scrutiny regarding business transactions, development projects, the management of loans, etc. Robin Theobold, for example, speaks of the "eerie silence, which prevailed [on the corruption issue] during most of the previous thirty years" (1999, 491–502). According to some critics, corruption among Third World allies was not only tolerated by successive U.S. administrations but also became an integral part of the U.S. alliance system (Chomsky and Herman 1979). The collapse of the Soviet Union, however, altered the strategic function of corruption. Whereas previously widespread corruption among Third World politicians, military figures, bureaucrats, and the local business class was calculated as part of the price of containing communism, now corruption represented a protectionist barrier that limited foreign investment and gave local actors unfair economic advantages. The transnational actors enlisted in the fight against corruption ostensibly promote government accountability, the rule of law, and the invigoration of civil society, but their mission also directly serves the interests of global capital. It is for this reason that Ivan Krastev suggests Transparency International "can be viewed as an instrument of a policy that was already agreed in [the] World Bank and US State Department" (2004, 13).

Given the prevailing discourse on corruption, it is instructive to consider a strand of thought from the 1960s literature on modernization and development that advocated a very different position. At this time, scholars such as Samuel Huntington (1968), Joseph Nye (1967), and James Scott

(1972) argued that corruption could, in some circumstances, actually facilitate political and economic development (see also Bayley 1966; Leff 1964;
Leys 1965). Collectively labeled the "revisionists," these thinkers were
themselves reacting to an earlier "moralist" tradition of thought that failed
to appreciate the multiple functions and unintentional effects of corruption
and could offer only an absolutist normative critique against it. Spurred on
by the practical problems associated with development, the revisionists
identified a number of political benefits that corruption could deliver, such
as providing an alternative form of interest articulation and inclusion for
the dispossessed, a means of accommodating or co-opting a recalcitrant
opposition, and furnishing additional instruments for the promotion of
elite unity and national integration.

In the last several years, revisionist insights have been revived by a hand-
ful of scholars who challenge the anticorruption discourse. For example, in
his celebrated study of "violent entrepreneurs," Vadim Volkov (2002) advances the compelling argument that organized crime played a vital role in
protecting private property during Russia's postcommunist transition. The
idea of the state as a "protection racket" or "organized crime" has in fact
inspired several studies that explore the links between corruption and the
general process of state-building (Reno 2002; Tilly 1986; Yarrington 2003).
Moreover, a growing number of scholars emphasize corruption comes in
many forms and contexts and therefore does not generate a single outcome
but several (Andreas 2004; Andvig and Fjeldstad 2000; Johnston 1986). In
the section below, revisionist ideas on corruption are resurrected and re-
molded into a framework for understanding how corrupt exchange among
rival ethnic elites can produce politically beneficial results.

Divided Societies, Multiethnic Coalitions, and the Limits of Corrupt Exchange

In his seminal study of the political patterns of ethnicity, Donald Horowitz
(1985) found little reason to expect that interethnic coalitions would be
durable and contribute to political stability. Based on his survey of plural
societies in Asia, Africa, and the Caribbean, Horowitz distinguished between two types of coalitions, those of convenience and those of commitment. A coalition of convenience is an alliance of two (or more) parties

representing different ethnic constituencies who coalesce for the purpose of forming government. The coalition of commitment comes together to establish government as well, but an additional motive is a political consensus among its member parties to ameliorate ethnic problems. Both coalition types are built on reciprocity, and both tend toward a quick disintegration, often due to intraethnic pressure. The average life of coalitions of convenience was slightly more than a year, while the one coalition of commitment Horowitz analyzed failed to last through a single election cycle.

Ethnicity poses a unique set of challenges for any political order. There is a wealth of literature on ethnic politics demonstrating its intense emotional quality, its zero-sum competitive logic, and its frustrating intractability. The "stateness problem," for example, poses a formidable obstacle for transitioning regimes (Dahl 1991; Linz and Stephan 1996; Rustow 1970). Peaceful conventional politics can hardly unfold when ethnic actors reject the rightness of the territorial unit of the state. The competitive dynamic of ethnic party systems also militates against interethnic cooperation and moderation. Ethnic parties have an ascriptive-based membership and voting constituency, which means they are furnished very little incentive to attract uncommitted "floating voters" as political parties often do in nonethnic party systems. Instead, the game of ethnic politics typically becomes one of competitive "outbidding" whereby opposition parties attempt to "outflank" parties in power by adopting more extreme positions. The existence of flanking parties puts pressure on dominant parties to shun moderation and interethnic negotiations lest they be branded with the stigma of selling out or betraying one's nation (Hislope 1996; Horowitz 1985, 340–64; Mitchell 1995; Rabushka and Shepsle 1972, 150–53).

Of course, the centrifugal tendencies of ethnic politics do not mean that interethnic cooperation is impossible to achieve, only difficult. Rational choice approaches to ethnic politics suggest that ethnic actors can find common ground because they are, no less than any other political elite, motivated by material benefits and personal gain (Chandra 2004; Fearon and Laitin 1996). Indeed, even scholars who stress the emotional and inherently divisive tendencies of ethnic politics tend to advocate rules and institutions they argue will steer ethnic actors into peaceful forms of coexistence (Horowitz 1985; Lijphart 1977; Sisk 1996). If ethnic elites were inherently impervious to electoral logic and instrumental calculations, then such institutional engineering would be in vain. Naturally, when elites adopt a public rhetoric based on extreme nationalism and chauvinism, the ground for compromises and flexibility narrows considerably. But even in these cases, elites may find compelling reasons to make compromises behind the scenes. Corruption is, after all, an illegal activity that is practiced not under the public gaze, where politicians can be reasonably monitored, but behind a veil of secrecy, in the realm of politics that Giovanni Sartori (1976) calls "invisible" (see also della Porta and Vannucci 1999, 99–100). What cannot be achieved visibly among rival ethnic elites, therefore, may be possible to secure invisibly, via corrupt exchange.

When political dissensus defines interethnic group relations, corrupt exchange among rival ethnic elites can purchase peace by giving each side a stake and personal interest in the system. The transformation of elite politics from disunity to consensual unity is of momentous historical importance in the political evolution of states and regimes. The democratic transition paradigms of the 1980s–1990s placed particular emphasis on the importance of elites from rival camps compromising and reaching settlements that structure political competition and lay the ground rules for a new democratic order (Di Palma 1990; Higley and Gunter 1992; O'Donnell and Schmitter 1986). Corrupt exchange contributes to this political transformation by fostering an elite instrumental unity and a demobilizing regime. Corrupt multiethnic coalitions are likely to create demobilizing regimes, as no coalition member has an interest in agitating and mobilizing its community against the other (Gagnon 1996, 2004). Such regimes hope to avoid interethnic confrontations; demobilizing elites thereby tone down their nationalist rhetoric and adopt a more pragmatic approach upon taking office. Although the bonds that unify elites are based on short-term payoffs and not on a fundamental political or value consensus, in the long term instrumental elite unity can contribute to elite structural integration or the development of overarching networks of influence and communication among elites (Higley and Gunther 1992). When ethnic party elites regularly interact, common norms and values can be discovered, friendships forged, and hostile stereotypes dispelled.

There is no absolute guarantee, of course, that the private vices of political elites will automatically produce public goods, even in the long term. After all, corruption is an illegal activity that requires trust among insiders and suspicion toward outsiders. The imperative of secrecy entails that corrupt networks will necessarily restrict access to valuable goods and services and this, in turn, can generate frustrations among those social forces out-side the arrangement.[4] In other words, when corruption occurs at the com-manding heights of the state, elites in control of resources must decide which associates to reward. Because the resources at stake are normally high-value items in limited supply (such as offices, foreign import licenses, proceeds from illegal contraband), and because the pool of potential recip-ients is large, intense rivalries and grievances can develop and thereby jeop-ardize system stability. As Donatella della Porta explains, with reference to the Italian experience: "In order to survive, the mechanism of corrup-tion must constantly extend participation, since it is precisely participation which strengthens the bonds of collusion. However, this produces an in-flationary spiral, reducing both the material and symbolic resources avail-able at the same time as it creates discontent among those excluded" (della Porta 1996, 368; see also Johnston 1986, 473). In sum, one must be attentive to the varying conditions of corrupt exchange and how different patterns can impact the political order with different combinations of centrifugal and centripetal pressures.

The Competitive Configuration in Macedonia

Of all the new states that emerged from the wreckage of Yugoslavia, none is more puzzling than Macedonia. Whereas Croatia, Bosnia, and Kosovo were overcome by internal and external ethnic challenges, and Slovenia experienced a ten-day secessionist clash with the Yugoslav Peoples' Army, Macedonia avoided serious conflict for the first ten years of its independ-ence (1991–2001). In regional terms, this young state overachieved in three distinct ways: it was the only Yugoslav republic to secede peacefully, to experience interethnic domestic peace, and to practice and maintain a mul-tiethnic coalition government. In international circles, Macedonia earned the epithets "oasis of peace" and "successful example of a well-functioning democracy in the Balkans."[5]

The basis of ethnic elite unity in Macedonia is an interesting intellectual puzzle given that very little consensus over the legitimacy and ethnic char-acter of the state existed prior to the resolution of the 2001 conflict. Mace-donia's two most politically significant ethnic groups are deeply divided along all the classic cleavage lines: language, religion (Orthodoxy and Islam, respectively), employment patterns, and traditions.[6] The political disputes between Albanians and Macedonians cover both material and symbolic matters, such as education, public employment, linguistic rights, cultural rights (such as the display of flags), and constitutional status (Hislope 2003; Koppa 2001). All these issues are emotionally charged, particularly as each community is against granting the kinds of rights the other is uniformly demanding. Given the level of dissensus in the republic, one would not expect interethnic coalition government to be possible, let alone durable. But this is precisely what occurred.

The key to Macedonia's success was the surprising durability of its multiethnic coalition governments. All of Macedonia's coalitions fit the convenience type. Across the Albanian-Macedonian divide, there was no vote pooling in parliamentary elections (1990, 1994, 1998), and the coalitions came together for the express purpose of governing (as opposed to developing a common platform). During the first multiparty coalition (1992–1998), several crises confronted the government, including the lack of international recognition, economic turmoil caused by trade sanctions, secessionist conspiracies by Albanian extremists, several episodes of interethnic violence, and a failed assassination attempt on President Kiro Gligorov in 1995.[7] Even more impressive was the staying power of the second coalition (1998–2002), which held together during both the spillover of 200,000 Kosovo refugees in 1999 and the 2001 conflict.[8] Although Macedonian junior coalition parties rotated in and out of the pre-conflict coalitions,[9] the Albanian parties never defected. In other words, the principal partners in each successive interethnic coalition survived every crisis they faced and served their entire mandate. The following table provides a snapshot of the main coalition partners between 1992 and 2002.

Dimensions of Corrupt Exchange in Macedonia

Among Macedonian and Albanian scholars, the term "sultanism" is widely used to describe the country's party system.[10] Sultanism denotes organizationally weak parties led by corrupt, authoritarian bosses. Once in power, such parties set in motion a "partization of the state administration" in

Table 8.1 Interethnic Coalitions in Macedonia, 1992–2002				
Main Coalition Parties	*Ethnic Affiliation*	*Ideology*	*Party Elites*	*Coalition Partner*
Social Democratic Union of Macedonia (SDSM)	Macedonian	Reform Communist Left-Wing	Kiro Gligorov Branko Crvenkovski Ljubomir Frckovski Vlado Popovski	PPD (1992–1998)
Internal Macedonian Revolutionary Organization-Democratic Party of Macedonian National Unity (VMRO-DPMNE)	Macedonian	Nationalist Conservative Right-wing Anticommunist	Ljubcho Georgievski Ljube Boskovski Dosta Dimovska	PDSH (1998–2002)
Party for Democratic Prosperity (PPD)	Albanian	Reform Communist Nationalist	Nezvat Halili Abdurahman Aliti*	SDSM (1992–1998)
Democratic Party of Albanians (PDSH)	Albanian Anticommunist	Nationalist Menduh Thaci	Arben Xhaferi (1998–2002)	VMRO-DPMNE

Note: In 1994 Halili was ousted and Abdurahman Aliti became the new Prosperity leader. Aliti stepped down after the 1999 presidential elections amidst repeated charges of corruption.

which ministries and state-owned enterprises are taken over and treated as the personal fiefdoms of the party. In the words of one Macedonian scholar, "unlike the ideal type of sultanism that does not allow political competition, in Macedonia it is being practiced [among] the actors in politics and transferred into [the] institutional culture when the party comes to power" (Bocevski 2002, 52; see also Buechsenschuetz 2001; Rusi 2003). Sultanism thrives in Macedonia because the country's political institutions are underdeveloped. Numerous NGO studies cite the sorry condition of Macedonia's political institutions, where accountability, professionalism, coordination of policy between the assembly and the executive branch, consultation with experts, and communication with constituents are sorely lacking. In addition, Macedonia lacks a strong civil society in which self-sustaining citizen-organizations apply a regularized form of pressure on political elites (Merritt 2001; UN Development Program 2001; U.S. Institute of Peace 2001).

Corrupt political relations in the postcommunist period first took shape during the 1992–1998 coalition between the Social Democrats and the Prosperity Party. The context for this development was a double trade embargo imposed on the country—one from Greece (1991–1995) over the right to use the appellation "Macedonia"; the other directed at Serbia by the international community (1992–1995), which cut off Macedonia from its most important trading partner. Beginning in 1993, reports began to surface in the international media about a vast network of sanctions-busting activities that had taken shape in Macedonia. Despite an official policy of compliance with the international embargo on the rump Yugoslavia, a clandestine political economy of smuggling developed (Landay 1993; *New York Times* 1993; Salome and Deans 1994).

State officials were intimately involved in these activities. Rumors circulated in Skopje about the riches amassed by individuals such as parliamentary speaker Stojan Andov and government ministers Jane Miljovski (without portfolio, later finance) and Ljubomir Frckovski (interior).[11] In 1994, Peter Goshev (of the small Democratic Party of Macedonia) singled out the ministers he felt were "disloyal, dishonest, and incompetent," including Iliaz Sabriu, Mohammed Halili, and Bekir Zhuta (from the Prosperity Party), Risto Ivanov (Liberal Party), Blagoj Handzhiski, Vlado Popovski, and Frckovski (all Social Democrats) (Macedonian Information and Liaison Service 1994). Menduh Thaci of the Democratic Party of Albanians (PDSH) chastised Prosperity leaders for being seduced by "money, favors and high positions" and thereby losing sight of "ethnic Albanian interests" (Kamm 1994). Apart from a 1997 pyramid bank scandal tied to the Social Democrats, corrupt activities at this time were shielded behind a wall of state protection. In the assessment of Balkan specialist Duncan Perry, "although there is little data, criminal groups, some of them believed to be associated with political parties, divided the economic territory to meet consumer demands. In effect, mafias proliferated and kept their people supplied. This contributed to internal stability by keeping the population fed; at the same time, the government winked at (and some members may have participated in) such activities" (Perry 1996, 113–17).

The primary effect of corruption between the Social Democrats and the Prosperity Party was coalition resilience in the face of several iterations of interethnic violence. Three episodes of violence occurred: the Bit Pazar marketplace, November 1992; the Tetovo university clashes, December

1994–February 1995; and the Gostivar flag crisis, July 1997 (Abrahams 1996; Human Rights Watch 1998).[12] The first instance involved a heavy-handed police approach toward the contraband cigarette trade, but the second two were more intense political confrontations between a Macedonian police force and PDSH-led Albanian protestors who were demanding an expansion of cultural rights in the republic. What is most amazing is how little these crises hindered the functioning of the ruling coalition. For example, only six days passed between a police demolition of a Tetovo university building (14 December) and the announcement of a new government (20 December 1994). The ease with which the Party for Democratic Prosperity (PPD) returned to power, as opposed to following an alternative strategy of principled opposition or imposing tough preconditions for their participation, reflected the party elites' overriding interest in maintaining its government seats. As President Gligorov remarked, "It wasn't difficult to have the Albanians enter Crvenkovski's new government, because PPD did not come out with any special conditions, and that means it was also an expression of their interests" (Macedonian Information Center 1994e; see also 1994a, 1994b, 1994c, 1994d). That this was not always an easy matter to sell to the Albanian public comes from Prosperity members themselves, who admitted they often had to visit towns and villages to explain to their constituency why they entered the government (Ordanoski 1992).

If corruption was rampant during the SDSM-PPD coalition, it rose to new, dizzying heights during the rule of the Internal Macedonian Revolutionary Organization (VMRO) and the Democratic Party of Albanians. Iso Rusi, an Albanian journalist, has written extensively on the corrupt pact between these two nationalist parties, which involved a two-thirds/one-third division of the state (Rusi 2002b, 2002d). Under this plan, Tetovo and western Macedonia (where Albanians are concentrated) became the exclusive province of the PDSH, while Skopje and eastern Macedonia were controlled by VMRO. The distribution of government positions, directorships of state enterprises, and revenues from government businesses were also divided according to the two-thirds (VMRO)/one-third (PDSH) formula (International Crisis Group 2002). Corrupt exchange between the parties occurred as well over the smuggling rackets that existed in the borderlands between Macedonia, southern Serbia, and Kosovo. Menduh Thaci reportedly controlled a portion of the trafficking business (ICG 2002;

Rusi 2002a),[13] and it was in cooperation with VMRO that the border areas remained weakly monitored and underpoliced.[14]

The political upshot of Macedonia's corrupt nationalist coalition was a demobilizing regime. While in opposition PDSH activists pursued a radical agenda, leading the political demonstrations that ended in violence in Tetovo and Gostivar. VMRO was equally nationalist. For example, in early 1998 Georgievski declared he saw "no reason for any Albanians to be part of the Macedonian Government. You can try repression with the Albanians, as in Serbia, and you can try tolerance, as we have in Macedonia. Nothing works. They still want to destroy the state and create a greater Albania" (Hedges 1998; see also Human Rights Watch 1998). But once the coalition deal was struck, both parties adopted a very different perspective. According to Xhaferi, "a small miracle occurred" when both party leaders realized that "strangely enough, we have no differences whatsoever" (O'Conner 1998, 6; see also *Radio Free Europe* 1999).

The 1999 Kosovo refugee crisis did cause considerable interparty strains. During the war between NATO and Serbia, 200,000 Albanians poured into Macedonia, overwhelming the state's economic resources and heightening the fears of Macedonians that the demographic balance in the country would be permanently altered. When the crisis began, Xhaferi gave VMRO notice that any attempt to transfer Albanians outside of Albanian-populated areas, such as Western Europe, would result in his party's departure from government. Still, PDSH ministers supported Georgievski when the latter criticized the international community for its inadequate response to the crisis. And once the crisis subsided, the PDSH continued to participate in the government (ICG 1998; Icevska 1999).

The beginning of the 2001 conflict was another critical moment when the PDSH demonstrated its commitment to the coalition. When the National Liberation Army (NLA) emerged from the shadows in February to begin its offensive against the Macedonian state, PDSH elites reacted with anger and disbelief. Xhaferi had only recently proclaimed that Macedonia had become a "stable state." In the aftermath of a terrorist attack against a police station at the end of January, Xhaferi confirmed that an Albanian rebel group was operating in Macedonia, but that Albanians did not support it and stability would prevail (Makfax 2001d). By March, however, the NLA had taken its insurgency to the Democratic Party's backyard, the Sar mountains above Tetovo. In response, Xhaferi and

Thaci attempted to discredit the rebels. Xhaferi dismissed the fighters as "psychologically damaged Rambos," while Thaci called them "criminals" and "traitors" whose demands were a "cosmetically modified plagiarism" of the PDSH program. Thaci even suggested that the government should crush the rebels, as "any government should exert its power in the entire region it governs" (Erlanger 2001a; see also Makfax 2001a; Raxhimi 2001; Smith 2001).

Overall, corrupt exchange within successive interethnic coalitions produced spectacular durability. The Social Democratic–Prosperity coalition endured numerous domestic and regional challenges, as did the VMRO-PDSH government. The latter coalition survived even the 2001 crisis and was only removed from office in the 2002 national elections.

Corrupt Exchange and the 2001 Crisis

Christopher Hill, the former U.S. ambassador to Macedonia (1996–1999), once poignantly described Macedonia as a "nice little country in a bad neighborhood" (McKinsey 1999). The fallout from the wars in Croatia, Bosnia, and Kosovo, not to mention the collapse of Albania in 1997, meant that Macedonia's regional setting was a very dangerous one indeed. One could in fact describe the whole region as locked into a corruption crisis, which is marked by the sudden influx of illegal resources, organized criminal groups, and the general social dislocations that stem from wars, state collapse, and economic sanctions (Johnston 1986, 471–73). Anarchy in Albania brought over half a million weapons into circulation, with much of that pouring into Kosovo and Macedonia (Perry 2000). The late 1990s witnessed the proliferation of both organized crime networks as well as paramilitaries throughout the region. The failure of NATO to disarm and disband completely the Kosovo Liberation Army (KLA) allowed a major security threat to develop at Macedonia's doorstep. The Liberation Army of Presevo, Medvedja, and Bujanovac (LAPMB), appeared first, in January 2000, setting its sights on the Albanian population in southern Serbia. Exploiting the same porous borders between Kosovo, Macedonia, and southern Serbia, the NLA opened its front in Macedonia in February 2001. For all of these reasons, the spillover effect from Kosovo stands out as the most immediate cause of Macedonia's crisis (Liotta and Jebb 2004).

Still, interethnic corruption in Macedonia did play an unintentional role in facilitating the NLA insurgency. Because VMRO and PDSH elites had de facto divided the territory, Macedonia's border villages became a safe haven for a burgeoning of Albanian paramilitaries. In 1998, Menduh Thaci admitted that the KLA had established bases in Macedonia and that the PDSH would help them in their struggle against Milošević (Brown 1998). One of those bases was Tanusevci, a remote, inaccessible, impoverished Albanian village that borders Kosovo. It served as a transit point and storage site for weapons destined for the KLA and later for the LAMPB in southern Serbia. That all these moves had the blessing of VMRO was confirmed in 1999, when the minister of the interior, Pavle Trajanov (a member of the Democratic Alternative Party), was told by Georgievski to ignore a mine shaft the police had discovered near Kumanovo that was full of weapons and uniforms (Makfax 2001b; Rusi 1999).[15] This decision would come back to haunt the coalition, as Tanusevci turned out to be the very location where the NLA and Macedonian police first traded gunfire (Naegele 2001a, 2001b).

It is ironic that the very mechanism that held Macedonia together for ten years contributed to its near undoing in 2001. Corruption was an integral part of interethnic exchange in Macedonia. It was rampant during the Social Democratic–Prosperity coalition and rose to new heights during VMRO-PDSH rule. The misfortune of the latter coalition was that the transactions coincided with turbulence in neighboring Albanian areas. The NLA insurgency against Macedonia was unintentionally aided by the decisions of coalition elites, such as the ignoring of Albanian paramilitary bases and inadequate border patrols. In this way, corrupt exchange served as both glue and dissolvent in Macedonia's postcommunist trajectory.

Alternative Arguments

There were, of course, other factors that shaped Macedonia's political path. One cannot lay too heavy of an explanatory burden on any single factor. As one corruption scholar notes, "whole systems will rarely stand or fall because of corruption alone" (Johnston 1998, 462). What other factors, then, steered elites in Macedonia toward cohabitation?

The regional balance of power was certainly an important backdrop that shaped the calculations of the Macedonian and Albanian political class. On the Albanian side, the exit options in the early 1990s all looked dreadful. Kosovo was under the brutal subjugation of Milošević, and Albania was preoccupied with recovery from its severe communist experience. Nevzat Halili of the Prosperity Party himself acknowledged this, noting that Albanians in Macedonia enjoyed political pluralism and faced none of the repressive measures inflicted on the Kosovars (Andrejevich 1991). Likewise, Servet Avziu, a top-ranking member of the PPD and government minister reasoned that "at the moment we live better (than Albanians elsewhere in the Balkans) because we managed to maintain peace in Macedonia. The people in power know what peace means and the price of peace" (Pope 1993, 2). Thus, in the eyes of most Albanian elites, the plight of Albanians outside Macedonia was more sobering than inspiring.

On the Macedonian side, the questionable motives and territorial appetites of neighboring states compelled party leaders to act cautiously. Internal anxieties also played a role. Unlike Kosovo, where an uprising by the majority Albanian population would not affect daily life in Belgrade, in Macedonia the Albanian population could not mobilize without creating political tremors. This political asset of being "inside," as Xhaferi explains, makes "Albanians dangerous because they can organize everything in Skopje. That is why there is a need for caution when acting as far as Albanians are concerned."[16] Indeed, while the Macedonian political class was capable of a show of force, it was not prepared to commit credibly to a coercive strategy. The weakness of the state, the insecure and precarious regional conditions, and the sheer size and disruptive potential of the Albanian minority all precluded a Milošević-style solution to the Albanian question. With the costs of repression too high for Macedonians, and the price of exit too great for Albanians, peace was maintained by Macedonian and Albanian elites mutually adjusting the terms of their partnerships.

The international community also helped bring Macedonian and Albanian elites together and keep coalitions intact. Quiet, behind-the-scenes pressure was often at work. Third-party involvement, such as the 1992 London Conference–mandated "Working Group," led by Geert Ahrens, provided timely "soft arbitration," which helped to bridge the otherwise great gaps in perspectives and policies between Macedonia's main ethnic groups (Ackermann 2000).[17] Into this mix can also be added the UN's first-ever use of preventive diplomacy. One thousand blue helmets (including 500 American soldiers), under the banner of the United Nations Preventive Force patrolled Macedonia's border with Kosovo, Serbia, and Albania between 1993 and 1999 with a mission to deter any spillover effect from the Yugoslav wars (Ackermann 2000; Lorenz 2002; Williams 2000). Equally important was the work of OSCE High Commissioner Max van der Stoel, who mediated the intractable higher education issue in Macedonian-Albanian relations (Erlanger 2001a).

Taken together, international pressure, Macedonian anxieties, and Albanian perceptions of the regional situation steered Macedonia toward a politics of interethnic bargaining. So what does corrupt exchange add to the story? Specifically, it provides the crucial link between low elite consensus and the stability of Macedonia's successive coalitions. International actors and regional conditions can bring elites to the bargaining table, but when fundamental dissensus exists on how to regulate majority-minority relations, elites must find sustained interaction compelling and self-serving. Access to the offices and resources of the state is a powerful incentive to put aside political differences. Macedonia's sultanistic parties and weak public institutions made corruption a low-risk, high-profit activity, providing the parties with a powerful stimulus to keep each coalition intact (Macedonian Information Agency 2006; Nikolov 2004).

The Demise of a Corrupt Coalition

The story of corruption in postcommunist Macedonia would be incomplete without a consideration of how the concerted pressure of transnational actors contributed to the electoral defeat of the VMRO-PDSH coalition in the September 2002 elections.

The International Crisis Group (ICG) is a nonprofit INGO that monitors political events in over thirty countries for the purpose of assessing the likelihood of conflict and making recommendations to policymakers. The ICG set up shop in Macedonia in the late 1990s and subsequently issued a series of reports on the political trajectory of the country. In August 2002, the ICG directly intervened in Macedonia's politics by publishing a detailed exposé on the corrupt dealings of the VMRO-PDSH government one month prior to the general election. The intention of the report was to put pressure on the ruling coalition and to warn international donors that financial aid would be wasted unless tied to domestic anticorruption reforms.

The ICG report, written under the direction of project director Edward Joseph, detailed at length how VMRO and the PDSH elites conspired to loot the assets of the state. Their malfeasance touched all spheres of the government, including graft in the customs services, a freight forwarder scandal, a health fund shakedown, the selling of import rights for personal profit in the ministry of economics, suspicious aspects of the privatization of the Okta oil refinery, VMRO's purchase of private businesses such as a bank, and government involvement in tobacco trafficking (ICG 2002, 7–23). Such revelations raised considerable political tensions in Macedonia. The release of the ICG report was preceded by an anticorruption conference in June, which was sponsored by the local branch of the Open Society Institute and organized by its director, Vladimir Milchin. During the conference proceedings, prime minister Georgievski made an impromptu visit where he rallied against the claims that his government was corrupt. With the Macedonian media present, a heated exchange transpired between Georgievski, on the one hand, and Milchin Edward Joseph, on the other (see Cvetkovska 2002; H. C. 2002; Macedonian Information Center 2002; Orgieva 2002; P. D. 2002; Rusi 2002c; Tupanchevski 2002).[18] Afterward, Joseph was viciously attacked in the press by VMRO interior minister Ljube Boshkovski and faced threats from right-wing Macedonian forces (Buechsenschuetz 2002; Petruseva 2002; Rusi 2002c). The entire spectacle exemplifies to what degree the ICG campaign against corruption touched a raw nerve in the VMRO leadership. In the end, the ICG report helped to bring down both VMRO and PDSH in the September elections.

TODAY, THE CONSENSUS in the international community is that corruption is overwhelmingly harmful and must be eradicated in developing and transitioning societies. World leaders condemn it, NGOs monitor it, IGOs sanction it, and global investors direct their capital away from countries that are mired in it. The prevailing scholarly opinion concurs that the costs of corruption far outweigh the benefits. This essay questions the purported political payoffs of the anticorruption consensus and advances an argument that corrupt exchange among rival ethnic elites can foster interethnic peace.

An argument inspired by the revisionist literature of the 1960s is developed that focuses on the role of weak party systems and underdeveloped political institutions. Because the institutions to mediate and contain conflict are often quite weak in the developing south and the transitioning east, revisionist insights carry explanatory promise in countries where peace and stability oddly coexist with severe ethnic cleavages, economic hardship, and/or a general lack of political consensus. As James Scott observed, "when violence becomes less common in a political system, corruption often becomes more common. The relationship is not simply fortuitous, but rather represents the substitution of bargaining for raw contests of strength" (Scott 1967, 511). This general argument is illustrated by an examination of corrupt exchange among ethnic party elites in Macedonia. I argue that corrupt transactions between Macedonian and Albanian party elites created a durable coalition government and a demobilizing regime, thereby enabling this nascent state to survive the multiple crises that beset it. Long-term stability was not achieved, however. Macedonia's bad neighborhood created conditions and opportunities for Albanian nascent elites and insurgents frustrated with the "invisible politics" of interethnic coalition government in Macedonia. Consequently, corrupt exchange purchased only a temporary peace.

9

USING AMERICA

AGAINST EUROPE

POLAND'S NATIONAL

REACTIONS TO

TRANSNATIONAL PRESSURE

David Ost

Oddly, such behavior goes down
well with some Poles, who like
to see their leaders putting snooty
foreigners in their place.

—*The Economist*, 13 May 2006

Why did Poland side so strongly with the United States in the conflict between Europe and America in 2002–2003, despite having far more economic ties in Europe?[1] Why did it give such support to the invasion of
Iraq? The common view is that it did so because Poles sympathized more
with America's position, due to their own long fight against oppressive
dictatorship. A close reading of the Polish foreign policy debate, however,
suggests something else. For what distinguishes this debate is how *little* it

concerned Iraq, or even America, and how much it concerned Europe. Support for America appears to have been caused more by dissatisfaction with the EU than by high regard for America. National policy seems to have been deeply affected by transnational pressure.

Mitteleuropa?

Understanding contemporary Eastern European foreign politics begins with a reading and deconstruction of a monumentally influential work whose ninetieth anniversary has just passed. Friedrich Naumann's *Mitteleuropa* sparked a huge debate in Europe in the quarter century after its initial publication in Germany in 1915. Indeed, with its call for a union of Germany with the Austrian empire and its assertion that there was no hope for small states in the region, many have seen it as a harbinger of the foreign policies of the Nazis.

This might suggest that it ceased to be relevant after 1945. Anyone reading the recent Polish press, however, would see that that is not the case. Writers and politicians of different persuasions evoke the specter of *Mitteleuropa* as the reason why Poland should be cautious in its dealings with the EU, and seem to hark back to the book's central assumptions when promoting their blunt pro-American intentions.

The EU as Naumann's *Mitteleuropa*? On the surface, nothing could be further from the truth. Its twenty-seven independent countries without an official leader seem to put the lie to any such association. But from an Eastern perspective it is not so far-fetched. As we shall see below, the enlargement process often looked like an effort by the West to increase its comparative advantage over the East. It was accompanied by a campaign for "deepening," with calls for a "core" Europe based around France and Germany to lead the way. Those two countries led the opposition to the United States over the invasion of Iraq, after which even German and French intellectuals, who might have been expected to be sensitive to Eastern concerns, called even more urgently for European unity based around this core, in opposition to the United States and without much concern about a revitalized Russia (Habermas-Derrida 2005).

Poland has begun formulating its own foreign policy only in the last several years. Not since 1989 but since 2002. After 1989, like all former communist East Europe, its only concern was to "join the West." That meant putting its energy into entering NATO and the EU. A rare political consensus emerged on this matter, and all governing parties followed through consequentially on the pledge. Poland entered NATO in 1999, and by 2002 it was assured of entering the EU two years later. But whereas in 1989 it appeared that joining both transnational organizations meant the same thing, that was far from clear in 2002. Europe's emerging clash with the United States, America's post-9/11 marginalization of NATO in favor of ad-hoc coalitions, "core" European hopes to build a new super-power, the debate over the European constitution—all this signaled that "the West" was no longer a single phenomenon, that it might become nec-essary to choose. Because of its size, as well as its deep national traditions, Poland alone could not *avoid* choosing. But which way would it go? With a population larger than all other nine incoming new member states put together, it would soon become the sixth largest country in the EU. This would seem to give it a crucial stake in a strong, united EU. Yet in the years just preceding Poland's entry, the EU began reorganizing itself in funda-mental ways, including devising new internal procedures that seemed to weaken Poland's position. Suddenly, the transnational agenda of the core EU began to clash with Poland's interests. But just as suddenly, the emerg-ing conflict with the United States gave Poland new leverage. Its decision to support the United States on Iraq was thus in large part a decision about its relation to Western Europe, and against the specter of a new *Mitteleuropa*.

It is now accepted "without argument," wrote Friedrich Naumann in 1915, "that neither now nor in the future can small or even moderate-sized Powers play any large part in the world. Only very big states have any significance" (Naumann 1917, 4). Between France and Russia, argued Naumann, there was room only for one state. For the small nations of Eastern Europe seeking their own states, this is unfortunate but inescapable. In their own interest, the East Europeans would have to give up their de-sire for independence. Isolation, he warned—by which he meant isolation from Germany—was no longer possible. For this is the age of "large-scale industry and of super-national organization." With "sovereignty . . . now concentrated at a very few places on the globe," even Germany is too small (4). The only hope, for all the peoples between France and Russia, is to bring together the German empire and the Austro-Hungarian empire, along with all the nations inside them, into one big power.

Naumann gives Poland particularly short shrift. It once had a state, he writes, but because its own people ruined it through "weakness and incapacity," Germany and Austria worked to dismantle it (79). This joint dismantling of Poland constituted the kind of beneficial "common task" that Naumann wished the two empires would engage in more often (3). Prussia had to save Poland from itself, and did: it "took compulsion in one hand and material prosperity in the other and demanded mental adhesion in exchange" (79). Though many Poles in 1915 might still wish they were independent, Naumann believes that facts on the ground were quickly changing that, because allegiance to state, he contended, is stronger than allegiance to nation. In the Great War, after all, Prussian Poles were fighting with the Prussians, Galician Poles with the Austrians, Russian Poles with the Russians. "The magnetic and material force of any State which rouses itself up to war is so enormous that no section can evade it" (80).

Small states have no future. What matters is who controls them. Naumann thus considered national particularities not bad but "impractical." "A Czech army, or a Croat General Staff or a purely Magyar Foreign Office, or a Slovenian economic policy or a Galician State Bank": their "impossibility . . . is obvious" (26). The entire region thus needs a *Mitteleuropa* formed from the union of the German and Austria-Hungarian empires. Ideally, France would be part of this too. Not only do Germans bear the French "no enmity," but "whenever the French are willing we shall be able to offer them the hand of friendship" (1–2). Ultimately, then, an all-European state standing up to Russia, and perhaps to the United Kingdom (the United States meant little for European power in 1915), is Naumann's aim. It is desirable because it is *necessary*. The age of small powers is over.

One of the characteristic features of *Mitteleuropa* is its insistence that it is not a call for German domination. Though he seeks a giant European state under German tutelage, Naumann insists he is no Great German chauvinist. *Mitteleuropa* is necessary not to defend the "German nation" but to defend Europe. Indeed, Naumann goes to pains to stress that his proposal entails sacrifices for ethnic Germans. Austrian Germans who supported it in order to get protection against their own nationalities would be disappointed. "With us in the German Empire . . . State policy comes before the policy of any nationality, hence we do and have done nothing which could seem like incitement to a German Irredenta" (21). Naumann begs forgiveness from his German readers but urges them to understand the bigger picture. *Mitteleuropa* will be run by Germans, but it is a state project on behalf of Europeans, not a national one on behalf of Germans.

This politically correct aspect of Naumann's pro-imperial contribution is surely its most maddening side for Central Europeans on the receiving end, meaning those who wish to retain their own nationality. Naumann, after all, is *sympathetic* to the plight of small nations. Just as he cautions Austrian Germans against treating *Mitteleuropa* as their salvation, he warns Prussians against seeing it as license to rule indiscriminately over others. He admonishes: "In exalting our nationality we ought at the same time to exalt theirs" (Naumann 1917, 11). Naumann does not *wish* other nationalities to die out. He just believes that they must, that their aspirations for sovereignty must remain unsated. Their decline is the work of History, not of those who aspire toward *Mitteleuropa*. We can, to be sure, provide nationalities with some autonomy. They deserve "a liberation from enforced Germanization" (80). But as state actors capable of exercising sovereignty, these nationalities have no chance—as they are indeed learning themselves. Naumann switches constantly in these pages between the role of advocate and prophet, between insisting that elites ought to create an overarching European state and arguing that that is what is happening anyway. German thought was of course suffused with Hegelian logic at this time, and so as Naumann puts it, "The intelligent man is he who does of his own free will what he recognizes as necessary" (5).

Return of the East

As we shall see, the specter of *Mitteleuropa* has returned as a central theme in Polish foreign policy debates, with the EU as the latest institution for asserting West Europe's (and particularly Germany's) control over the East. Due to a combination of West European hesitance and protectionism, asymmetrical power imbalance, and historical Polish suspicions that savvy parties knew how to exploit, the EU, in its increasingly federalist phase of the early 2000s, came to be seen as the latest pretender in a long line of West European aspiration for hegemony over the East.

But how has this transnational pressure affected national politics? It did so in three different ways. First, it elicited a strong *reaction* in Poland. Poles adopted a pro-U.S. foreign policy due to the asymmetrical and deeply humiliating nature of the EU accession process. Second, it strengthened the *realist* tendency in Polish foreign-policy thinking. To the extent it appeared that EU policies only masked the interests of leading Western states, particularly Germany and France, it pushed even those decision makers sympathetic to the EU to embrace pro-American policies and take an obstinate line against EU reform measures. And, third, it generated a *bargaining* standpoint on the part of domestic elites. Since most of these elites understood that Poland's clout was real but limited (it was the largest of the new members, the only one without which enlargement would make no sense, but still with a comparatively poor economy more needy of the EU than vice versa), they came to believe that a defiant foreign policy stance could help them extract concessions that might otherwise not be forthcoming.

Of course, it was not the EU alone that shaped domestic choices. Perceptions of NATO, of its actions concerning Eastern Europe, also played a key role here. In short, Poles' *national* decisions followed from their perceptions of the actions of *transnational* actors. Domestic actors found they could play off the differences between the two transnational actors for their own political advantage.

The pro-U.S. and anti-EU tilt in Polish domestic politics became particularly prominent and public only in 2002. Until then, post-1989 Polish politics was marked by a widespread agreement across most of the political spectrum to refrain from taking sides, to hold off criticism of either side, to treat the two equally as emblems of democratic "Westernness" to which all Poles subscribed.

What brought about the change? Three things. First, they had finally all but been "admitted" to "the West." Together with Hungary and the Czech Republic, Poland had entered NATO in 1999 and was now on the verge of full entry into the EU. Some technical issues of compliance still needed to be worked out, but the hard work had been done, and there was no longer any realistic possibility that Poland would be left out. As Vachudova (2005) writes, EU leverage on the Eastern states "drastically diminished two or three years before [the 2004] accession, once full membership seemed like a done deal." It was the first time Poles could *risk* taking sides in a transatlantic dispute or simply state forcefully their own position.

It was also the first time they *had* to take sides. While the end of the cold war brought some tensions to the alliance between America and Western

Europe—their respective elites no longer had a common foe, while the unparalleled military power of the United States raised fears about how it would be used—it was only in 2002 that those tensions came out into the open (Anderson 2002). The proximate cause, of course, was the planned invasion of Iraq. The EU had balked neither at the NATO intervention in the former Yugoslavia nor the American invasion of Afghanistan, but saw an unprovoked attack on Iraq as an extraordinary violation of international law, a security danger to their own countries with large Muslim populations, and a sign of a United States potentially out of control. More precisely, EU public opinion saw it that way, as did the governments of the two countries most important for shaping the EU—France and Germany. But the governments of Britain, Italy, and Spain took a different position; there was still no European foreign policy center; and ten countries were about to join the EU imminently. So America, seeking allies to offset charges of unilateralism, set about lobbying the "new" Europe intently. If 2002 was the first moment in which Poland could choose, it was also the first moment it had to choose.

Third, this was the period of the EU's constitutional convention, with various proposals for "deepening" integration gaining steam. The convention began in February 2002 and concluded in July 2003. The future of the organization that these states were about to enter was up for grabs, with the federalist tendency increasingly prominent. The point was not only that since big issues were being decided about the future of Europe, the countries about to become member states could no longer remain silent. For Poland, it was also a matter of defending gains that had already been made. One of the main aims of the constitutional convention was to revise the treaty agreed on at the 2000 European Council meeting in Nice. Nice gave Poland a large number of votes in the European Council that the draft constitution sought to take away. Having had so little role in shaping EU institutions so far, Poland was reluctant to give up the few advantages it happened to have obtained. This too pushed it to play a greater international role than it had been willing to play before.

For a number of reasons, then, this post–9/11 moment constituted a unique opportunity in which Poles not only *could* but also *had* to speak with a voice of their own. They needed to make clear that they existed, that they could not be taken for granted, and that future transnational politics would have to include them too.

"Asymmetry"

Poland's exasperation with West Europe has its roots in old history. In the sixteenth century Poland was the largest country in Europe, more democratic than its neighbors. In the eighteenth it was devoured up by Prussia, Austria, and Russia, acting together. Even Immanuel Kant approved: "Such a people must be educated by force" (in Krzemiński 2005, 150). From then on, Poland simultaneously looked to West Europe for help in winning back its independence and suspected the West was not interested in that independence at all—not just out of deference to Russia but because it was inconvenient to their own plans for the region, as the partitions had demonstrated.

This historical background constitutes the unstated framework against which contemporary suspicions gain their force. First, there was the enduring Prussian and Austrian occupation, often though not always less onerous than the Russian one, but lasting just the same till 1918. French intellectuals could be counted on for their moral support, but for French policy makers the "Polish Question" figured chiefly as an issue for managing relations with the two German-speaking empires on their borders. While Napoleon carved out a rump Polish independence during his march to Russia, he abandoned it as he retreated, and it did not return to the fore of French strategic thinking until the end of World War I, when the collapse of all its occupying powers thrust Poland back into statehood with strong French support, including a promise to guarantee the new state's security. But because of French fears that Poland could not survive the tensions of its many minorities, and British worries about Poland's own imperial designs in the region that were already bringing in new Ukrainian minorities, these two (and, at the time, only) West European powers ended up treating the revived Poland as a kind of protectorate, a juvenile state whose betters needed to nurse it along. They imposed the Polish Minority Rights Treaty on the country, which even those Polish liberals who thought it might save the country from itself nevertheless still opposed as a mark of continued Western domination over the East, if only because no such obligations had been imposed on Germany or Italy, to say nothing of Europe's colonies. As Mark Mazower puts it, "the Great powers were happy for the League [of Nations] to interfere in the internal affairs of 'new' states, but not in their own" (Mazower 2002, 57).[2] And by the early 1920s, the league's control meant French and British control, as the United States had already retreated.

Then came World War II, and while Britain and France duly declared war on Germany when the Nazis invaded Poland—fulfilling treaty obligations they had reneged on months earlier vis-à-vis Czechoslovakia—they dropped their concern for Poland's integrity after the Soviet Union entered the war and stood by as the Soviets installed their own government and system. Never mind that there was not much Britain and France could do about this (and of course the United States stood by as well). For many Poles, it stood as yet another example of disregard, if not betrayal.

Since Western Europe was itself occupied in 1945, and clearly was no longer the center of world power, it became hard as time went on to hold them culpable for continued Polish misfortune. Nevertheless, Easterners were disappointed at the eagerness with which West Europeans embraced the various "thaws," "peaceful coexistences," and "détentes" that constituted the bulk of Soviet reform projects till the late 1980s, while treating popular uprisings in the region with caution. Liberal Westerners, of course, thought Easterners irresponsibly minimized the dangers of war in this nuclear age, and also believed that détente was the best the East could get in a stuck cold war world. But oppositionist Easterners considered—no doubt more accurately, and not just in hindsight—Soviet warnings about the possibility of continental war in the event of political upheaval as a bluff designed precisely to reduce European support for their protests, and also believed they could achieve much more than détente.

The rise of Solidarity in 1980 did change things. The emergence of a peaceful workers' movement challenging the communist regime with demands with which even radical West European leftists could sympathize (now that few Western leftists saw the Soviet model as representing an authentic left), led to unprecedented popular West European support for an East European opposition movement. But though that support continued in the immediate aftermath of the imposition of martial law in December 1981, it began to dwindle when Ronald Reagan became its chief spokesperson. More accurately, support for Solidarity turned into opposition to Reagan, whose proposal to place nuclear weapons in Europe many Westerners saw as a more immediate threat. When former West German Chancellor Willy Brandt visited Poland in 1985 without calling on Lech Walesa in Gdansk, many in the East—including those who would soon become the East's new leaders—thought the West had abandoned it yet again.[3]

Long-simmering resentments leave their mark on contemporaries only when the ambers of anger are continually stoked. This is what has happened in the most recent period. For while 1989 was greeted as a magical year by the Western mass public—a new springtime of nations auguring a long-term peace—for policy makers it meant trouble. Not insurmountable trouble, but trouble nonetheless, mandating a rethinking of the European future at the very moment that the European Community, as it was then called, was finally proceeding with its own "deepening" process, set in motion with the passing of the Single European Act in 1986. The West's first reaction to 1989, then, was to stave off new entreaties. East Europe's first postcommunist governments knew they would not join the EU soon, but they did expect the latter to endorse the idea of membership, if only because the notion of a united Europe had been at the heart of the European integration process from the start. But the EU pointedly refused to do so. Starting in 1990, it offered Association Agreements ("Europe Agreements") instead, with confusion even among the signing countries over whether these were "an end in themselves or a stepping stone to future membership" (Czubiński 2000). The EU began various aid projects as well, most notably the PHARE program and the European Bank for Reconstruction and Development. But without a clear commitment that full EU membership would follow, all these measures had the effect only of forcing hopeful Eastern states to open themselves up completely to the West. They would carry out all EU "suggestions," do whatever the EU-15 told them to do, in the hope of securing a promise that membership was in the offing.

It was, in short, a humiliating position. In the presence of EU officials—which basically meant all West European officials—Easterners had to play the role of compliant, amenable petitioners eager to lap up advice and implement it back home. It did not matter if the advice was sage or silly; benefactors needed to be placated. EU membership depended on it (see Sajo 1998; Wedel 1998). If the relationship entailed only hurt feelings, it would have been easier to bear. The problem is that it meant acquiescence in unequal economic policies too.

What were those policies? As Gowan puts it, the Central European states "without exception . . . faced severe protectionist barriers from the EC under the Europe Agreements. The CAP was not modified significantly and the bulk of agricultural exports from Poland and Hungary—grain, livestock and dairy—[were] in core CAP sectors. Chemicals continued to be subject to . . . anti-dumping measures; textiles and apparel were subject to a form of managed trade which would be very damaging to the Visegrad textile industry; steel would face restrictive price agreements and anti-dumping instruments, and other sectors like Polish cars were subject to so-called Voluntary Export Restraints (in other words, quotas)" (Gowan 1995, 26).

None of these rules were imposed on West European states. That is, although the West did reduce tariffs on most Eastern imports, it left in place the nontariff barriers, while at the same time insisting that the East abandon these too. In 1992, while the East had to open up its markets to Western goods, the EU imposed antidumping duties on steel products from the region, while a number of individual countries imposed quotas as well. The West, in other words, imposed on the East a whole host of rules it would not impose on itself. The balance of trade quickly changed: the East's $1.5 billion trade deficit with the EU in the first half of 1992 ballooned to $7.2 billion in the comparable period in 1993 (Gowan 1995, 27). While only 3 percent of the EU's 1993 imports came from Poland, Hungary, and the former Czechoslovakia, nearly 70 percent of Poland's imports that year came from the EU (Czubiński 2000).

Thanks to these arrangements, the EU kept out of *its* markets many of those goods in which the East might have been competitive, such as heavy industrial goods, agricultural products, or beef and pork. The EU insisted that the East's prospective members refrain from protectionism and demonstrate their bona fides, while simultaneously demonstrating by their own behavior that they did not feel similarly bound.

Gowan's claim that all this was done on behalf of West European industry, as a way of eliminating competition, underplays the role of the East's domestic elites, who were as anxious to decimate their own industrial economies and thus "Westernize" their countries as anyone in the West might have been (see Appel 2004). Still, the effect of all these policies was to make it hard for anyone in the East to see the altruistic rhetoric of the Europe Agreements as more than a facade. Just as in the East's first period of independence after World War I, the West played the role of tutor, the educator who needs no education, and if it wanted to be considered for entry into the EU the East had to sit tight and accept the imbalances.

Later studies of the East-West relationship confirm this early pattern. As Dorothee Bohle wrote in 2005, "Rather than exporting a solidaristic model of capitalism to Eastern Europe, the EU has preferred to protect its own political economies as far as possible against disruptive influences of enlargement" (Bohle 2005). András Sájo put it differently, comparing the relationship between West and East Europe to one between "missionary and savage," while Wade Jacoby, continuing the religious simile, described it as "priest and penitent" (Jacoby 1999; Sájo 1997). Both these accounts capture not only the irrational aspects of the relationship—manifested in the reluctance of Easterners to talk about their real needs and weaknesses in order not to provide additional reasons for the West to delay accession as it had done for most of the 1990s—but even more, its *humiliating* aspects.

The European Constitutional Convention that began in February 2002 brought forth a new issue into the humiliation paradigm: the effort to supplant Nice. In 2000, the EU's Intergovernmental Council meeting in Nice promulgated new internal voting arrangements in preparation for the enlargement from fifteen to twenty-seven members. The Amsterdam Treaty of 1997 had first introduced the principle of nonunanimous decision making, but the subsequent commitment to enlargement meant that those rules needed to be updated. The trick was how to allocate votes so that binding decisions could be made by both a super-majority of states and a super-majority of people, with the more hidden but obvious aim of simultaneously satisfying what was emerging as a "core" Europe focused around France and Germany—so-called not just because of their central role in the EU from the beginning but because of their desire to move toward deeper integration, which they felt the new members might understandably not be ready to support. At Nice it was agreed that the four biggest countries would all have the same number of votes in the Council of Ministers —twenty-nine each. Spain, which had only two fewer votes under the Amsterdam arrangement, managed to keep that differential in Nice, and with Poland the same size as Spain, Poland was also allocated twenty-seven votes. Binding decisions would require a triple majority: 72.3 percent of the votes plus a majority of countries with at least 62 percent of the total population.

Nice was negotiated in a hurry. Most of the delegations left thinking it would have to be revisited prior to enlargement. For Germany in particular it was a bad deal: despite being the most populous country in Europe with the strongest economy, it had the same number of votes as three other countries, and just two more votes than two countries half its size. The subsequent Constitutional Convention thus proposed fewer votes for Poland and Spain and a different system of voting, according to which binding decisions would require only a double majority: 55 percent of the countries representing 65 percent of the people. As various calculations demonstrated, the new arrangement would make it harder for Poland to block deals it did not like and would put Germany in a stronger position.

Some of the Polish commentary on the constitutional treaty acknowledged that Nice was an accident, not something Poles should expect the entire EU to agree on. One journalist called Nice "an incredible deal for Poland, warranted neither by our size nor our economy, which came about only due to fleeting French fears of a too strong Germany" (Kurski 2003). Still, many had the disappointing sense that the sequence was all too predictable: Poland gets a good deal in the EU, and the EU works to take it away. As Jacek Saryusz-Wolski, Poland's first plenipotentiary for European integration, put it, "We entered the EU on poor economic terms, but good political terms. And now, suddenly, it turns out that the political terms are changing for the worse" (in Kurski 2003). The humiliations, it seemed, were everywhere.

"America" to the Rescue

Humiliation breeds a desire to strike back, and there is no question that much of the pro-Americanism appearing in the Polish press stemmed from this desire to stick a thorn in Europe's eyes. The foreign policy clash between America and Europe presented the opportunity to do so. As the most significant country of the new states joining both NATO and the EU, Poland could not avoid taking a position in this dispute. Unable to express its anger directly, since it needed Europe both to finalize EU admission and to contribute more aid, the intra-Western dispute between the United States and the EU allowed Poland the opportunity to express its anger *indirectly*. That anger and a desire for payback animated the response is evident from the delight many Polish commentators so obviously took in articulating their pro-American position. Just as during the communist era, when Poles commonly expressed anger at the regime by supporting its enemies—for example, by lauding Israel in its fights with the Arab world since the Soviets sided with the latter—so, in the early 2000s, they articulated anger with Europe by supporting America. The advantage of this indirect expression of anger is that it is safe. By supporting your adversary's opponent, your desire for retribution is sated without openly antagonizing the adversary who can still do you harm.

But if pro-Americanism served as a safe outlet for expressing frustrations with Europe, it soon began to be taken up by strategic thinkers as a way of defending Poland's interests. Here is where the realists and the bargainers emerged. Realists emerged to the extent that strategists began to see EU decisions as a mask for pro-French and pro-German policies. *If* the EU was a cover for large countries protecting their national interests, then Poland should challenge EU policies in order to avoid becoming subordinates to those large countries. Pro-Americanism could thus be useful as a way of challenging the two dominant EU countries and simultaneously gain some leverage, both with the EU and with the United States, which might vie for Poland's support. Such, in any case, was the wish of the realists.

That Western Europe engaged in an enlargement strategy that humiliated the new member states is what one would expect from Andrew Moravcsik's (1998) account of European politics, according to which each state uses the resources it has to get the best deal for itself. As Moravcsik and Vachudova put it, the pre-enlargement EU-15 leaders "promot[ed] accession because they consider[ed] enlargement to be in their long-term economic and geopolitical interest" (2003, 43). And they got a better deal because they had less to lose if the deal did not get through. Such are the benefits of "asymmetrical interdependence": countries that are less dependent on others have less incentive to make concessions, meaning that the strongest stay strongest. Countries that need alliances the most, meanwhile, must make the most concessions, leading them to be resentful precisely of the organizations they most want to join.

But if asymmetrical interdependence made Poles upset, it also gave them certain opportunities. For although both East and West were perfectly aware who had the power in this enlargement dance—as Westerners liked to put it, "they're joining us, we're not joining them"—*within* the East the Poles clearly counted most. Their clout stemmed from Poland's size, location, and the moral weight of its claims. Poland had the largest economy and most people of all the East European states. It would soon be the EU's sixth largest country. It would soon have the EU's longest border with the former Soviet Union. These assets made it the only new member NATO military strategists took seriously. They also made Poland of vital importance for any European Defense and Security Policy, one of the key "deepening" reforms being pushed by France and Germany. That France and

Germany took Poland more seriously than any other prospective entrant was made clear by the formation, already in 1991, of the so-called Weimar Triangle, a loose arrangement that brought together these three countries' foreign ministers and defense ministers for periodic informal encounters (Geremek 1998).

Poland's clout also stemmed from its *moral* symbolism, due to its long history fighting for authentic independence as well as to Solidarity, the social movement that first made European unity seem possible. Moral right constituted an important asset within the EU precisely because enlargement did have a powerful moral dimension. The Western *discourse* of enlargement had always stressed this dimension. Western elites said they were reaching out because it was the right thing to do, because it fulfilled age-old dreams of Europeans, because a continent united on the basis of common values could be a harbinger of world peace. Western leaders *wanted* to be seen as promoting enlargement because it bestowed upon them credibility and prestige.[4] And the bottom line was that no enlargement would have been seen as morally legitimate if it did not include Poland. Since its size and location also made Poland the key strategic country of enlargement, the result was that Poland quickly emerged as the decisive player within the "new Europe."

But how to realize that role? How to turn its assets into tangible resources? It was America that presented the opportunity. By pressing for an invasion of Iraq, scornfully dismissing key allies' objections, and then making clear that it would carry out the invasion nevertheless, America forced all countries, particularly those in NATO, to take sides. The Eastern states were in a difficult situation. Do they alienate France and Germany, their main trading partners and the ones still setting the terms for EU entry? Or do they alienate the United States, which had guaranteed their security? With the EU divided and America uncompromising, there was greater pressure to stand with America. Easterners were aware that American critics of NATO enlargement had argued that enlargement was not in America's interests (see Blank 1998). Here was a chance to prove them wrong. The pressure was particularly strong for those countries (all but Poland, Hungary, and the Czech Republic) which had not yet been admitted to NATO. But while all East European countries signed onto the famous two Open Letters, which expressed support for President Bush and his plans for the invasion,[5] all of them hedged their bets except for

Poland. The Hungarian prime minister, for example, clumsily explained that he signed the letter only because he thought the West European countries were doing so too. The Czech parliament forbade the prime minister to sign it, so the president did.

Poland, however, did not apologize or hedge the issue in any way. Even before it announced that it would send 2,500 troops and lead an occupation zone in conquered Iraq, it made clear that it was in the American camp. The sharp party divide between former communists and Solidarity successors disappeared on this issue; both the president and the prime minister were former communists, and the president, Aleksander Kwaśniewski, quickly became one of President Bush's closest allies. Their public statements focused on the issues the American government focused on: Saddam Hussein's weapons of mass destruction were a danger to world peace and to the West in particular. Liberal supporters of the war added on the moral dimension as well: we know what dictatorship is like, and introducing democracy (they were persuaded that America knew how to do this) is a humanitarian gesture that should be supported on grounds of human rights.

Yet the key to the alacrity and eagerness with which Poles signed on to American plans was not these moral arguments but the desire to make a symbolic gesture breaking from the tutelage of France and Germany, and the recognition by realists that this unexpected opportunity to do so offered potential good bargaining benefits to Poland both from Europe and from America.

Aleksander Smolar first called attention to the "reaction" and "bargaining" aspects of Poland's emerging foreign policy, and the plethora of responses his critique elicited only seemed to confirm its accuracy. Smolar is the most pro-EU political and strategic thinker writing in Poland today, probably the result of his having spent most of his adult life in France. He moved there in exile after the student protests and subsequent antisemitic purges of 1968, but stayed closely involved with Polish opposition politics, founding in 1974 the émigré journal *Aneks*. Since the early 1990s he lives in both Poland and France, serving as head of the Stefan Batory Foundation in Warsaw and as senior research fellow at the National Center for Scientific Research in Paris. In 2002 he recognized that a number of developments—the EU's constitutional debate, Poland's imminent entry into the EU, its membership in NATO, the strengthened position of Germany after the end of the cold war, Russia's close post–9/11 alliance with America, and the impending invasion of Iraq already precipitating a crisis in the Atlantic alliance—were forcing Poland to become an important European foreign policy player. But he believed that instead of undertaking a serious discussion about what that foreign policy should entail, Poland was being pushed to an overly deferential attitude to America and a confrontational approach to Europe that was ultimately damaging to Poland vis-à-vis both transnational powers. He first made this argument in a tightly argued September 2002 essay titled "Gulliver and the Lilliputians," which set in motion a raging foreign policy debate that has been going on ever since (Smolar 2002).[6]

Smolar begins by defending Europeans from the charge of spinelessness, then in vogue as a result of Robert Kagan's broadside, and argues that the United States was pursuing a new and dangerous foreign policy, one of whose chief characteristics was pulling back on the alliance with Europe in pursuit of global hegemony. Due to Poland's location in and economic interests with Europe, and its security relationship with America, Poland, Smolar argues, *should* be working to minimize the conflict between the two. Instead, he laments, Poland had become one of the engines of this conflict, pushing one-sidedly toward an alliance with America and distancing itself from Europe because of differences over the EU enlargement process. He cites numerous Polish commentators bubbling enthusiastically about the benefits of alliance with America. In this view, Poland would become a regional power whose special relationship with America would convert it into the Eastern equivalent of Great Britain. But too few, he says, ask just what America is looking for in Poland. Some seem completely uninterested in this question, taking the view that "it's not important why they want us, what's important is that they do." But such an approach, he argues, hurts Poland not just in Europe—with whom, because of location, Poland was condemned to live in much closer relations than it ever could with the United States—but even in America. He cites former American ambassador to Poland Dan Fried's comment that one does not have to kneel down to America in order to be its friend, and alludes to the widespread opinion in Washington that America is so assured of Polish support that it never needs to give anything in return.

In Smolar's view, Poland is useful to America chiefly as something with which to fight the EU. "The conflict between America and Europe has its roots long before September 11th, namely in the United States' [post–cold war] fears that the integration process in Europe represents a threat to America." Because Poland needs both Europe and America, however, Smolar says Poland must do what it can to mitigate these differences, not lean to one side in a way that hurts it with both.

The publication of "Gulliver and the Lilliputians" marked the beginning of Poland's first foreign policy debate to be carried out in public since before World War II. Smolar's argument that Poland needed good relations with both Europe and America elicited a gush of responses arguing that Poland must in fact opt for America, because of the dangers represented by Europe and because Europe was allegedly treating Poland so badly. Smolar's essay, in other words, broke a taboo: it finally became possible to challenge the premise that all sides had accepted since 1989, namely that Poland needed both Europe and America equally.

Maciej Łętowski, a prominent conservative politician and writer, offered one of the first responses: "Either Poland will be a regional power, or it won't be anything at all. It would stay on the map of Europe, but solely as the periphery of the Western world, the economic vassal of a powerful Germany" (Łętowski 2002). For Łętowski, the one bit of consensus politics in Poland since 1989 has been that Poland should have "the closest relations possible" with the United States. Smolar had challenged that by demanding Poland be loyal to Europe. In fact, writes Łętowski, it is Europe that is Poland's real danger. Yes, Germany has been the most forceful proponent of Eastern expansion. But where Smolar sees that as a sign of West European goodwill to the East—the West, writes Smolar, "has taken on the enormous burden of incorporating countries at a significantly lower stage of development, such as Poland"—Łętowski sees such interest as the warning sign of *Mitteleuropa*. The only way to avoid becoming Germany's "vassal" is to become a local power instead, and the only way to do that is through the closest possible alliance with America.

Even a moderate left-wing politician, former government minister Michał Strąk, cautioned against too much loyalty to Europe on the grounds that it might hurt Poland with America. Strąk recalled a 1994 meeting in Washington with Senator Claiborne Pell, then chairman of the Senate Foreign Relations Committee, who told him "We in America know that in 50 years time Germany and Russia will exist, as two strong states. Will Poland exist too? We don't know that yet" (Strąk 2002). Germany's embrace of us, in other words, might not serve us well, and we must continue to prove, over and over, that we are America's great friend.

In the months ahead, others developed this theme about the dangers posed by Western Europe. It was as if now that Poland's entry into the EU was finally assured, many Poles needed to voice their distrust and dissatisfactions, while others made clear how the expression of dissatisfaction could bring real benefits. Smolar thus brought out both the angry and the strategic. The tenor of the subsequent debate suggests that dissatisfaction with Europe, more than approval of American policy, pushed Poland toward its ardent pro-American position in the dispute over Iraq.

EU as Danger

"The history of Europe . . . is the history of political or cultural kidnapping." So begins the most serious anti-EU polemic published in Poland's recent foreign policy debate, Marek Cichocki's *The Capture of Europe* (2004, 7). Its central theme is as its title announces: that Europe has been stolen, used by its dominant powers for their own purposes. Particular European countries, according to Cichocki, have always sought to endow Europe with universal significance in order to use it for their own purposes. For the French, Europe was once the Enlightenment; for the Germans, the *Sonderweg*. Today, for both of them, it is the EU.

That the EU agreed to take in new members changes nothing. On the contrary, says Cichocki, the dominant countries did this in a way that preserves their own dominance, as demonstrated by the constitutional convention. The convention's departure from Nice "is consistent with the interests of Germany. . . . It is also consistent with the French interest, according to which nothing should be possible within the EU without France. The object of the new arrangement . . . is to secure the leading political role of France and Germany in an enlarged EU" (Cichocki 2004, 22).[7]

Though writing mostly in a cool, analytical style, Cichocki, who would go on to become a key adviser to the 2005–2007 government of Jaroslaw Kaczyński, does not refrain from conspiratorial intimations. The constitutional convention, he says, was going smoothly, doing nothing to change the Nice accords, until the French and German foreign ministers began showing up in Fall 2002 "in order to gain greater control over the convention's work" (108). Only then did the convention propose to scrap Nice in favor of a "double majority" system with a new allocation of votes in the European Council that would give Germany the main power to promote new EU rules and France the main power to block them.

In Cichocki's view, Germany poses the greatest threat to Poland, as it presents its regional-dominating plans in benign language: in this case, the language of enlargement. "Soft colonization," he calls it (71). And thus he returns to Naumann's *Mitteleuropa*. "Naumann did not hide his nationalist motives. *Mitteleuropa* was above all a strategy to politically subordinate Germany's eastern borders in the interests of German security." But it also had its "soft" side; *Mitteleuropa*, after all, was said to be in Poland's interests too, as it would become integrated, with autonomy, into a larger power capable of obtaining what was best for its citizens.

Historically, says Cichocki, the German attitude to Poland has been of indifference or disgust on the one hand, and the desire to "civilize and stabilize" on the other (69). Both tendencies were obvious with Naumann. But Cichocki sees them in German policy in the 1990s as well: enlargement had as its goal the "civilizing" of the areas to Germany's east, but also the evening out of economic disparities, through financial aid and by "tying Poland closer to Germany. . . . It's no accident that Germany was the strongest proponent of enlargement" (75).

For Cichocki, the EU is but the latest iteration of *Mitteleuropa*. From 1914 to today it is the "same old play—only the times, costumes, and decorations have changed" (76).

Zdzisław Krasnodębski, one of the more prolific Polish writers on European affairs, and soon to become another close adviser of the Kaczyński government, sees the EU as *Mitteleuropa* finally realized. Didn't Naumann himself write that "whenever the French are willing we shall be able to offer them the hand of friendship" (Naumann 1917, 1–2)? Well, since World War II, the EU has been exactly that: the instrument for the would-be Franco-German domination of the continent. The EU, according to Krasnodębski, was set up in order to save France, and ended up rehabilitating Germany. France freed itself from German control, Germany freed itself from British control, and "today, Germany together with France stand at the head of a 'European directorate'" (Krasnodębski 2005). Though born in Poland, Krasnodębski has lived and taught in Germany since the early 1990s, and the main thrust of his writing is his admonition to Poles to beware of the EU: it is a transnational institution in image only, and otherwise is aimed at securing French and German dominance of an anti-American and pro-Russian Europe.

Others urge Poles to be wary of the EU not because it is a tool of a particular power, but because it stymies Poland's power at the very moment when it might otherwise finally be expressed. Jacek Saryusz-Wolski, for example, the first Polish plenipotentiary for EU integration and currently an influential member of the European Parliament, speaks only in a slightly more nuanced way than Cichocki or Krasnodębski. For Saryusz-Wolski, the transnational actor that is the EU must be treated with the same hard line with which it continually treats Poland. "In international politics," he says, "you are treated the way you behave," and so Poland will be taken seriously only if it acts tough. Saryusz-Wolski thus makes explicit the *bargaining* potential of the anti-EU approach. Toughness, he says, is "central to the EU canon. That is how Britain got its rebate [and] Spain its structural funds." Poland, however, because it took whatever was offered, has found itself continually demeaned, with developments since Nice only the latest example. For Saryusz-Wolski, the EU is not the transnational actor its proponents suggest. "So the question before us is: are we one of the large countries with whom others must talk, or one of the small ones you can ignore—which is how the 'Big Four' still treat us." Ever the realist, he concludes, "We are fighting now for our place in Europe" (in Kurski 2003).

By late 2003, conservative realists had made their case so powerfully, and without much opposition, that even the social democratic government started sounding like the Euroskeptics they were not. There were of course exceptions to the anti-EU approach, most prominently Aleksander Smolar and former Foreign Minister Bronislaw Geremek. In 2003, Smolar complained that Poland was acting as if it had no interests in Europe. He warned against Poland's growing EU reputation, six months before it was to join, as a troublesome country that makes demands without giving in return. "It is unacceptable for us to demand aid from the EU, because those are our principles, yet speak out against the EU in matters important to them, because those are our interests." Adopting a realist approach himself, Smolar argued that Poland's stance was exacting heavy long-term costs both politically and economically. "In politics, slogans such as 'Nice or Death!' do not go unpunished" (Kurski 2003). Geremek, meanwhile, just days before Poland's EU entry, lamented that Smolar had been proved right:

"Poland has never had as bad a reputation [in the EU] as it does today. We've fallen into unprecedented isolation" (Geremek 2004).

For the critics, "isolation" meant only that Poland had shown itself unwilling to capitulate to French and German dictates. Liberal pro-EU Poles retorted that France and Germany did not control European policy. The EU may have been *started* because of French and German concerns, acknowledges Smolar, but now it is trying to establish a new, post-power politics based on "compromise, consensus, and principles of solidarity." "Even Robert Kagan," he pleads, acknowledges this (in Kurski 2003). Yet the case of Poland's EU defenders was made weaker by the publication of the famous Habermas-Derrida manifesto in May 2003, which calls for Europe to move faster toward becoming a postnational state, yet says only a "core" of Western countries can now begin the process (Habermas-Derrida 2005). This relegation of the East to being at a lower stage of development, coming from a prominent German and prominent French intellectual, smacked of just the kind of condescension that Smolar was saying the West had given up. Though the letter expressed understanding that the East was "not yet ready to place limits on the sovereignty they have so recently gained," it nevertheless seemed to confirm charges of anti-EU Eastern critics that Westerners have a vision of Europe that does not include "us." It came to be seen as the left-wing version of Jacques Chirac's infamous quip, in early 2003, that by coming forth with their own position on Iraq, the East European countries "missed an excellent opportunity to shut up."

Continued missteps like these help explain the ability of this anti-EU line to become so dominant in Poland. Because there is no question that it did. For although the harsh critiques cited above were presented mainly by political figures associated with the political right, moderate liberals and even the social democratic government followed their lead. The slogan "Nice or Death!" in fact, was coined in 2003 by Jan Rokita, co-chairman of the liberal Civic Platform, which previously had been very supportive of the EU. And whereas the Social Democrats ran in 2001 on a strong pro-EU platform, by 2003 it too was denouncing any departure from Nice and making a great deal of anti-EU noise. All this was a result of the built-up frustrations with the West's handling of the accession process ever since 1989: the years of putting off a commitment to enlarge, the unequal economic arrangements, the "priest and penitent" nature of the negotiations. As Saryusz-Wolski noted, Poland was compelled first to "accept an asymmetrical association agreement, and then to accept membership on terms far below what was expected"—and below what previous members were awarded (in Kurski 2003). Even EU supporters had to acknowledge this. "Western Europe did a great deal to cool our affections," wrote Aleksander Smolar in 2004. "The negotiations to join Europe were carried out just the way Europe is: overly technical, lacking in symbolic gestures, without warmth or pathos. They never expressed much enthusiasm for us new members" (Smolar 2004). It is no wonder that the harsh critics shaped the political climate, now that membership was finally assured. Recent relations with the transnational EU made toughness, now that it could not be used against them, a compelling political position.

The critics were a motley group. Some denounced the idea of a "core Europe" because they wanted the EU to be nothing more than a loose conglomeration of states with open trade. Others criticized it for being run by France and Germany, whereas their aim was for a core that included Poland, too. The point, however, was that each of them advocated strong support for America as a way of gaining bargaining power within Europe.

Recall Maciej Łętowski's argument on behalf of Poland becoming a regional power with a special relationship to the United States: because otherwise, he says, Poland will remain "the economic vassal of a powerful Germany." For Krasnodębski, the EU's universalist ambitions, which the notion of a "core" Europe has accelerated, are contrary to Poland's need to build itself up as a strong country, both because of the dominating role of France and Germany in the EU and because such universalism makes them perpetually fascinated by Russia. Poland must stand with America in order to offset Europe, for "Anglo-Saxon culture, after all, has always had troubles with universalism" (Krasnodębski 2004).

Saryusz-Wolski, meanwhile, has always stressed that the aim of his harsh criticism of the EU is for Poland to secure its place *within* it. Thus, he does not challenge Smolar's claim that America has its own anti-EU interests in reaching out to Eastern Europe, nor does he defend America's position. He simply accepts that a strong alliance with America bolsters Poland's position within the EU.

Indeed, a striking thing about all the most vehement arguments for a strong pro-American position is how little they actually defended America. Whereas liberal idealists, such as Adam Michnik, supported the American invasion of Iraq because they appreciated the commitment to topple a malevolent dictatorship, and believed the United States could carry it out in the easy way it advertised, the conservative realists quoted here refrained from paeans about America's commitment to democracy (Ost 2004). They supported the invasion simply because America was doing it, and they hoped to use America to further their own aims within Europe.

Marek Cichocki said it best: "The consolidation of Poland's position in the transatlantic configuration through a special relationship with the United States must not be an aim in itself but . . . a necessary means to achieve the fundamental objective: a change in the balance of power within the EU upon enlargement, and preventing the scenario of the Franco-German core from [coming into] being" (Cichocki 2004, 33).[8]

The NATO Contrast

Why this belief that they could use America for their own purposes? Probably because the experience of joining NATO contrasted so sharply with the experience of joining the EU.

Poland's effort to get into *this* transnational institution was quite different from the one to get into the EU. For here, the United States supported East European entry without demanding much in return. There could be no characterization of priest and penitent here. Once the United States decided to expand NATO, accession came quickly and painlessly. The new member countries got the world's premier security guarantee, in return for which they promised to modernize their militaries and coordinate plans with the United States.

Of course coordination meant subordination. This was a transnational institution clearly under United States' control. Unlike for the EU, no Poles griped that some ran things secretly. Here, the United States ran things openly. But the benefits were such that no one else could provide. Unlike with the EU, the very *idea* of NATO was that the Eastern states would be subordinate to the United States. And since the asymmetry was so obvious, NATO enlargement went through without the indignities typical of EU accession. Whereas Western Europe issued stern reports of reproach to entering countries not following through on their responsibilities, the United States set the plans, pushed the new countries to follow through, and did not get too upset when they dallied. A year before joining

NATO, for example, Poland had serious deficiencies throughout its military. It still needed to change communication and command and control systems to NATO standards, modernize air defense, increase ammunition stocks, improve naval and air force training, and dramatically increase the English-language training of officers (Simon 2004). Even so, the United States did not threaten or even bluff that Poland might thus not be admitted, as happened frequently in EU negotiations. It simply restated its conditions and pushed Poland to follow through.

Indeed, if Eastern efforts to enter the EU too often seemed to bump up against European self-interest, its efforts to enter NATO seemed to put them into contact with stereotypical unselfish American idealism. In fact, that is precisely what American *critics* of enlargement objected to: that it was not, they charged, in America's interest. The critics charged that the costs to America would be high, and that the new countries had little to contribute. (As the largest country by far of the new members, only Poland was seen as being at all useful militarily.) They noted that President Clinton was not even promoting enlargement on the grounds that it would serve clear United States interests. It was "foreign policy as social work," as Michael Mandelbaum (1996) quipped, in an article with that title (see also Rubinstein 1998).

That characterization is surely inaccurate. Enlargement fit well with American plans to maintain its global dominance and forestall any challenge. It did come with costs, more than proponents were willing to acknowledge. But since World War II America has often been willing to pay to maintain its dominance. This would be no exception. For Eastern Europe, however, it *was* an exception. This was the first time they were the recipients of such American largesse. The contrast with EU accession was obvious.

Once President Clinton decided on enlargement—and his aim to maintain unquestioned American dominance was shared by his Republican rivals—East Europe was going to be accommodated. This allowed for the region to have a very different experience than it did with the EU. As a result, for the East European public, as well as for elites, it was easy to be pro-American. And easy to use pro-Americanism as a way to put pressure on the EU, particularly on France and Germany, which from 2002 to 2004—the very moment of EU expansion—had such differences with the United States.

What this means, then, is that transnational actors affect domestic politics not only by providing incentives and posing constraints, which assumes that national preferences are constant. They also themselves structure preferences. "National interest" is not a fixed concept, and what we see in postcommunist Europe is the way that the behavior of transnational actors helped elites decide what was in their interest. Of course, as I have shown, the historical record of relations between individual countries also matters. But the behavior of the EU allowed old suspicions to linger, and thereby facilitated the crystallization of recent foreign policy choices.

In the end, recent East European support for the United States does not signify permanent, long-term attraction. Rather, these countries have sought to use the United States to make gains within Europe. And it has probably been useful, too. Poland is not a very popular country in the EU today. It has the reputation of a country difficult to please, full of demands, cantankerous, and very pro-American. But it also has the reputation of being a tough country, whose opinions cannot be easily dismissed. Indeed, even Aleksander Smolar, Poland's strongest voice against his country's pro-American and anti-EU orientation, said in 2005 that all these policies had probably helped Poland more than hurt, gained it respect within Europe, even if grudgingly.[9] Polish demands within the EU are less likely to be ignored today. Indeed, they have not been ignored. The new Reform Treaty of Lisbon, signed in December of 2007, certifies the maintenance of the Nice rules until 2014, and it allows Poland to insist on using them in particular votes for another three years after that.

If, as Witold Gombrowicz once wrote, "God is the pistol [Poles] use to shoot Marx," we can say that America is the pistol they use to shoot Europe.

10

FROM TRANSITION

TO HEGEMONY

EXTENDING THE CULTURAL
POLITICS OF MILITARY
ALLIANCES AND
ENERGY SECURITY

Michael D. Kennedy

There is great value in trying to figure the relative influence of and relationship between transnational and domestic actors in policy making and agenda setting. Much good work has been undertaken, notably in this volume, in specifying how that balance shifts across particular networks of influence and policy domains, and how these levels of action combine in various ways in relatively complex systems. I believe, however, that this kind of institutional analysis can direct our attention away from the foundations in broader power relations and global transformations that enable these institutional politics and foci to work. I propose, therefore, that a more critical engagement of those deeper structures of power and change might be important to highlight in a new transnational scholarship. Simply put, a middle-range focus was understandable in the decade after communism's collapse in East Central Europe, but now it is time to put questions of global control over key resources and various degrees of national influence in that project back to the center of our analysis of global and post-communist transformations.

As questions of military contest and energy security become more central in public discourse, questions of hegemony and empire become manifestly more apparent. When consumer protection and health care reform in the process of accession to the EU shape our approach to assessing the balance of transnational and national influences, big power relations and stark alternatives hardly seem to matter. Of course more critical theorists will ask why certain regional references become sites for emulation, and others sites for alienation, even in these cases. But the parsimonious theorists among us are unlikely to ask about the conditions that make directions of change obvious until those conditions that lead us to normalize those trajectories shift. That shift has begun.

I have already proposed that such a shift began in 1999, during the course of NATO's intervention in the Wars of Yugoslav Succession (Kennedy 2002), but that shift has become much more substantial following the Rose and Orange Revolutions and the American-led intervention in Iraq in 2003. It is of course possible to interpret the colored revolutions in the same ways that we might discuss adoption of particular sections of the *acquis communautaire*; we can look at the particular microprocesses, distributions of resources, and patterns of strategic influence to assess the relative importance of Western versus indigenous sources of change. If one were to propose Western hegemony in the revolutions, or in East Central European accession to the EU or NATO, some might also suspect political sympathies with antidemocratic transnational or xenophobic domestic forces. Such groans only make my last point of departure more important.

Cultural politics are not just the stuff of protest marches or identity politics. Attempts to influence and transform the meanings, identities, values, and representations accompanying the exercise of power and influence inflect the questions and frames we bring to our scholarship, not only what activists bring to the streets. For that reason, we need to be particularly attentive to how our research programs reinforce normatively defensible hegemonies, or regrettably augment ethically dubious ones. I don't presume to categorize these hegemonies, much less offer a new and revised theory of hegemony and transition strategy, but I do wish to raise questions that might not sit easily with any of them by asking how our research on transnational and national influences on social change articulates the deeper power relations and alternative futures around which I believe we should organize more of our research.

Most discussions of transnational and national postcommunist European politics and social change seem to fit in a broader transition culture. Attending to the cultural politics of military alliances and energy security within Poland raises issues that transition culture does not pose very well, especially when in one case, a matter of security, energy, and democracy contributes to the fall of a government, while in another case, it hardly bears public discussion. The analytical implications of this shift in focus toward the cultural politics of more consequential power relations and global transformations raise essential questions.

Transition Culture in the New Transnational Agenda

In 1999, we could still speak without difficulty of the march of progress toward democracy and markets in the transition away from communist rule. For example, the following appeared on the World Bank Web site: "Since the fall of the Berlin Wall in 1989, countries in Central and Eastern Europe and Central Asia have been undergoing a dynamic process of economic and social transformation in their effort to create market economies. Throughout the region, countries have varied in the pace at which they have been able to put in place the components of a successful transformation to a market economy—and in their economic performance" (World Bank 1999).

This brief account was typical in the 1990s as analysts and politicians worked to give meaning to that decade's remarkable transformations. I have argued that such reflections were more than neat descriptions; they were part of a powerful transnational sensibility that I called "transition culture." This culture mobilized actors around certain logical and normative oppositions, valuations of expertise, and interpretations of history. It of course emphasized the opposition of socialism and capitalism, and the exhaustion of the former and normative superiority of the latter, but it also highlighted the value of generalizing expertise around the workings of market economies and democratic polities. In this culture, publics were perceived to be damaged by socialist rule, and thus not to be trusted. Consequently, resources and research were focused on elites in particular institutional niches and the institutional design around them. Global integration was taken to be a given, and only a matter of debate about what course it might take and who would benefit most from it. Transition culture became, in the cultural sociological sense, a tool kit with which actors variously located could realize their interests and define their frustrations. It also wound up helping to reconstitute East Europeans' interests and strategies in addition to inspiring volumes of social scientific research about this transformation.

I established this cultural formation with reference to cultural artifacts, focus groups, and business practices, but it may be useful to consider its explicit articulation with the dominant frame for interpreting transnational politics that shapes this volume. For our choice may be to do more than add another dimension of transition; we might also consider directly what theory of power and change articulates the research agenda we elaborate.

Orenstein, Bloom, and Lindstrom characterize the new transnational scholarship with reference to five interlocking claims, with emphases on multiple trends in various fields with multiple outcomes; nonstate actors; the nondiplomatic transnational ties of states themselves, notably in the production of international norms; networked, rather than hierarchical and territorial forms of interaction; and the mutual formation of ideas and interests. Although they refer principally to political scientists in establishing this trajectory, it certainly fits with the way sociology tends to approach power relations within and across societies (see Latham and Sassen 2005). Unlike much sociology, however, this agenda searches for ways to highlight the growing complexity of organizational forces without focusing on how deeply structured power relations constitute this space and shape its trajectories.

It is useful for political science to pluralize the range of issues that might be studied, but it is also important to keep in mind how one agenda might set the terms for other agendas. It is novel to consider the relative independence of international organizations from states, but it is also good to keep in mind the layers of influence powerful states can manage when it matters. I also like to consider the ways in which the transnational policy community can do more than reflect power, and work with other players on the scene to create possibilities, but I want to know the limits of action within which this can take place. As most sociologists would, I like appealing to the multiplicity and complexity of global systems, but in that movement I am concerned not to lose sight of the question of whether there are dominant axes that shape more particular contests.

Although moved to ask genuinely new and interesting questions, I can see in this new agenda transition culture's extension. I don't think that such an extension is as important, even with an emphasis on these five interlocking points, as it might be to consider transition culture's power-laded constitution.

In an eloquent comparison of places and issues, Wade Jacoby (2004) has found that in the explanation of transnational policy adoption and implementation, one must attend more to the latter than to the former in order to understand outcomes.[1] In particular, one should attend to the density of recipient actors, and of international organizational rules, in particular issue areas. For example, when domestic actors and foreign rules are both sparse, as in consumer protection, there are relatively few policy innovations and outcomes. When those rules are few but those actors are many, more indigenously driven continuous learning tends to take place, as in health care. When there are more foreign rules than existing domestic actors organized to care about them, he notes a kind of scaffolding, as when EU regional policy helped to make domestic regional interests and actors. Open struggle between transnational and national actors emerges, however, when there are both lots of rules and many previously constituted actors, evident in the reform of agriculture for the EU and of the military as it moved into NATO. But just as the East European political elites treated it as obvious, so Jacoby treats the wish to emulate and join transnational organizations as points of departure, rather than questions in their own right.

It is important to keep in mind against what Jacoby is arguing—this is no simple transfer of know-how and of policies. One must treat all of the actors in the process of adapting to various kinds of transnational organizations as informed and empowered, ready to resist when their interests are challenged, and to use transnational resources to realize other desires. But their politics, and Jacoby's analysis, function within the frame of transition culture itself.

Transition culture is organized around the notion that democracies recognize the value of contest and markets the value of competition, if within the terms established by the deeper structure of the system in which those contests are embedded and as they are articulated by those privileged within it. This is not even a point of debate when it comes to accession, for, after all, the powerful are in the position to decide whether or not those who wish to join them can. In Jacoby's terms, these penitents must be sufficiently distant from the dysfunctional and immoral past they must escape, while assuming the basic functionality, and morality, of the system they aspire to join. Transition culture seems to allow the naming of priests and penitents, so long as the alternatives under discussion are the ones sanctified by the system itself. One begins to depart from the terms of transition, however, when the sins of the sacred become more apparent, as they are in Zsuzsa Gille's work.

Gille traces the transformation of the waste economy in Hungary, through various periods of socialist management in which reuse, rather than disposal, realized some prominence in waste management (Gille 2007). But the Hungarian reforms of the 1980s helped to produce not only new market mechanisms but also new ways of conceiving efficiency and profit, with additionally harmful environmental consequences. One effect of this was to develop a new technology around incinerators for the elimination of waste, whose substantial toxic effects were publicly acknowledged only after 1989. Acknowledgment of social problems was not the only fruit of communism's end, however.

As Hungary and other EU acceding postsocialist societies sought to affirm their Western credentials, they sometimes had to take in more than lessons in marketing and human resource management. Gille documents how a small capacity incinerator in Garé, Baranya County, won new foreign investments and technology, but in order to make them sufficiently profitable, they had to import additional waste, conveniently from the West, in order to make the technological and economic investments cost effective. By providing the technology, the investments, and the waste, and even by modeling the legislation that allowed it, the EU in effect created a new landscape in Hungary in this specific instance that can be seen across the whole of the postsocialist world. It is filled with more landfills, incinerators to deal with them, and the environment resulting from it. Gille therefore argues that transition's radiant European future became a bit more toxic than accession promised and EU environmental policy would suggest.

Although both Jacoby and Gille thus lay out the complicated interplay of domestic and transnational forces in establishing outcomes, focus on nonstate actors in outlining contests, and highlight the mutual formation of ideas and interests, among other parts of the new transnational scholarship, the cultural politics they extend are different. Jacoby works within transition culture itself, explaining how variations take place within the broad stroke of adaptation to larger structures beyond broad reformulation, although subject to manipulation within its terms. Gille does not find terrific agency to create meaningful alternatives either, but she highlights the hegemonies at work in her explication of how explicit alternatives mask the deeper impositions involved in joining the EU, where the residents of Garé must choose between public health and economic well-being, while West Europeans rejoice in the export of that very choice.

In short, as we consider the new transnational agenda, we should become even more attentive to how the complexity of the system and the mutual constitution of ideas and interests are articulated with the deeper power structures that constitute our views of what is possible and what is not, and who wins and who loses, within and beyond the postcommunist space itself. Much as Gille suggests in her analysis of the waste economy, not all deep power structures are so obvious, and therefore it is important to recall her work to illustrate just how deeply buried some trajectories are in our transnational and national systems. But some of those deep structures are now coming right to the surface, making our attention to control and contests over the major means of power all the more necessary. Indeed, Jacoby himself highlights that possibility.

Geopolitical Foundations of Transition and Its Sequel

Noting that Poland, Hungary, and the Czech Republic entered NATO very shortly before the bombing of Serbia in 1999, he references the delicate cultural politics Hungarian and Czech elites managed in supporting their newfound military allies. He finished writing his book shortly after the last war in Iraq began and highlights similar dilemmas facing political elites as they moved with the United States, against France and Germany, and without the majority support of their publics. By so doing, he highlights one of the underlying conditions that enabled transition culture to be compelling. Transition culture depended on the containment of violence and therefore the vision of one world into which postcommunist societies might transition.

One of the principles that enabled transition culture to develop thus was complementary behavior by those with control over the means of violence and the use of force. This much I have already said (Kennedy 2002): First, the Soviet Union had to be "willing" to allow the transformations within Eastern Europe. Second, domestic actors with control over the means of violence within these countries had to eschew violence or be prevented from using it. Finally, those who wished to launch transition had themselves not only to resist temptations to use violence, but also to be wary of provocations that would justify state violence. Transition depended on peaceful change and the perception that this peace was in the interests of all nations. With this vision, it could avoid the cycles of violence likely to be found with the exercise of force.

Of course there were some regions in the 1990s that were embedded in violence. Both the Caucasus and the Balkans had violent contest built into their transformations and thus never simply fit into the story of transition. The passions, loyalties, and legal contests of wartime and postwar post-communist social change cannot be addressed adequately within the framework favored by transition culture, one that minimizes attention to the cultural politics of power and change. But these war stories were critical for the cultural politics of transition itself.

War was a danger that might be identified for those, especially in ethnically mixed areas, who did not take the path of transition and instead took the path of nationalism. War could be treated as an anomaly, something that normal Western societies did not undertake (Williams 2007).[2] It was contrary to the trend toward an integrated and peaceful globalized economy. But when the West became directly involved in military action against Serbia, that presumption could be challenged. The West erased the possibility of constructing itself as an integrated and simply transcendent party in the unfolding of global change. Regardless of whether one believed that intervention to be the first war launched in the name of human rights or not, the use of force to establish change fundamentally changed the conditions of transition culture. The cultural contest over the exercise of force came to the fore, first of all with naming the quality of power associated with the military power of the United States. Transition culture now, instead of dealing with the decentered power relations of globalization, had to contend with questions of American militarism and imperialism (see Giddens 1990; Pieterse 2004; Steinmetz 2005).

This worry is not uniformly held. After all, it was the use of force that enabled, in Serbia, the stirrings of democratic change, which itself was contagious. Just as in 1989 we saw the export of roundtable negotiations, in the start of the new millennium we saw the export of youth movements mobilizing democratic revolutions. Serbia's Otpor activists helped Georgia's Kmara youth movement, which in turn instructed Ukraine's Pora movement of young people. And of course this revival of transition culture is visible among the heads of governments themselves; the 11 January 2005 joint declaration by President Mikheil Saakashvili of Georgia and President Viktor Yushchenko of Ukraine sounded like a script out of transition culture itself: "We are certain that the revolutions in Georgia and Ukraine are shaping the new wave of liberty in Europe. . . . They will usher in the ultimate victory of liberty and democracy across the European continent."[3] Indeed, Karatnycky echoes that which is a powerful sentiment, within the region and in the West: "the orange revolution had set a major new landmark in the postcommunist history of eastern Europe, a seismic shift Westward in the geopolitics of the region. Ukraine's revolution as just the latest in a series of victories for 'people power'—in Poland, Hungary, and Czechoslovakia in the late 1980s and, more recently, in Serbia and Georgia" (Karatnycky 2005, 35).

This account is certainly true in the revolutionary sense, but profoundly misleading at the geopolitical level. The foundations of force have shifted fundamentally over this period, with, I would propose, major consequence.

First, in 1989, while the USSR was falling behind the West in military technology, it was still clearly a bipolar world. The USSR could let Eastern Europe go because it was sufficiently confident of its own communist allies' popularity within their countries. At the same time Russia saw this new peace offensive as a way of countering the military advantage accruing to the United States. The Soviets sought a new strategy to ally with Western Europe against the American buildup. The return of Eastern Europe to Europe was designed as a way to open the door for Russia to Europe. Of course we could, with Jacques Levesque (1997), marvel at the Leninist arrogance of the Soviets in thinking their parties could realize influence and that Russia might become closer to Europe than the Americans. But in little more than a decade, Gorbachev's foreign policy aims might ultimately be right, even if they are realized on very different foundations.

Oil and gas have become newly central, or at least evident, in geopolitics. Michael Mann (2004) and David Harvey (2003), for example, make the control over oil central to their argument about the contours of American empire today. With control over oil and gas increasingly central to the world economy, and to military efficacy, and with its trade in dollars critical to American financial interests, direct American control over Iraq not only assures American control over a key productive asset, but also extends American power vis-à-vis Europe and China in the relative extension of those two in their own regional trading blocs in the larger world economy.

Russia of course has as much interest, if not more interest, in the global political economy of oil and gas. The World Bank has estimated that in 2003 about 25 percent of Russian GDP depended on the oil and gas sector; in that same year, Russia was behind only Saudi Arabia in the number of barrels of crude oil produced.[4] In terms of foreign policy, therefore, Russia must take care about its energy interests as much as anything else, which means that it must attend to Central Asia, the Caucasus, and the transit countries that funnel its oil and gas to its wealthy European consumers.[5]

While the EU is equivalent to the United States in economic activity, it is far more dependent on foreign sources of energy, with two-thirds of its energy imported; oil is the leading resource, providing over 40 percent of all power.[6] Russia and the EU are especially closely tied; in 2001, "over 19% of total net European Union oil imports and over 40% of European Union gas imports came from Russia. During the same year, energy exports accounted, in value, for nearly 50% of total Russian exports to the European Union."[7] While Gorbachev's peace offensive opened a much wider road to Europe, energy exports now help to pave that road. "Russian oil and gas exporting companies that already all but dominate Europe's energy supplies. . . . According to the International Energy Agency, by 2020, natural gas will account for 62 percent of Europe's energy consumption, and Russia will supply two-thirds of that gas. . . . Germany already gets 35 percent of its oil and 40 percent of its gas from Russia, figures that will steadily increase as Germany pursues its policy of winding down its nuclear power industry," cautions one American observer.[8] Apparently, German policy itself viewed this energy dependency as a way to integrate Russia into Europe on commercial and geopolitical terms (Alexander Rah in Landler 2006).

Some authors have gone further to wonder whether a European/Eurasian trading bloc is emerging, designed to challenge American superiority in economic affairs (see Harvey 2003). In this, the EU and Russia could find common ground with the euro as the currency that denominates cooperation.

And of course this growing role for the euro runs contrary to American interests, as does growing Russian influence over the European energy market.

By looking at the Rose Revolution and Orange Revolution in these terms, we see something more than transition culture's extension. We see not only an extension of freedom but also critical transformations in energy geopolitics that can reduce Russian influence and enhance U.S. control over the distribution of energy, with consequent maintenance of American economic influence in the formation of a European/Eurasian trading bloc.

It is difficult, therefore, not to find at least compatibility between American strategic interests in energy and its support for Georgia before and within the Rose Revolution.[9] Azerbaijan's "deal of the century"—that extraordinary investment in Azerbaijani oil production—required a means to transport the Caspian Sea oil to the West (see Gökay 2001). The Americans refused to countenance an Iranian pipeline, and the Azeri war with Armenia made the most direct route impossible, requiring a Georgian transit. Indeed, even Armenian enclaves within Georgia were avoided in the construction of this pipeline from Baku through Tblisi to the Turkish terminal in Ceyhan.[10] This BTC pipeline was officially launched on 10 May 2005.[11]

The pipeline proved a difficult sell, for a combination of economic, environmental, and political reasons (Fuller 2004). Environmental risks accompanying inadequate safety coating for the line led the major private investor, Italy's Banca Intesa, to pull out.[12] Even more worrisome, however, were potential terrorist attacks on the pipeline. Perhaps laying the pipelines beyond Armenian enclaves was a reasonable security measure, but these detours were not the only cost. The extensive American antiterrorist training of Georgian troops is not only designed for war on Al Qaeda, but to assure the pipeline's security. The Americans, and Georgians, must do all they can to keep the Caucasus peaceful, in order to make this alternative pipeline realize its economic potential. The disruption of this pipeline would not be nearly so costly to Russian geostrategic interests, of course.

Practically speaking, therefore, the Russians could do what they can to disrupt the pipeline or to gain economic control of it. In 2005, Gazprom tried to buy the main north/south import line bringing gas to Georgia and to Armenia from Russia,[13] reinforcing the strategy they have undertaken in Armenia to use their ownership of the means of energy production to assure control over the Armenian economy. This only reinforces the interest the United States has in making the Caucasus energy independent of Russia and squeezing Russia out of Caspian oil and gas transit.

This contest in the Caucasus is a great place to explore the importance and utility of thinking in terms of imperial contest rather than transition culture or globalization, but since the Orange Revolution its utility has become even more obvious in Ukraine.

Of course it did not take colored revolutions for strategic thinkers to recognize how Ukraine could become a key ally for containing Russia. For example, Zbigniew Brzezinski characterized Ukraine as a "geopolitical pivot": "Ukraine, a new and important space on the Eurasian chessboard is a geopolitical pivot because its very existence as an independent country helps to transform Russia. Without Ukraine, Russia ceases to be a Eurasian empire. Russia without Ukraine can still strive for imperial status, but it would then become a predominantly Asian imperial state, more likely to be drawn into debilitating conflicts with aroused Central Asians, who would then be supported by their fellow Islamic states to the south" (Brzezinski 1997, 46). Significantly, this is not only a matter of continental location but, critically, of energy geopolitics. As it is, Ukraine is, in the eyes of energy experts, an ideal corridor for oil and natural gas to transit from Russia and the Caspian Sea region to European markets. But does a pivot function well as a corridor? Russian leaders clearly did not think so before the Orange Revolution, and most vividly do not think so now. In a dispute over prices for natural gas, Russia cut off its supply to Ukraine and, Ukrainian leaders argue, cut as well the supply to Europe that crosses Ukrainian territory. Russian leaders accuse Ukrainians of stealing that gas, while Europeans and others castigate the Russians for their unreliability as energy partners (Kramer 2006).

Given these politics, one can see why Ukraine seeks to decrease its energy dependence on Russia and to turn to the Caspian region. They must bet on a new Odessa-Brody pipeline and the Pivdenny maritime terminal, which would ultimately allow it to transmit Kazakh oil through Poland to Plock and then to Gdansk, where it would be exported. On 1 March 2005, Ukrainian Prime Minister Yulia Tymoshenko and her Georgian counterpart Zurab Nogaideli announced that the Odessa-Brody pipeline would carry oil shipments from Kazakhstan and Azerbaijan to Western Europe.[14] And here, finally, we find Poland's place, and ultimately the challenge of cultural politics around energy security and military alliances, in their American affinity.

Poland is a small transit country for Russian oil, although it does transfer Russian oil to Germany. Poland has been actively involved in Ukraine, with the EU, to develop this corridor. It is using EU funds to build the pipeline that will connect to Plock sometime in the next several years. By building a pipeline connecting Caspian oil from Georgia and Ukraine, Poland is therefore actively involved in helping to reduce Russian energy power over Europe. While Russian oil and gas might be cheaper, in the end, business leaders argue, it is critical to diversify sources of oil and gas to assure not only security but good bargaining leverage. This is not just a matter of Polish or European interest, however; it is also a critical question for American influence in Europe and ultimately, then, a question of military alliances and economic trading blocs.

Such an interest in deep structures of power relations and their implications for global change is less today a matter of theoretical preference. Of course it remains important to be able to identify why some fields of emulation are more contentious than others by referring to the various compositions of rules and resources in particular fields. But it is more important today than it was in the days of transition to attend to the hegemonies at work in structuring those very contests, for the relative consensus underlying transition is fading before a world increasingly torn by the explicit use of violence and its proxy in control over energy.

Although my critical sociological affinities are apparent in *Cultural Formations of Postcommunism*, I did not rely explicitly on the concept of hegemony to elaborate transition culture. I found within transition culture sufficient spaces for hope to make the emphasis on transition culture's power-laden limitations of action misplaced. Theorizing transition culture first as hegemony would locate the critical disposition at a greater distance from transition's immanent potentials than I found useful. Inspired by the kind of cultural historical sociology associated with Sewell (2005), I sought to identify what transition culture's multiplicities, intersectionalities, and transposable schemas offered to the constitution of a more critical theory and practice of transition (see also Kennedy 1999). But, in retrospect, this comfort within transition culture's frame also reflected its considerable hegemony during the 1990s.

Hegemony has a complex genealogy (Laclau and Mouffe 1985), but it generally refers to some kind of authority based on consent by subjects whose implication in the constitution of that authority is not simply voluntary. In contrast to Weber's legitimate domination whose recognition depends on voluntary acquiescence to authority, hegemony's consent is itself embedded in the rules of institutions whose allocation of resources create real incentives for accepting the authority of others. By referring to hegemony, we are motivated to explain how the acquiescence of subjects to authority is itself constituted.

Building on David Laitin (1986), Jan Kubik and Amy Linch (2007) are especially helpful in breaking this notion of hegemony apart by referring both to its semiotic and psychosocial dimensions. On the one hand, they argue that hegemony is constituted when a certain discourse saturates the public space, making alternative formulations hard to articulate. Hegemony is limited, however, if that saturation does not resonate with those supposedly formed by it. In Poland, for example, communist discourse saturated the public space for most of the party's rule, but it did not resonate with most of the Polish people. Thus, in order for us to analyze how hegemony works, we need to attend both to the production and organization of the discourse that is hegemonic, but at the same time understand its reception and use by those supposedly constituted by it. There is, however, another level of hegemony's analysis that we need to unpack before proceeding.

Cultural schema, or generalizable procedures, operate at all sorts of depths, from superficial etiquette like the rules of the queue to deep structures like Levi-Straussian binary codes. Hegemony can operate at all of these levels, but we typically reserve the term for those levels of cultural structure that are themselves mutable, where counterhegemonies are in practice or at least imaginable. For example, despite capitalism's historical and geographical variety, Sewell (2005, 150) notes that "the core procedure of capitalism—the conversion of use value into exchange value or the commodification of things—is exceptionally transposable" and durable. It is important, when we analyze hegemony, to recognize the power of these deepest structures, the way in which they help to shape variations in more mutable structures, and the contests accompanying them.

The hegemony of transition culture operates, therefore, at many different levels. The hegemony of commodification within transition culture is not now the principal axis of contest in transition culture's wake, even in the realm of energy where one might argue that energy's commodification has itself produced the very contests we ought to analyze more closely (Gille

2007). However, the way hegemony works in the suturing of democracy, markets, Western alliances, and peace is manifestly at risk. Those at work in setting the terms of change seem to think so, too.

The Cultural Politics of Military Alliances and Energy Security

Although such a meeting is hardly unprecedented, I learned an exceptional amount during one session at Cambridge University in which the British Ministry of Defense and other organizations, alongside academics, struggled to define the principal challenges to human security in these times. While we can agree that terrorists and their motivations are critical to understanding these challenges, we are not so clear, when we work at a transnational level, about the more fundamental sources of human insecurity. Some raised the question whether the wish to export democracy was, or was not, a destabilizing influence; others doubted whether the enduring and deep Anglo-American alliance could survive the growing divergence of national interest and values between Europe and America. But most striking, some wondered whether foreign policy is becoming too democratic, destabilizing the alliances that need to be made in order to keep the world secure (University of Cambridge 2003).

When questions like that are posed, we should also rethink the broader narratives used to think about global change. Does the idea of increasing global integration and growing democratization capture what we need to address when we think about the tensions between democracy and good foreign policy? Can we, for example, use Craig Calhoun's formulation of the qualities of a rational critical public sphere to assess the quality of discussion around the conditions of energy security and military alliances? Calhoun writes the following: "We need to ask how responsive public opinion is to reasoned argument, how well any potential public sphere benefits from the potential for self correction and collective education implicit in the possibilities for rational-critical discourse. And we need to know how committed participants are to the processes of public discourse and through that to each other. Finally, and not least of all, we need to ask how effectively the public opinion formed can influence social institutions and wielders of economic, political, or indeed cultural power" (2003, 246). Can we think about these terms when security is the topic for discussion?

When going to war in Iraq, American leaders could not apparently discuss the real threats Iraq posed and instead focused on issues that were resonant with public opinion—ties to Al Qaeda and possession of weapons of mass destruction—that ultimately proved to be unfounded. The real power Saddam Hussein enjoyed around oil production in the eventuality of a larger energy crisis could not be put directly on the democratic table. In part, I would propose, this was because of the effective conquest of the public discourse by terms like "no blood for oil." This slogan became one of the dominant cultural frames organizing public protest across the world to the American-led invasion of Iraq. In fact, one can also find this slogan at the extensive Web site in Poland dedicated to this very issue.[15] But as much as America's political elites hardly debated the move toward war, Poland's political authorities also failed at such an exercise in democratic deliberation, if for very different reasons (Shelton 2004).

AMERICAN VALUES

The meaning of the Polish soldiers in Iraq for the public, and for the elite, is strategically ambiguous, with the tension between principles and pragmatism animating discussion. For example, Włodzimierz Cimoszewicz, then minister for foreign affairs, said that this decision to join America was based exclusively on normative grounds: "We did not expect to make political profits or economic gains. The decision to support the invasion of Iraq was mainly based on our understanding of the true meaning of alliance and solidarity" (Little 2004). At the same time, this is all done with a wink, because within parliament, there were implied "paybacks" for this support, whether with regard to changing the terms of visas for Poles visiting America or for other kinds of preferred treatment, like contracts for postwar Iraqi reconstruction. To treat this alliance in public as a quid pro quo would in fact diminish the value of the alliance, but it is useful to examine how the returns on the Polish investment in the alliance might be viewed.

For example, the U.S. Diplomatic Mission to Warsaw displays on its Web site several such successes—the export of 240 flatbed rail cars to the Iraqi Republic Railways Company by the Wagony Swidnica company. Its majority owner is a U.S. company called Greenbrier, the Web site notes (U.S. Department of State 2005a). In July 2005, Bumar, a state-owned Polish defense company,[16] signed a $100 million contract (*Defense News* 2005) with the Iraqi Ministry of Defense to supply 600 Dzik-3 armored vehicles and 115 BTR 80 transports to the Iraqi army (U.S. Department of State 2005b). This follows other deals previously negotiated that were worth about $236 million in the supply of helicopters, weapons, ambulances, and fuel and water systems (Hołdanowicz 2005).[17] But these are relatively small investments in comparison to what one might expect. It might be more useful, therefore, to consider the transaction that has been called the "deal of the century" in Poland: the $3.5 billion purchase of forty-eight F-16 fighter planes from Lockheed Martin (Little 2004), the biggest military purchase since the end of the cold war by any postcommunist country (Stylinski 2003).

This deal, signed on 18 April 2003, offers incredible terms, at least on paper. Not only is payment delayed for eight years, at below interest rate expectations, and guaranteed by the U.S. Congress, but it also provides offset payments to Poland. The terms of the deal assure that, over ten years, at least $6 billion in U.S. investments would go to Poland, with estimates sometimes going up to $7.5 billion and $12 billion, depending on how one values the multiplier associated with the initial economic outlay. It is not a simple win/win outcome, however, especially for Polish/European relations.

Poland was also considering other planes for their purchase, planes made in the EU, the Swedish-British Gripen jet and the French-made Mirage 2000.[18] Poland has paid for their American choice, with vary degrees of openness. Some speculate, for instance, that PSA Peugeot-Citroen chose Slovakia over Poland for the construction of a new factory as payback (Trebski et al. 2005). Sometimes it is more explicit. President Chirac, on the occasion of the visit by Vice Minister and Minister of the Economy Jerzy Hausner to Paris on 28 February 2005, reminded him that he should buy Airbus rather than Boeing 787s when Poland considers adding six planes (a $500–$700 million contract) to its commercial fleet in Polish Airlines (the government owns 68 percent of the stock in LOT). This, he implied, would help Poland overcome the damage that came from buying the American fighter planes. And if they do not buy Airbus, they could suffer when it comes to the EU budget in 2007.[19]

This whole public debate is misleading at one level. After all, the fighter jet deal is only one of many, and the only one, in one recent list, that went to an American firm rather than a European or Israeli firm, but this particular aircraft deal strikes a chord because it is tied so closely to military alliances, and the perception that Poland is insufficiently European, and is a Trojan horse, or even a Trojan donkey, for America in Europe (Trebski et al. 2005). That perception has of course been heightened recently by the speculation that Poland hosted secret detention camps for prisoners taken in the American-led war on terrorism. Transatlantic and East/West European tensions grow, too, with this very uncertainty, leading EU spokesman Frisco Roscam Abbing to warn that Poland would face sanctions if any breach of European treaty rules had been made (Dempsen and Kanter 2005).

Although we witnessed a major shift in the Polish political authorities with parliamentary and presidential elections in the fall of 2005, it is not obvious that there will be any major changes in this Polish/American alliance. Indeed, the new government announced that instead of bringing Polish troops home early in 2006, as the previous government intended, they would remain through the end of the year (BBC 2005).

There are, nevertheless, many reasons why we should imagine such a shift: the Polish-American alliance has been developed at the cost of Poland's European relationships; it has depended on muted discussion in the Polish public, distorting democracy's vigor; it has cost seventeen Polish lives in a conflict most Poles do not believe they should engage in, even one that violates Catholic sensibilities (see Bortnowska et al. 2004); and, finally, it is based on a quid pro quo that is increasingly perceived to be dubious at best.[20] Poland still does not enjoy the visa situation its West European neighbors enjoy, and the deal of the century looks a bit less dramatic. In short, we need to ask why Polish/American alliances remain so firm when there are plenty of reasons one could imagine their attrition.

One might simply argue that a strong Polish/American alliance is necessary to assure Poland's place in Europe and its security overall, but the cultural politics reinforcing that security might enjoy many layers. For example, when French President Chirac chastised Poles and other East Europeans as if they were children, telling them that "they missed a good opportunity to keep quiet" in the debate over the invasion of Iraq, we find not only an illustration of West/East European cultural tensions (CNN 2003); we also find, in this faux pas, a terrific opportunity for East Europeans to respond with outrage and to use their American affinities to remind the arrogant that they are nobody's inferiors.

In brief, the cultural politics of Poland's military alliance with America in general, and particularly around Iraq, deserves more extensive analysis on many different levels. We could try to explain it as Polish leaders do, with reference to high-minded notions of solidarity and commitments to liberation, forged in the domestic struggle against communism with abiding American assistance. Those norms are clearly operative. We could try to explain it with reference to the significance of ties made around the military industrial complex, by considering how the Pentagon, Lockheed Martin, and U.S. foreign policy worked to assure Polish loyalties, but we would have to explain how European countervailing pressures failed to win out over American preferences. We might dig even deeper and wonder to what extent our Polish colleagues were thinking not only about postwar military contacts but also energy security in the long run, recognizing the dangers of Russian dependency in ways that their EU neighbors to the west hardly appreciated.

We may not find the answers to these questions by assessing what takes place in democratic public deliberations, however, because their very formulation requires an expertise, and a sense of future risks and needs, that can hardly be developed in democratic public spheres. That, at least, could be one reason why Polish political elites are wary to subject the alliance with America to much democratic deliberation. They are not so wary, however, when it comes to identifying the threats posed by Russia. Here we often find that superficial interpretations of public expressions capture the basic problem. This was especially evident in 2005 around Orlengate and Jan Kulczyk.

RUSSIAN THREATS

Jan Kulczyk is Poland's richest man, about four times richer than the second richest person, with a personal fortune worth around $4 billion. His investments include a 14 percent stake in TPSA, the partially privatized former state telecommunications company, and 10 percent in PKN Orlen, the Polish oil refinery based in Gdansk. But he misstepped. While the story was still not complete on my writing, I rely on what I learned during my visit to Poland in March 2005, for my ethnographic present.

In 2002, Jan Kulczyk proposed to Prime Minister Leszek Miller that they could merge the Gdansk Refinery with Orlen and sell both of them. Although formally illegal for anyone other than someone from the Ministry of the Treasury to negotiate about selling state property (Andrusz and Bartyzel 2004), Kulczyk met in October with Wagit Alekpierow, the chief of Lukoil, in London and tried to sell him this idea.[21] He also learned, he said, that the Russians tried to bribe the minister of the economy and the chief of the plant, which he reported to the proper Polish authorities. Still a few months later, when meeting with a Russian spy, Vladimir Alganov (whose friendship with Józef Oleksy caused the latter to resign as prime minister on 24 January 1996, and who as first secretary in the Russian embassy in Warsaw spied on the country for years but who is now retired and a representative for the Russian oil industry), in Vienna,[22] he supposedly discussed the possible sale of Orlen and Gdansk Refinery. Present at the meeting were Polish intelligence agents who took notes indicating that Kulczyk reportedly said that he could reach "pierwszy," or the number one, whom those investigating assumed to be President Kwaśniewski, to get his full support for the sale.[23]

This controversy becomes important for two reasons. Kulczyk had dealt previously with foreign interests and major privatizations, including that of TPSA and French Telecom. But this time, he was dealing with Russians, and with energy, something that affects security much more than telephone services and that inspires political passions like nothing else.[24]

This charge led to the formation of a parliamentary commission of investigation dedicated to Orlen in July 2004.[25] Ultimately, the original concerns motivating the commission's foundation paled in comparison to the intrigues that grew out of this investigation. As the left would have it, the commission was motivated by a political agenda led by right-wing parties. Its leading actors included Zbigniew Wassermann of Law and Justice (Prawo i Sprawiedliwość) and Roman Giertych of the League of Polish Families (Liga Polskich Rodzin) (both of whom are exceptional interrogators, the first of whom is a former prosecutor and the latter of whom is the vice chair).

The commission extended its mandate to investigate ties between the president's chancellery and business leaders, and who was connected with whom.[26] Connecting charges of corruption to questions of patriotism itself, the man who would ultimately lead his party to parliamentary victory in the fall of 2005, and whose twin brother would become president, charged Kwaśniewski with having a file in Russia.[27] Building on these questions of corruption and treason, and faced with potentially incriminating evidence of his own complicity in the corruption scandal, Włodzimierz Cimoszewicz, the presidential candidate most clearly associated with

President Kwaśniewski, resigned on 14 September 2005 from the race for president. On 25 September 2005, the 146-page report was submitted to the Marshal of the Sejm, in which Roman Giertych proposed that President Kwaśniewski sought to sell the Polish fuel sector to the Russian agents (*Gazeta Wyborcza* 2005a).

Such tensions overwhelmed the Polish public sphere in the middle of 2005. They reflected an invigorated public sphere, raising questions of military alliances, energy security, and democracy in ways that, while highly politicized, would no doubt have won critical acclaim from other quarters had such questions been raised around energy security, military alliances, and democracy in the decision to ally with America in the occupation of Iraq. My point is not, however, to make the obvious one that the Polish public sphere can be mobilized by Russophobia, while problematic aspects of its American alliance are handled with a relative wink. That is, in a certain sense, obvious given sympathies and suspicions in the Polish electorate (Bernstein 2005).

Instead, I wonder whether we can judge the quality of these matters of energy security in the terms that Calhoun offers—is the Orlengate affair superior because of the extensive debate offered around questions of energy needs and national security, or inferior because it was so clearly tied to a political agenda designed to weaken the left in Polish politics? Or is the public discussion around the Polish alliance in Iraq and the purchase of F-16 fighter jets superior because it ceded so much to political authorities who claim to understand the character of threats, and the value of military alliances, better? Does the nature of one's answer simply depend on a priori political affinities, or can we develop methods and critical approaches that will identify the conditions under which relative consensus reflects an accurate assessment of the real state of needs, and when raucous debate is not just good for its own sake but might even be a distraction from what needs to be discussed? In short, can we address the conditions of hegemony not only in terms of how it masks the exercise of power, but also in terms of the degree to which it reflects realistic assessments based on rational-critical discussion within appropriate publics? That, it seems, is the key question within national and transnational public spheres. And that requires a different extension of transition culture, moving its exploration into not only a transnational sphere but also more directly into a question of power and culture.

From Transition to Hegemony?

The conditions that enabled transition culture's questions to be central are disappearing. Colored revolutions reanimated its political passions and appeared to invigorate transition culture's scientific terms. Proving the domestic sources for democracy's embrace in struggles against dictatorships is a good thing, but it also distracts us from the nightmare questions that the 1990s enabled us to overlook. Control over the major energy resources enabling economic development remain highly concentrated, and can serve as a reason for war and as a substitute for military occupation in the direction of East European change. Debating who orchestrated orange and rose changes does not help us imagine how imperial contests will be resolved when the bloom has left the revolutionary flower; it especially will not tell us how the location of pipelines will affect economic futures and national sovereignties.

How do we figure the politics of these fundamental contests beyond transition culture then? Empirically, we can compare how particular military alliances and energy security matters are discussed in publics and how these agendas are presented to different policy communities. As I have suggested, it is useful to compare how quickly one might search for evidence of corruption when Russians seek to influence energy security in Poland with the debates over Polish decisions to go to Iraq in support of America. But before political cultures are invoked as sufficient explanations, we can consider just how much these dispositions, and other actions like the purchase of Lockheed Martin jets, fly in the face of our assumptions about Polish wishes to be European.

These empirical investigations can also challenge our cultural political sensibilities. While there are few in American academic circles who embrace the dispositions of the League of Polish Families or the Law and Justice party, this right-wing disposition may have been correct to emphasize the dangers of Russian influence over Polish energy infrastructures in light of what happened in the beginning of 2006 between Russia and Ukraine. Transition culture's optimism around the rationality of global market integration may have made analysts and politicians both a bit overly dismissive of East European nationalist skepticism of Russian commercial commitments. Too, it fits nicely with European anti-American sensibilities to wonder about Poland's role as Trojan horse, but it is not obvious that, in light of the growing combustibility of energy politics, Polish elites were not right in anticipating the value of gaining control over Iraqi energy resources and gaining American support to move the Orange Revolution ahead on energy security grounds alone. The Trojan horse might just save Europe! At least that would be how those within the horse would like us to think.

One might be dubious that "securitizing" energy will save Europe (Buzan et al. 1998), however the cultural politics of energy security need not satisfy an objective need, but rather constitute the hegemonic discourse of the problem.[28] The Trojan horse might manage those very maneuvers that will make other Europeans skeptical of Russian trustworthiness as an energy partner and maneuver Russia into subsequent practices and policies that give the Russoskeptics evidence for their claims about the imperial use of energy resources. Regardless of interpretation, whether Russian energy suppliers and potential energy distributors are untrustworthy, or their critics unreasonable, these very points about energy security and military interventions could, and should, be debated. And that, I believe, is what questions of empire, and of hegemony, raise beyond the terms of transition culture itself.

I find Michael Mann (2004) and others to be quite right to wonder about the articulation of military power with economic, political, and cultural power in the development of America's incoherent empire. But we should also pose the same questions around Russia and rethink the place of the EU in the middle of it all.

Of course, we cannot speak about the EU in singular terms, even though the conventions of disciplines and of our language might enable us to speak of American and Russian strategies without gasp. It is clear, however, that we should be considering the ways in which different national leaderships are struggling to maneuver within the EU to shape its own response to recurring rival American and Russian use of military and energy resources. We should also consider, therefore, how power relations within the EU shape national dispositions in those rivalries.

In the end, it is not only a matter of geopolitical contest around oil and guns, even if that has been my focus. I also find that we should be attending, as Zsuzsa Gille suggests, to those deeper structures of power and change that lie beneath the surface, ones that interface not only with the means of energy production and violence, but also with environmental capacities to secure public health and sustain environmental well-being, and to entertain, therefore, even those questions about how to treat energy's exchange and use values themselves. For that reason, we should not only consider how the new transnational agenda might be explored within particular sectors, or even how it might articulate with emerging imperialist contests. We should also explore those issues that endanger security even when publics and politicians have little room on their immediate agendas for their address. A focus on energy, fortunately, allows that very engagement and invites us to consider the ways in which ideas and interests around environmental security might inspire new visions of military alliances and energy needs. But it will not realize this vision by working within the terms of transition culture itself.

Even as we explore the articulation of increasingly complex transnational and national levels of policy and practice, we might also inquire directly into the ways in which competing hegemonies work in this era. It might not always be apparent if we view the articulation of power only in terms of who does what, but we may appreciate those hegemonies more if we also consider how those actions reproduce, or transform, the major axes of power in the world system. Maybe we could take military alliances and energy security for granted in discussions of European accession, but in a time of war and increasing competition for energy security, it is no longer obvious how the world will be integrated or whose hegemony will reign, much less how those choices resonate with long-term environmental security. We might, however, in the spirit of a more critical transition culture, consider whether more open public discussion of those very issues in a transnational public sphere would contribute, or not, to better solutions than those that seem to prevail today.

NOTES

Chapter 2

1. For the purpose of this article, East Central Europe denotes the following post-communist states: Bulgaria, the Czech Republic, Estonia, Hungary, Latvia, Lithuania, Poland, Romania, Slovakia, and Slovenia. All of these states joined the EU in 2004, except for Bulgaria and Romania, which joined in 2007.

2. Judith Kelley's groundbreaking book *Ethnic Politics in Europe* (2004) was the first to systematically test rationalist and constructivist mechanisms side by side. Kelley argues that the political conditionality used by European institutions was surprisingly effective at getting postcommunist governments to adopt policies to accommodate ethnic minorities, while softer diplomatic pressure alone rarely worked. For studies that also privilege rationalist mechanisms, see Schimmelfennig et al. (2003) and Vachudova (2005). For the argument that Kelley's research design and findings do not disprove constructivist explanations of compliance with ethnic minority rights criteria, see Epstein (2005b). Whether and how constructivist mechanisms play an important role is also raised in Kubicek (2003) and Schimmelfennig and Sedelmeier (2005).

3. A few references here must stand for many: Bunce (1999); Cameron (2005); Ekiert (2003); Ekiert and Hanson eds. (2003); Fish (1998, 2005); Grzymała-Busse (2002); Kitschelt (2003); Orenstein (2001); Rupnik (1999); Vachudova (2005); Vachudova and Snyder (1997).

4. As Robert Keohane and Joseph Nye (1977) have shown, power in an interdependent relationship flows from asymmetry: the one who gains more from the relationship is the more dependent. See also Moravcsik (1998).

5. On the credibility of conditionality and factors that make it more or less effective, see also Grabbe (2006); Hughes et al. (2004); Kelley (2004); Pridham (2005); Schimmelfennig and Sedelmeier (2005); Sedelmeier (2006); and Smith (2003).

6. Several scholars have identified aspects of political competition as pivotal in determining the quality of democracy in postcommunist states. See Fish (1998); Frye (2002); Grzymała-Busse (2007); Hellman (1998); McFaul (2002); O'Dwyer (2006b); and Vachudova (2005). For the similar measure of political openness versus closure, see Fish (2005).

7. Interviews with the author, 1997–2002.

Chapter 3

1. This chapter was prepared with the research assistance of Jelena Djordjevic.

2. Campbell (1998) differentiates among "programs," "paradigms," "frames," and "public sentiment" on the basis that programs and paradigms operate at the cognitive level, and frames and public sentiments at the normative level. Campbell also suggests

that programs and frames are located in the foreground of policy debate, while paradigms and public sentiments are located in the background. While this conceptual differentiation is useful, this analysis follows Hall in analyzing ideas and outcomes that are readily observable—or, in Campbell's terminology, those in the *foreground* of policy debate.

3. Proponents of ideational analyses differ with respect to how much emphasis they place on agency. In other words, some analysts stress how policy actors can self-consciously and deliberately manipulate existing collective beliefs to promote and legitimize particular policy strategies, while other "thicker" constructivists focus on the broader interpretive frameworks that frame understandings of elites and the public alike.

4. STOP is short for "Incentive and exchange programme for persons responsible for combating trade in human beings and the sexual exploitation of children." DAPHNE is short for "Programme for Community action to prevent and combat violence against children, young people, and women and to protect victims and groups at risk."

5. Trafficking Victims Protection Act (22 U.S.C.7101 et. seq.) and Trafficking Victims Reauthorization Protection Act (Public Law 108-193).

6. These insights are based on personal interviews and participant observation carried out in Belgrade from 2002 to 2005.

7. The underground nature of trafficking is portrayed in Lukas Moodysson's 2002 film *Lilja 4-Ever*. In this fictional account, a young Russian woman, unemployed and living in poverty in a Russian province, is recruited by an acquaintance with the promise of working legally. She arrives by plane in Stockholm, is driven to a provincial Swedish industrial city, raped by her handler, and held captive in a private apartment in a nondescript housing bloc.

Chapter 4

1. This chapter uses "external" and "outsider" as synonyms to represent Western IGOs whose practices or policies affect postcommunist choices about institutional design. Similarly, "internal," "domestic," and "insider" are synonyms for postcommunist actors whose choices are affected by the policies or practices of the Western actors. "Institutions" are formal rules, laws, and official policies.

2. Also see Kopstein and Reilly (2000).

3. I develop this approach more fully in Jacoby (2006).

4. See Schoppa (1997) for IR literature akin to the minority traditions approach.

5. Obviously, the wisdom of IMF policies is a separate (and crucial) issue. The focus here is simply on the degree to which IMF policy advice was accepted by various PCR factions. Stone generally defends IMF policy prescriptions. A much more critical view is Stiglitz (2003).

6. On the other hand, the Hungarian military was never deeply politicized under communism in the way Poland's was, and during the protracted transition from communism, the military was never poised for violent intervention as it was in, say, Czechoslovakia or East Germany.

7. But like EU on the ethnic minority rights case, it did have the support of individual member states, who often had bilateral programs that supported the broad NATO guidelines.

8. In October 1990, the president refused the prime minister's request to call the military into a transport strike. In September 1991, the constitutional court ruled that the president, as commander-in-chief, could issue only guidelines, and not orders, to the military. In 1992, a defense reform bill removed the president from the normal chain of command but did not bring the HDF chief of general staff under MOD control. Under the Social Democrats, the MOD defied the Hungarian constitution by ordering Hungarian pilots to participate in NATO live-fire exercises without parliamentary approval.

9. That is, they were least available in the ethnic minority rights case and most available in the civil-military relations case.

10. Volkov (2002) stresses the Russian police's extraction of rents as a reaction to security gaps rather than their cause. Once established, however, such rents might be hard to eliminate without making the security situation even worse (see also Taylor 2004).

11. Here the idea of enhanced legitimacy is particularly worthy of further research since many PCRs are clearly devoted to their reform ideas—which may or may not owe a debt to Western assistance—and yet often struggle to justify their novel ideas to the voting public.

12. On the virtues of rapid reform, see Fish (1998) and Hellman (1998). On change teams, see Greskovits (1998).

Chapter 5

I would like to thank the National Bank of Hungary and the Czech National Bank for their gracious cooperation in this research. In addition, many thanks to Hilary Appel, Andrew Barnes, Stephen Bloom, Phil Cerny, Ágnes Csermely, Tony Deutsch, Benjamin Forest, Péter Karádi, Mitchell Orenstein, and three anonymous reviewers for the *Review of International Political Economy* for their helpful comments on earlier versions of this chapter. Thanks also to the *Review of International Political Economy* for permission to reprint this article here. The Canadian Social Sciences and Humanities Research Council (SSHRC), the National Council for Eurasia and East European Research (NCEEER), and the National Fellows program at the Hoover Institution have generously funded my research on postcommunist central banking.

1. The larger project involves both a broad analysis of international efforts to transform postcommunist central banks and comparative case studies of central bank development in Hungary, the Czech Republic, Russia, and Kyrgyzstan. I conducted over one hundred open-ended interviews for this project between February 2000 and June 2005, including interviews with Western central bankers and officials of international financial institutions (the donors) and with postcommunist central bankers (the recipients). I also administered surveys to two hundred central bank managers in Hungary and Kyrgyzstan, sat in on training sessions, and gathered statistical data on various training programs.

2. Although Kapstein (1989, 1992) has argued that central bankers represent at best a nascent epistemic community, he makes his claim based on central bank beliefs and behavior regarding banking supervision and regulation. However, central bankers typically consider monetary policy, not regulatory policy, to be their primary task (and, indeed, many central banks do not have responsibility for banking supervision at all, ceding this task to a separate government agency or agencies).

3. See Marcussen (1998, 2000) for a more extensive discussion of central bankers' shared state-level beliefs.

4. These requirements themselves reflected the preferences of European central bankers, and in particular the Bundesbank. They were adopted only after the European central bankers were able to persuade their governments of the general value of these policies, encouraging the governments to tie their own hands for the sake of macroeconomic stability in the EU (Marcussen 1998).

5. Thelen argues persuasively that identifying institutional reproduction mechanisms should represent a central theoretical concern for historical institutionalists, especially since historical institutionalists take issue with functionalist arguments that infer past institutional origins from the coordination tasks they perform in the present.

6. While inflation did rise in East Central Europe after the transition began, legislation granting independence to the central banks predated it. According to Maxfield (1997), the average level of statutory central bank independence in fourteen postcommunist states from 1990 to 1994 (using Cukierman et al.'s coding) was .45, comparable to Western Europe's .46 ranking.

7. Indeed, the one Czech central bank researcher who had consistently argued against early euro adoption, Stanislava Janáčková, "retired" from the CNB in 2000 and began working for President Václav Klaus (Janáčková 2002; Janáčková and Janácek 2004).

8. Mongelli (2002) defines an optimum currency area as "the optimal geographic domain of a single currency, or of several currencies, whose exchange rates are irrevocably pegged and might be unified. . . . *Optimality* is defined in terms of several *OCA properties*, including the mobility of labor and other factors of production, price and wage flexibility, economic openness, diversification in production and consumption, similarity in inflation rates, fiscal integration and political integration."

9. Indeed, Špidla was forced to resign by his own party in June 2004 in the wake of high and persistent unemployment numbers.

Chapter 6

1. Among industrialized countries, three are outliers. Ninety-nine percent of New Zealand's banking assets are foreign owned and 95 percent of Luxembourg's are. As a financial center, foreign ownership in banking is also high in the UK for European standards, approaching 46 percent (Barth et al. 2006).

2. Note that in the early 2000s, Slovenia had a very low foreign presence in its banking sector at 15 percent (Naaborg et al. 2003, 26).

3. The Dutch financial group ABN Amro was attempting to buy Banca Anton-Veneta in Italy. Fazio was recorded talking to the head of a midsized Milan bank, Giampiero Fiorani. Together they allegedly orchestrated an Italian counteroffer to the ABN-Amro bid as a way of preserving Italian ownership, but in violation of European competition rules.

4. By depressing interest rates through regulation, the state can create an excess demand for credit, thereby becoming the lender of last resort for private enterprise. Thus the state is in a strong position to choose which projects will receive financing. The costs of financial repression are spread across depositors, as their returns, in keeping with the overall policy, are suppressed (see Fry 1995, 3–19).

5. Mitchell Orenstein argues that economic and political liberalization have coincided in central and eastern Europe, contrary to some scholars early expectations, largely because of the peculiar dynamics of political competition there (Orenstein 2001).

6. Author's interview with Stefan Kawalec, 4 November 1999.

7. This discussion is based on the author's interview with Anthony Doran, former International Finance Corporation official, Warsaw, 8 October 1999.

8. Author's interviews with Doran and Stefan Kawalec, former undersecretary of state at the Ministry of Finance in the Republic of Poland, Warsaw, 2 November 1999.

9. ING invested both in Bank Slaski S.A. in Katowice (controlling) and Bank Powszechny Handlowy (BPH) in Krakow (14 percent as of 1999). UniCredito eventually bought a controlling share in Pekao SA.

10. Stefan Kawalec, the same Polish Ministry of Finance official who originally contacted the IFC to act on Sachs's proposal, was also the chief architect of Poland's bank bailout scheme. One part of the plan caused some friction between Polish officials and their Western advisers. While the Poles wanted a decentralized system of Work-Out Departments (WODs), the Bretton Woods institutions were urging a clearinghouse model based on experiences in other countries. Eventually Poland prevailed in this debate—largely on the logic of Polish anticentral planning sentiments. Author's interviews with Piotr Rymaszewski, economic adviser to the Polish Ministry of Finance, Warsaw, 18 October 1999; Kawalec; and his assistant Robert Konski in Warsaw, 9 June 1999 (see also Kawalec et al. 1994).

11. The original złoty stabilization fund was $1 billion. It was never used, however, because in the course of macroeconomic stabilization, there was never a run on the Polish currency. The amount set aside for the bank recapitalization fund was $600 million.

12. According to former Prime Minister Jan Krzysztof-Bielecki, there was very little political controversy around the plan. Author's interview with Krzysztof-Bielecki, London, 26 May 1999.

13. Note that the World Bank was initially skeptical of the idea because it had not been tested, and also, in all likelihood, because it was coming from the IFC, which has a long-standing rivalry with the World Bank. Author's interview with Doran.

14. The first consultative gathering in which first-tier Western banks gathered under the direction of Paul Volker was a failure. This set of Western banks used the

opportunity to air their concerns about Poland's failure to make good on outstanding debt payments and expressed no interest in training or investing.

15. The SLD and PSL did not initially embrace the idea of developing stronger ties to NATO, for example, although once in power they quickly changed their position. See Kostrzewa-Zorbas (1999). It should also be noted, however, that despite public skepticism toward rapid reform and international institutions, when the World Bank and IMF surveyed the political parties on the eve of the 1993 elections, they found the SLD to be the best prepared, technically, to develop economic platforms. Author's interview with Ian Hume, former World Bank Resident Representative in Poland, Warsaw, 11 November 1999. On the legacy of technocratic competence, see Bozóki (1997).

16. Regional banks tended to support the consolidation initiative and government intervention (*East European Banker* 1995), as did some high profile Polish economic policy makers, including the head of the central bank (*Życie Warszawy* 1996). The management at Bank Przemysłowo-Handlowy (BPH), already partly privatized, was less enthusiastic, however (*Gazeta Wyborcza* 1995).

17. The foreign business press quoted critics who called the plan a "collectivization move," and who further compared it to 1945, "when the communists gave peasants small pieces of land, only to take them back again." Sean Bobbit, "BPH Consolidation Stuns Investors" (see *Economist* 1995). Further, a journalist from Poland's leading newspaper, *Gazeta Wyborcza*, asked Kołodko at a press conference in Washington why he was "re-communizing" Poland's banks. Author's interview with Kołodko.

18. For what the U.S. Treasury and David Lipton were saying about Poland's proposed bank consolidation, see *Gazeta Wyborcza* (1996a). The following discussion is based on the author's interview with a high-level Polish Ministry of Finance official who attended a series of meetings with U.S. officials over this period.

19. The United States had contributed $200 million of the $600 million bank bailout fund administered by the IMF, formerly the złoty stabilization fund.

20. Although some bank consolidation around Pekao SA did take place, the government failed to administrate it (Balcerowicz and Bratkowski 2001, 18–19, 29). Consolidation was rather market driven and then the banking group was subsequently sold to UniCredito of Italy and the German insurer Allianz in 1999.

21. Author's interview with Kołodko, 18 February 2000.

22. Hungary also had conditionality agreements with both the IMF and the World Bank between 1990 and 1994 (the first phase of reform), but those agreements were not explicitly tied to bank privatization as in Poland. An IMF $394 million loan was predicated on cutting the budget deficit, however, which could have been linked to increasing privatization receipts—in part by privatizing banks.

23. The Romanian Banking Institute was established in 1991 and 1992 to provide technical training to Romanian bankers. In addition, the European Union, through its PHARE program, provided funding for assistance in bank auditing, the establishment of work-out units and strategic banking development and training. The early blueprint for banking reform was provided by the IMF and the World Bank (Tsantis 1997, 173).

24. Author's interview with Daniel Daianu (10 November 2004).

25. Manufacturers Hanover Trust Co, Société Général, Frankfurt Bukarest Bank AG and Misr-Romanian Bank had all established operations in Romania under state socialism.

Chapter 7

1. All of the pope's speeches on this trip were made available at the Holy See's Web site at http://www.vatican.va.

2. The First Vatican Council declared in 1870 that when the pope "defines a doctrine concerning faith or morals to be held by the whole church . . . such definitions of the Roman Pontiff are of themselves, and not by the consent of the Church, irreformable" (see Tanner 1990).

3. The Polish constitution can be viewed at http://www.sejm.gov.pl.

4. I interviewed a number of bishops and activists on theses questions. For greater detail, see Byrnes (2001).

5. For a concise account of Stepinac's role in Croat history, see Ramet (1996) and Alexander (1979).

6. This was the *London Times*'s interpretation of President Tudjman's spin on the pope's visit (see Kennedy 1994).

7. This was the claim of Nikola Stanjojevic, of the *Belgrade Tanjug*, translated and reproduced in *FBIS-EEU-94-177* (12 September 1994).

Chapter 8

1. Several prominent Macedonians, including the first president, Kiro Gligorov, told the author this joke during a research visit in 2000.

2. For a collection of the contending definitions of corruption, see Heidenheimer and Johnston (2002). Although the concept of corruption invites "inevitable indeterminacy" in historical and cross-cultural terms (see Philp 2002), the current international anticorruption campaign promotes a Western-based conception as a common standard. This is essentially the public office–centered definition, whereby political corruption is understood as a transaction in which a public agent violates the formal rules of office by trading the resources of that office (decisional power, privileged information, economic goods) for private gain.

3. The World Bank, for example, regards corruption "as the single greatest obstacle to economic and social development." World Bank president, James D. Wolfensohn, spoke of the "cancer of corruption" in his 1996 annual speech. http://www1.worldbank.org/publicsector/anticorrupt/index.cfm.

4. "Even when everybody knows that corrupt practices exist, the need to keep them secret imposes a limit on their extent" (Elster 1989, 271). For an argument on the economic costs that secrecy involves, see Vishny (1993).

5. The second phrase is from Lord Robertson, NATO secretary general (*New York Times* 2001).

6. According to the 2002 census, Albanians represent 25 percent (509,083) of the

population and Macedonians constitute 64 percent (1,297,981). Albanians are concentrated in an arc of territory contiguous to the Albanian-inhabited lands of southern Serbia, Kosovo, and Albania. The single largest concentration of Albanians is in the capital, Skopje, where over 71,000, or 14 percent of the total Albanian population, live (State Statistical Office 2003).

7. In October 1995, a car bomb killed the president's driver and blinded the president in one eye. To this day, the perpetrators have not been caught. Conspiracy theories abound, as the timing of the assassination took place days before a Macedonian-Greek rapprochement and one day after a Gligorov-Milošević meeting on mutual recognition.

8. During the crisis, a grand coalition involving all the major parties was constructed with the support of the international community. It lasted from May to November 2001.

9. The Liberal Party was dropped from the first coalition in 1996 and the Democratic Alternative, a partner in the second coalition, disintegrated in 2000.

10. Personal interviews with the professors Gjorge Ivanov and Teuta Arifi (Skopje, November–December 2000).

11. In 2000, during my first visit to Macedonia, talk still lingered about the illegal earnings and dealings of politicians during Social Democratic rule.

12. Overall, seven people were killed and hundreds injured.

13. Interview with employee of Macedonian secret services, Skopje, 20 November 2002.

14. The Macedonian police presence in these Albanian-populated regions was never that pronounced. From 1993 to 1999, UNPREDEP blue helmets patrolled the borders. With the end of this mission, however, Macedonian police were not deployed to pick up the slack (Balalovska et al. 2002; International Crisis Group 2002).

15. Personal interview with secret service employee, 20 November 2002.

16. Interview with Arben Xhaferi in Tetovo, Macedonia, 13 December 2000.

17. The Working Group mission ended in early 1996.

18. This author attended the conference and his work was denounced by Georgievski as well, who called it "an alibi for the international community" and a "good example of political corruption."

Chapter 9

1. Thanks to Stephen Bloom and Abby Innes for their close reading and very helpful advice.

2. Mazower's chapter, "Empires, Nations, Minorities," is especially good on how the West's support for Central European independence went hand in hand with a caretaking mentality that perpetuated the theme of West/civilized vs. East/barbaric.

3. On the dialogue between Eastern and Western oppositionists during the Reagan years, see Kenney (2003), especially chapter 2.

4. Elena Gadjanova makes this point as part of her review of P. Ludlow's book *The Making of the New Europe* in *Journal of Common Market Studies* 44, no. 1 (2006): 224.

5. First came the "Letter of Eight," signed by eight NATO countries, published 30 January 2003. A week later, ten east European countries not yet in NATO published the "Letter of Ten."

6. The essay comes in the form of a interview with *Gazeta Wyborcza* journalist Artur Domoslawski.

7. This first chapter is available in English as "An Old or a New Europe? A Sketch on the Philosophy Underlying Polish Policy in Europe," Center for International Relations, Warsaw, 2003, http://www.csm.org.pl/en/files/raports/2003/rap_i_an_0203a.pdf.

8. This from the chapter available in English at http://www.csm.org.pl/en/files/raports/2003/rap_i_an_0203a.pdf.

9. Conversation with Smolar, New York City, May 2005.

Chapter 10

I thank Geneviève Zubrzycki, the late Marian Kempny, Markku Kivinen, Donna Parmelee, Mitch Orenstein, and Steven Bloom, as well as those various audiences hearing previous versions of this essay at the Budapest-based National Science Foundation workshop on the Cultural Politics of Globalization and Community in East Central Europe, May 2005, at the Aleksanteri Institute in Finland in March 2005 and at Syracuse University in September 2005, for their comments. I also wish to thank the European Commission for its support of the ongoing work of the EU Center for Excellence at the University of Michigan on the cultural politics of energy security in Europe and Eurasia.

1. For my full review of his work, see my 2006 review in *Contemporary Sociology*, from which I draw for this section.

2. Since writing this, I have found Williams (2007) to be especially helpful on this problem, most notably in regard to the discipline of the democratic peace (42–61).

3. See http://www.brama.com/survey/messages/36904.html.

4. See http://www.eia.doe.gov/emeu/cabs/russia.html.

5. Of course the geopolitical strategies followed by Russia in oil and gas production and transit and alliances with Central Asia have become only more significant since the time of this writing.

6. See http://www.eia.doe.gov/emeu/cabs/euro.html.

7. See the communication from the commission to the council and the European parliament on the development of energy policy for the enlarged European Union, its neighbors and partner countries, 26 May 2003. http://ec.europa.eu/dgs/energy_transport/international/doc/2003_communication_en.pdf

8. See Irwin M. Stelzer, "The Axis of Oil: China and Russia find a new way to advance their strategic ambitions," *Weekly Standard* 10, no. 20 (2005), http://www.freerepublic.com/focus/f-news/1346965/posts.

9. See http://www.eurasianet.org/departments/business/articles/eav120103.shtml#.

10. For a project summary of the Baku-Tbilisi-Ceyhan (BTC) Oil Pipeline, see http://www.bicusa.org/bicusa/issues/bakutbilisiceyhan_btc_pipeline_project_azerbaijangeorgiaturkey/index.php.

11. "Linefill of the BTC pipeline began at the Saganchal oil terminal in Azerbaijan on 10 May 2005 and the first export of oil from the Ceyhan marine terminal in Turkey is due to commence during the second half of the year." http://www .caspiandevelopmentandexport.com/ASP/BTC.asp.

12. See http://www.carbonweb.org/documents/PR011204.htm.

13. See http://www.rferl.org/featuresarticle/2005/02/8f1205e3-2826-4470-811a-bc9d9ef577a3.html.

14. See http://www.themoscowtimes.com/stories/2005/03/01/053.html.

15. See http://www.irak.pl/index1.html.

16. See http://www.bumar-waryski.com.pl/html.informacje.html.

17. It is interesting to see how the Iraq Development Program portrays this deal: Iraqi Defense Minster Ziad Cattan reportedly said at the signing ceremony for this event, "Poland has helped us a great deal, so we're trying to build strong links between companies form our two countries." The note concludes with this observation: "Several Polish companies have complained about being shut out from lucrative Iraqi reconstruction contracts despite the country's leadership of a multinational division in the stabilization force and its contribution of 2500 troops" (http://www .iraqdevelopmentprogram.org/idp/news/new600.htm). Ziad Cattan, who now lives in Poland, was in charge of procurement for the Iraqi military until 2005, when the Iraqi Justice Ministry charged him with corruption (Moore and Miller 2005). See also http://www.corpowatch.org/article.php?id=12758; http://www.ziadcattan.com/ en/historia.html.

18. There are some other military deals, of course. For example, Polish defense officials signed a $1.2 billion deal for the delivery of 690 Finnish-made troop carriers over the next ten years.

19. Ironically, the whole article is about how European politicians use their political influence to sell their nation's products. This is not corruption, just the nature of the business, it seems. Of course it is not just about planes; the business of government investments extends much further (Trebski et al. 2005).

20. See http://icasualties.org/oif. In response to the question, "Do you support the participation of Polish soldiers in the operation in Iraq, or not," about 70 percent of the population has expressed a negative opinion between June 2004 and March 2005, with 20–30 percent offering their support (Badan 2005).

21. See http://biznes.interia.pl/news?inf=569750.

22. See http://www.agentura.ru/english/press/about/jointprojects/mn/sutyagin/.

23. From Polonia. Also see http://eb.eiu.com/index.asp?layout=oneclick& country_id=1730000173. For the story that prompted Aleksander Kwaśniewski to refuse attending the commission meeting, see Butkiewicz and Dzierzanowski (2005).

24. See http://biznes.interia.pl/news?inf=569823.

25. Its members include Roman Giertych (LPR), Andrzej Celiński (SdPL), Bogdan Bujak i Andrzej Różański (SLD), Zbigniew Wassermann (PiS), Konstanty Miodowicz (PO), Andrzej Grzesik (Samoobrona), Andrzej Aumiller (UP), Józef Gruszka (PSL), Zbigniew Witaszek (FKP) i Antoni Macierewicz (RKN). http://biznes.interia.pl/ news?inf=522583.

26. Ordynacka is one association that appears prominently in the speculations. Its members were mainly members of the Zwiazek Studentow Polskich from the mid-1980s, the networks among whom are described in Pinski and Trebski (2005), in which Andrzej Kratiuk and his role in Mrs. Kwaśniewska's foundation is discussed.

27. Jaroslaw Kaczynski said, "Moskwa dysponuje takimi dokumentami dotycza-cynmi prezeszlosci prezydenta, ktore go czynia nie suwerennym w jego decyzjach Ewa Milewicz" (*Gazeta Wyborcza* 2005).

28. I am indebted to Mikko Palonkorpi for his introduction to this literature, and to my other colleagues at the Aleksanteri Institute—Pami Alto, David Dusseault, and Markku Kivinen—for their continued collaboration on this work around energy security.

REFERENCES

Abbott, Kenneth, and Duncan Snidal. 1988. "Why States Act through Formal International Organizations." *Journal of Conflict Resolution* 42:3–32.

Abrahams, Fred. 1996. A Threat to "Stability": Human Rights Violations in Macedonia. Special issue, Human Rights Watch (June).

Abramson, Kara. 2004. "Beyond Consent, Towards Safeguarding Human Rights: Implementing the United Nations Trafficking Protocol." *Harvard International Law Journal* 44:473–502.

Ackermann, Alice. 2000. *Making Peace Prevail: Preventing Violent Conflict in Macedonia*. Syracuse: Syracuse University Press.

AFX International Focus. 2004. "Czech PM Spidla Sees No Euro Entry Before 2009." 17 February.

Agustin, Laura. 2005. "Migrants in the Mistress's House: Other Voices in the 'Trafficking' Debate." *Social Politics: International Studies in Gender, State and Society* 12:96–117.

Albert, M. 1993. *Capitalism vs. Capitalism*. New York: Four Walls Eight Windows.

Alderson, K. 2001. "Making Sense of State Socialization." *Review of International Studies* 27:415–33.

Alexander, Stella. 1979. *Church and State in Yugoslavia since 1945*. Cambridge: Cambridge University Press.

Amsden, A., J. Kochanowicz, and L. Taylor. 1994. *The Market Meets Its Match: Restructuring the Economies of Eastern Europe*. Cambridge, MA: Harvard University Press.

Anderson, Perry. 2002. "Force and Consent." *New Left Review* 17 (September/October): 5–30.

Andonova, Liliana B. 2003. *Transnational Politics of the Environment: The EU and Environmental Policy in Central and Eastern Europe*. Cambridge: MIT Press.

Andreas, Peter. 2004. "The Clandestine Political Economy of War and Peace in Bosnia." *International Studies Quarterly* 48 (1): 29–51.

Andrejevich, Milan. 1991. "Resurgent Nationalism in Macedonia: A Challenge to Pluralism." *Report on Eastern Europe* (17 May): 26–29.

Andrews, D. 2003. The Committee of Central Bank Governors as a Source of Rules. *Journal of European Public Policy* 10:956–73.

Andrusz, Katya, and Dorota Bartyzel. 2004. "Spy, Tycoon, LUKoil Stir Up Polish Politics." *Moscow Times,* 25 October.

Andvig, Jens Chr., and Odd-Helge Fjeldstad. 2000. *Research on Corruption: A Policy Oriented Survey*. Norwegian Agency for Development Cooperation (December).

Appel, Hilary. 2004a. *A New Capitalist Order: Privatization and Ideology in Russia and Eastern Europe*. Pittsburgh: University of Pittsburgh Press.

———. 2004b. "Western Financial Institutions, Local Actors, and the Privatization Paradigm." *Problems of Post-Communism* 51 (September/October): 3–10.

Arai, Adriana. 2004. "Czech Ctrl Bk Downplays FX Crisis Risk in EU Newcomers." *Dow Jones,* 19 April.

Aris, Ben. 2005. "Muddling through Deficit Troubles." *Euromoney* (1 April): 1.

Badan, Komunikat Z. 2005. "Opinie o Obecnosci Polskich Zolnierzy w Iraku I o Innych Interwencjach Zbrojnych." CBOS, Warsaw (April). http://www.cbos.pl/SPISKOM.POL/2005/K_075_05.PDF.

Balalovska, Kristina, Alessandro Silj, and Mario Zucconi. 2002. *Minority Politics in Southeast Europe: Crisis in Macedonia.* Rome: Ethnobarometer.

Balcerowicz, E., and A. Bratkowski 2001. Restructuring and Development of the Banking Sector in Poland: Lessons to Be Learnt by Less Advanced Transition Countries. CASE Reports 44. Warsaw: Center for Social and Economic Research.

Balcerowicz, Leszek. 1994. "Understanding Postcommunist Transitions." *Journal of Democracy* 5 (4): 75–89.

———. 1995. *Socialism, Capitalism and Transformation.* New York: Central European University Press.

Banker. 1993. "Romania: Isarescu to the Rescue." 143 (June 1).

Barany, Zoltan. 1998. "Hungary: Appraising a New Nato Member." *Clausewitz Studien* 14 (4): 1–31.

Barnett, Michael, and Martha Finnemore. 2004. *Rules for the World: International Organizations in Global Politics.* Ithaca, NY: Cornell University Press.

Barth, James R., Gerard Caprio, and Ross Levine. 2001. *The Regulation and Supervision of Banks around the World.* http://www.worldbank.org/research/interest/worddocs/Database%20WP_050701_all.pdf.

———. 2006. *Rethinking Bank Regulation: Till Angels Govern.* New York: Cambridge University Press.

Bates, Robert. 1974. "Ethnic Competition and Modernization in Contemporary Africa." *Comparative Political Studies* 6 (4): 457–83.

Bayley, David H. 1966. "The Effects of Corruption in a Developing Nation." *Western Political Quarterly* 19 (4): 719–32.

BBC. 1991a. "Pope Calls for Tolerance of All Nationalities." *BBC Summary of World Broadcasts.* 24 August.

———. 1991b. "Romania: New Legislation on Foreign Investment." *BBC Summary of World Broadcasts.* 25 April.

———. 2004. "Hungarian Central Bank Official Expects Flexible EU Approach on Euro Zone Entry." *BBC Monitoring European.* 15 January.

———. 2005. "Poland Postpones Iraq Troop Withdrawal." *BBC News.* http://news.bbc.co.uk/1/hi/world/europe/4562838.stm.

Benford, Robert, and Snow, David. 2000. "Framing Process and Social Movements: An Overview and Assessment." *Annual Review of Sociology* 26: 611–39.

Berman, Jacqueline. 2003. "(Un)Popular Strangers and Crises (Un)bounded: Discourses of Sex-Trafficking, the European Political Community and the Panicked State of the Modern State." *European Journal of International Relations* 9:37–86.

Berman, S., and K. McNamara. 1999. "Bank on Democracy." *Foreign Affairs* 78 (2): 2–8.

Bernstein, Carl, and Marco Politi. 1997. *His Holiness: John Paul II and the Hidden History of Our Time*. New York: Henry Holt and Co.

Bernstein, Richard. 2005. "Corruption, Russophobia Weigh on Poland." *Moscow Times*, 28 January. http://www.themoscowtimes.com/stories/2005/01/28/201.html.

Blahó, Miklós. 2004. "Járai: Kulturálatlan javaslat [Járai: An uncultured proposal]." *Népszabadság*, 29 October.

Blank, Stephen J. 1998. "Rhetoric and Reality in NATO Enlargement," in *European Security and NATO Enlargement: A View from Central Europe*, ed. Stephen Blank. Strategic Studies Institute of the U.S. Army War College. http://www.strategicstudiesinstitute.army.mil/pdffiles/PUB142.pdf.

Blankenburg, Erhard. 2002. "Judicial Anti-Corruption Initiatives: Latin Europe in a Global Setting." In Heidenheimer and Johnston, 911–23.

Blinder, A. 1998. *Central Banking in Theory and Practice*. Cambridge: Massachusetts Institute of Technology.

Bloom, Stephen. 2004. "Economic Reform and Ethnic Cooperation in Post-Soviet Latvia and Ukraine." Ph.D. diss., University of California, Los Angeles.

Blyth, Mark. 1997. "Any More Bright Ideas? The Ideational Turn of Comparative Political Economy." *Comparative Politics* 29: 229–50.

Bocevski, Ivica 2002. "Analysis of Election Results—Stabilization of the Party Systems." *Macedonian Affairs* 4 (4): 45–76.

Bockman, Johana, and Gil Eyal. 2002. "Eastern Knowledge as a Laboratory for Economic Knowledge: The Transnational Roots of Neoliberalism." *American Journal of Sociology* 108 (2): 310–52.

Bohle, Dorothee. 2005. "The EU and Eastern Europe: Failing the Test as a Better World Power." In *Socialist Register 2005: The Empire Reloaded*, ed. Leo Panitch. New York: Monthly Review Press.

Bonin, John. 1998. *Banking in Transition Economies: Developing Market Oriented Banking Sectors in Eastern Europe*. Cheltenham, UK: Edward Elgar.

Bortnowska, Halina, Marek A. Cichocki, and Krzysztof Mądel. 2004. "Moralnosc po Iraku: 'za wasza I nasza wolnosc'?" *Wiez* 3 (545): 11–26.

Börzel, Tanja, and Thomas Risse. 2003. "Conceptualizing the Domestic Impact of Europe." In *The Politics of Europeanization*, ed. Kevin Featherstone and Claudio Radaelli, 57–81. Oxford: Oxford University Press.

Bozóki, A. 1997. "The Ideology of Modernization and the Policy of Materialism: The Day after for the Socialists." *Journal of Communist Studies and Transition Politics* 13 (3): 56–102.

Brock, Peter. 1979. *The Slovak National Awakening: An Essay on the History of East Central Europe*. Toronto: University of Toronto Press.

Brown, Justin 1998. "War Next Door Tugs at Macedonia." *Christian Science Monitor*, 25 August.

Bruch, Elizabeth. 2004. "Models Wanted: The Search for an Effective Response to Human Trafficking." *Stanford Journal of International Law* 40:1–46.

Brusis, Martin. 2005. "The Instrumental Use of European Union Conditionality: Regionalization in the Czech Republic and Slovakia." *East European Politics and Societies* 19 (2): 291–316.

Bryant, C. G. A., and Mokrzycki, E., eds. 1994. *The New Great Transformation? Change and Continuity in East-Central Europe.* London: Routledge.

Brzezinski, Zbigniew. 1997. *The Grand Chessboard: American Primacy and Its Geostrategic Imperatives.* New York: Basic Books.

Buechsenschuetz, Ulrich. 2001. "Macedonia Divided." *Radio Free Europe/Radio Liberty* 5 (33).

———. 2002. "Macedonia's Ruling Coalition Enraged over Corruption Charges." *Radio Free Europe/Radio Liberty* 6 (23 August).

Bull, Hedley. 2002. *The Anarchical Society: A Study of Order in World Politics.* 3rd ed. New York: Columbia University Press.

Bunce, Valerie. 1999. "The Political Economy of Postsocialism." *Slavic Review* 58 (4): 756–93.

———. 2000. "Comparative Democratization: Big Bounded Generalizations." *Comparative Political Studies* 339 (6/7): 703–34.

———. 2003. "Rethinking Recent Democratization, Lessons from the Postcommunist Experience." *World Politics* 55(2): 167–92.

Butkiewicz, Tomasz, and Marcin Dzierzanowski. 2005. "Aleksander K." *Wprost* (13 March): 18–21.

Buzan, Barry, Ole Waever, and Jaap de Wilde. 1998. *Security: A New Framework for Analysis.* Boulder: Lynne Riener.

Byrnes, Timothy A. 2001. *Transnational Catholicism in Postcommunist Europe.* Lanham: Rowman & Littlefield.

Cafruny, Alan, and Magnus Ryner, eds. 2003. *A Ruined Fortress? Neoliberal Hegemony and Transformation in Europe.* Lanham, MD: Rowman and Littlefield.

Calhoun, Craig. 2003. "Information Technology and the International Public Sphere." In *Digital Directions,* ed. D. Schuler, 229–51. Cambridge, MA: MIT Press.

Cameron, David. 2001. "The Return to Europe: The Impact of the EU on Post-Communist Reform." Paper delivered at the Annual Meeting of the American Political Science Association, San Francisco, August.

———. 2003. "The Challenges of Accession." *East European Politics and Societies* 17 (1): 24–41.

———. 2005. "The Quality of Democracy in Postcommunist Europe." Paper presented at the Annual Meeting of the American Political Science Association, Washington, DC.

Campbell, John L. 1993. "Institutional Theory and the Influence of Foreign Actors on Reform in Capitalist and Post-Socialist Societies." In *Institutional Frameworks of Market Economies,* Hausner, Jerzy, Bob Jessop, and Klaus Nielsen, eds., 45–67. Aldershot: Avebury.

———. 1998. "Institutional Analysis and the Role of Ideas in Political Economy." *Theory and Society* 27:377–409.

Carothers, Thomas. 2004. *Critical Mission: Essays on Democracy Promotion*. Washington, DC: Carnegie.

Carothers, Thomas, and Marina Ottaway, eds. 2005. *Uncharted Journey: Promoting Democracy in the Middle East*. Washington: Carnegie.

Carpenter, Michael. 1997. "Slovakia and the Triumph of Nationalist Populism." *Communist and Post-Communist Studies* 30:205–20.

Central and Eastern Eurobarometer. 1991. No. 2. Brussels: Commission of the European Communities.

Cernat, L. 2006. *Europeanization, Varieties of Capitalism and Economic Performance in Central and Eastern Europe*. London: Palgrave Macmillan.

Chandra, Kanchan. 2004. *Why Ethnic Parties Succeed: Patronage and Ethnic Head Counts in India*. Cambridge: Cambridge University Press.

Chang, H. J., and Nolan, P., eds. 1995. *The Transformation of the Communist Economies: against the Mainstream*. New York: St. Martin's Press.

Chapkis, Wendy. 2003. "Trafficking, Migration and the Law." *Gender and Society* 17:923–37.

Checkel, Jeffrey. 1998. "The Constructivist Turn in International Relations Theory." *World Politics* 50:324–48.

———. 2000. "Compliance and Conditionality." ARENA Working Paper 00/18, University of Oslo.

———. 2001. "Why Comply? Social Learning and European Identity Change." *International Organization* 55 (3): 553–88.

Chomsky, Noam, and Edward S. Herman. 1979. *The Washington Connection and Third World Fascism*. Boston: South End Press.

Cichocki, Marek A. 2004. *Porwanie Europy*. Krakow: Osrodek Mysli Politycznej.

Cirtautas, Arista Maria. 2001. "Corruption and the New Ethical Infrastructure of Capitalism." *East European Constitutional Review* 10 (2/3): 79–84.

CNN. 2003. "Chirac Lashes Out at 'New Europe.'" *CNN.com*, 18 February. http://www.cnn.com/2003/WORLD/europe/02/18/spj.irq.chirac/.

Cohen, Roger. 1994. "In Croatia, a Frail Pope John Paul II Urges a 'Culture of Peace.'" *New York Times*, 11 September.

Condon, Christopher. 2004. "Hungary Sets New Euro Entry Target." *Financial Times*, 13 May.

Cooley, Alexander, and James Ron. 2002. "The NGO Scramble: Organizational Insecurity and the Political Economy of Transnational Action." *International Security* 27:5–39.

Crawford, Beverly, and Arend Lijphart. 1995. "Explaining Political and Economic Change in Post-Communist Eastern Europe: Old Legacies, New Institutions, Hegemonic Norms, and International Pressures." *Comparative Political Studies* 28 (2): 171–99.

Croft, Stuart, John Redmond, G. Wyn Rees, and Mark Weber. 1999. *The Enlargement of Europe*. Manchester: Manchester University Press.

Csajbók, 2004. "Towards the Euro in Hungary: A Bumpy Road to Heaven?" Paper presented at the Tenth Dubrovnik Economic Conference.

Csajbók, A., and Á. Csermely. 2002. "Adopting the Euro in Hungary: Expected Costs, Benefits, and Timing." *NBH Occasional Papers* 24.

Csermely, Á. 2004. "Convergence Expectations and Convergence Strategies: Lessons from the Hungarian Experiences in the pre-EU period." *Comparative Economic Studies* 46:104–26.

CTK Business News. 2003a. "Government Puts off Euro Strategy Talks on CNB Governor No-show." 8 October.

———. 2003b. "Klaus Says Deflation in Czech Republic Not Good, Blames CNB." 22 April.

Cvetkovska, Violeta. 2002. "In Macedonia a Governing Coalition of Corruption. Bitter Debate About Corruption in the Country." *Utrinski Vesnik* (22–23 June): 4.

Czech National Bank. 2002. "The Czech Republic and the Euro—Draft Accession Strategy." 23 December. http://www.cnb.cz.

———. 2003. "The Czech Republic's Euro-area Accession Strategy." September. http://www.cnb.cz.

Czubinski, Zbigniew Anthony. 2000. "The European Union and NATO from the Polish Perspective." Jagiellonian University Centre for European Studies, Krakow. http://www.ces.uj.edu.pl/european/papers.htm.

Dahl, Robert A. 1991. "Democracy, Majority Rule, and Gorbachev's Referendum." *Dissent* 38 (4): 491–96.

Dahrendorf, Ralf. 1990. *Reflections on the Revolution in Europe.* New York: Times Books.

Dawson, Stella. 2004. "Promise of Euro Years Away for Most EU Newcomers." Reuters, 29 April.

De Grauwe, P. 2003. "The Euro at Stake? The Monetary Union in an Enlarged Europe." *CESifo Economics Studies* 49 (1): 103–21.

De Nevers, Renee. 2003. *Comrades No More: The Seeds of Change in Eastern Europe.* Cambridge: MIT Press.

"Decree on the Bishops' Pastoral Office in the Church." 1966. In *The Documents of Vatican II,* ed. Walter M. Abbott, S. J. Gallagher, and Joseph Gallagher, 424–25. New York: Guild Press.

Dědek, O. 1998. "Echoing the European Monetary Integration in the Czech Republic." *Prague Economic Papers* 3:195–225.

———. 2002. "The Czech Economy and the Euro." *Politika Ekonomie* 50 (3): 361–75.

———. 2004. "Adopting the Euro—Brake On or Engine for True Convergence?" *Eastern European Economics* 42 (2): 45–62.

Defense News. 2005. "Iraq to Take Delivery of 22 Polish Armored Vehicles." http://www.defensenews.com/story.php?F=1310771&C=landwar.

della Porta, Donatella. 1996. "Actors in Corruption: Business Politicians in Italy." *International Social Science Journal* 48 (3): 7–9.

della Porta, Donatella, and Alberto Vannucci. 1999. *Corrupt Exchanges: Actors, Resources, and Mechanisms of Political Corruption.* New York: Aldine de Gruyter.

Dempsen, Judy, and James Kanter. 2005. "EU Looking into Report of Secret CIA

Jails." *International Herald Tribune,* 4 November. http://www.iht.com/articles/2005/11/03/news.cia.php

Denton, N. 1993a. "The Hole at Hungary's Banking Heart." *Financial Times* (20 May): 15.

———. 1993b. "Hungary Pledges Help for Troubled Commercial Banks." *Financial Times,* 21 May.

Di Palma, Guiseppe. 1990. *To Craft Democracies: An Essay on Democratic Transitions.* Berkeley: University of California Press.

Dimitrova, Antoaneta. 2002. "Enlargement, Institution-Building and the EU's Administrative Capacity Requirement." *West European Politics* 25 (4): 171–90.

———. 2005. "Europeanization and Civil Service Reform in Central and Eastern Europe." In *The Europeanization of Central and Eastern Europe,* ed. Schimmelfennig and Sedelmeier, 71–90.

Doezema, Jo. 2000. "Loose Women or Lost Women? The Re-Emergence of the Myth of 'White Slavery' in Contemporary Discourses of Trafficking in Women." *Gender Issues* 18:23–50.

Doltu, C. 2002. "Banking Reform in Romania." In Šević, 285–308.

Dow Jones International News. 2003a. "Hungary's Central Bank to Propose 2005 ERM II Entry—Paper." 26 May.

———. 2003b. "Hungary to Introduce EUR from Jan 1 2008." 16 July.

———. 2004a. "Hungary's Fin Min: Stability Pact Criteria Too Rigid." 10 March.

———. 2004b. "Hungary's Ruling Party Accepts EU Convergence Plan Terms." 6 July.

Dumke, R., and H. Sherman. 2000. "Exchange Rate Options for EU Applicant Countries in Central and Eastern Europe." In *Essays on the World Economy and Its Financial System,* ed. B. Granville, 153–95. London: Royal Institute of International Affairs.

Dunay, Pál. 2002. "Civil-Military Relations in Hungary: No Big Deal." In *Democratic Control of the Military in Postcommunist Europe: Guarding the Guards,* ed. Timothy Edmunds, Anthony Forster, and Andrew Cottey, 64–87. London: Palgrave.

Dyson, Kenneth. 2000. "EMU as Europeanization: Convergence, Diversity and Contingency." *Journal of Common Market Studies* 38 (4): 645–66.

Dyson, Kenneth, and K. Featherstone. 1996. "Italy and EMU as a '*Vincolo Esterno*': Empowering the Technocrats, Transforming the State." *South European Society and Politics* 1 (2): 272–99.

———. 1999. *The Road to Maastricht: Negotiating Economic and Monetary Union.* Oxford: Oxford University Press.

Dyson, Kenneth, Kevin Featherstone, and George Michalpoulos. 1995. "Strapped to the Mast: EC Central Bankers between Global Financial Markets and Regional Integration." *Journal of European Public Policy* 2 (3): 465–87.

East European Banker. 1995. (November): 6.

———. 1996. (June): 11.

Easterly, William. 2006. *The White Man's Burden: Why the West's Efforts to Aid the Rest Have Done So Much Ill and So Little Good.* New York: Penguin.

Economist. 1995. "Plan Spatski" (9 December): 75.

———. 1999. "Eastern Promise." (28 August).

———. 2006. "A Survey of Poland." (13 May): 6.

Economist Intelligence Unit. 2003. "Hungary: Euro Freaks." *Business Eastern Europe.* (28 July): 6–7.

———. 2004. "Country Watchlist: Hungary." *Business Eastern Europe* (7 June).

Égert, Balázs, Thomas Gruber, and Thomas Reininger. 2003. "Challenges for EU Acceding Countries' Exchange Rate Strategies after EU Accession and Assymetric Application of the Exchange Rate Criteria." *Focus on Transition* 2:152–72.

Eigen, Peter. 2002. "Controlling Corruption: A Key to Development-Oriented Trade." *Carnegie Endowment for International Peace* 4. http://www.ceip.org.

Ekiert, Grzegorz. 2003. "Patterns of Postcommunist Transformation in Central and Eastern Europe." In Ekiert and Hanson, 89–119.

Ekiert, Grzegorz, and Stephen E. Hanson, eds. 2003. *Capitalism and Democracy in Central and Eastern Europe: Assessing the Legacy of Communist Rule.* Cambridge: Cambridge University Press.

Ekiert, Grzegorz, and J. Kubik. 1999. *Rebellious Civil Society: Popular Protest and Democratic Consolidation in Poland, 1989–1993.* Ann Arbor: University of Michigan Press.

Elster, Jon. 1989. *The Cement of Society: A Study of Social Order.* Cambridge: Cambridge University Press.

———. 1993. "The Necessity and Impossibility of Simultaneous Economic and Political Reform." In *Constitutionalism and Democracy: Transitions in the Contemporary World*, eds. Douglas Greenberg, Stanley Katz, Melanie Beth Oliviero, and Steven Wheatley, 267–74. New York: Oxford University Press.

Engelberg, Stephen. 1991. "Pope Calls on Poland to Reject Western Europe's Secular Ways." *New York Times,* 8 June.

EOS Gallup Europe. 2005a. *Flash Eurobarometer 125: The Euro, Four Years after the Introduction of the Banknotes and Coins.* Brussels: European Commission.

———. 2005b. *Introduction of the Euro in the New Member States, Wave 2.* Brussels: European Commission.

Epstein, Rachel. 2005a. "Diverging Effects of Social Learning and External Incentives in Polish Central Banking and Agriculture." In *The Europeanization of Central and Eastern Europe,* ed. Frank Schimmelfennig and Ulrich Sedelmeier, 178–99. Ithaca, NY: Cornell University Press.

———. 2005b. "NATO Enlargement and the Spread of Democracy: Evidence and Expectations." *Security Studies* 14 (1): 63–105.

———. 2005c. "The Paradoxes of Enlargement." *European Political Science* 4:384–94.

———. 2006a. "When Legacies Meet Policies: NATO and the Refashioning of Polish Military Tradition." *East European Politics and Societies* 20 (2): 254–85.

———. 2006b. "Cultivating Consensus and Creating Conflict: International Institutions and the Depoliticization of Postcommunist Economic Policy." *Comparative Political Studies* 39 (8): 1019–42.

———. Forthcoming. *In Pursuit of Liberalism: The Power and Limits of International Institutions in Postcommunist Europe.* Baltimore: Johns Hopkins University Press.

Erlanger, Steven. 2001a. "Albanian Rebels Declare a Cease-Fire in Macedonia and Ask for Talks." *New York Times,* 22 March.

———. 2001b. "Another Balkan Battle: Higher Learning." *New York Times,* 25 March.

European Commission. 2003. *Regional Strategy Paper, 2002–2006: CARDS Assistance Programme to the Western Balkans.* Brussels: European Commission. http://www.ear.eu.int/agency/main/Agency-a1a2c3.htm.

European Council. 1999. *Presidency Conclusion.* Tampere: European Council.

———. 2002. *Framework Decision of 19 July 2002 on Combating Trafficking in Human Beings.* OJ L 203, 01.08.2002.

European Parliament. 1996. *Resolution on Trafficking in Human Beings.* OJ C 32, 05.02.1996.

Evans, Peter. 1997. "The Eclipse of the State? Reflections on Stateness in an Era of Globalization." *World Politics* 50: 62–87.

Fearon, James. 1998. "Commitment Problems and the Spread of Ethnic Conflict." In *The International Spread of Ethnic Conflict: Fear, Diffusion, and Escalation,* ed. David Lake and Donald Rothchild, 107–126. Princeton: Princeton University Press.

Fearon, James D., and David D. Laitin. 1996. "Explaining Interethnic Cooperation." *American Political Science Review* 90 (4): 715–35.

Featherstone, K. 2001. "The Political Dynamics of the *Vincolo Esterno*: The Emergence of EMU and the Challenge to the European Social Model." *Queen's Papers on Europeanization* 1:1–22.

Finance East Europe. 1994. "BLB and EBRD take MKB." (5 August).

Fish, M. Steven. 1998. "The Determinants of Economic Reform in the Post-Communist World." *East European Politics and Societies* 12 (1): 31–78.

———. 2001. "The Dynamics of Democratic Erosion." In *Postcommunism and the Theory of Democracy,* eds. Richard Anderson, M. Steven Fish, Stephen E. Hanson, and Philip Roeder, 54–95. Princeton: Princeton University Press.

———. 2005. *Democracy Derailed in Russia: The Failure of Open Politics.* Cambridge: Cambridge University Press.

Foreign Broadcast and Information Service. 1994. "State Official on State Rapport, Constitution." FBIS-EEU-94–148. 2 August.

Frait, Jan. 2003. "EU Accession, EU Membership, and Challenges for the Central Bank." Austrian National Bank, 15 December. http://www.cnb.cz.

Frenkel, M., and C. Nickel. 2005. "How Symmetric Are the Shocks and the Shock Adjustment Dynamics between the Euro Area and Central and Eastern European Countries?" *Journal of Common Market Studies* 43 (1): 53–74.

Friman, Richard, and Simon Reich, eds. 2007. *Human Trafficking, Human Security and the Balkans.* Pittsburgh: Pittsburgh University Press.

Fry, M. 1995. *Money, Interest and Banking in Economic Development.* Baltimore: Johns Hopkins University Press.

Frye, Timothy. 2002. "The Perils of Polarization: Economic Performance in the Postcommunist World." *World Politics* 54 (3): 308–37.

Fuller, Liz. 2004. *RFE Report.* 24 September.

Gagnon, V. P., Jr. 1996. "Ethnic Conflict as Demobilizer: The Case of Serbia." *Institute for European Studies Working Paper 96* (1).

———. 2004. *The Myth of Ethnic War: Serbia and Croatia in the 1990s.* Ithaca: Cornell University Press.

Gaspari, M. 2004. "Interview with Mitja Gaspari, Bank of Slovenia." In *EU Enlargement and the Future of the Euro,* ed. Pringle and Carver, 195–202. London: Central Banking Publications.

Gazeta Wyborcza. 1995. "Rządowy niewypał." 30 November.

———. 1996a. "Przymknięta furtka." 30 January.

———. 1996b. "Wielka wyprzedaż." 10 October.

———. 2005a. "Jest Raport Komisji ds. Orlenu." 27 September. http://serwisy.gazeta .pl/kraj/1,58300,2936969.html.

———. 2005b. "Po co on tak jezdzi do Moskwy?" 11 March.

Geremek, Bronislaw. 1990. "Pour l'Europe." *Liber,* 10 March.

———. 1998. "The Weimar Triangle." *Central European Review,* 20–21 February. http://www.medianet.pl/~ceurorev/numer21/23.htm.

———. 2004. "Niech wrzask ustapi racje." *Gazeta Wyborcza,* 3–4 July.

Gerschenkron, A. 1962. *Economic Backwardness in Historical Perspective: A Book of Essays.* Cambridge, MA: Harvard University Press.

Gheciu, Alexandra. 2005. *NATO in the "New Europe": The Politics of International Socialization after the Cold War.* Stanford: Stanford University Press.

Giddens, Anthony. 1990. *The Consequences of Modernity.* Stanford: Stanford University Press.

Gilbert, Geoff. 1996. "The Council of Europe and Minority Rights." *Human Rights Quarterly* 18 (1): 160–189.

Gille, Zsuzsa. 2007. *From the Cult of Waste to the Trash Heap of History: The Politics of Waste in Socialist and Postsocialist Hungary.* Bloomington: Indiana University Press.

Gilpin, Robert. 2001. *Global Political Economy.* Princeton: Princeton University Press.

Global Alliance against Trafficking in Women (GAATW). 2001. *Human Rights and Trafficking in Persons: A Handbook.* Bangkok: GAATW.

Gökay, Bülent, ed. 2001. *The Politics of Caspian Oil.* Basingstoke: Palgrave.

Goldsmith, Benjamin. 2005. *Imitation in International Relations: Observational Learning, Analogies and Foreign Policy in Russia and Ukraine.* New York: Palgrave.

Goodman, J. 1989. "Monetary Politics in France, Italy, and Germany: 1973–85." In *The Political Economy of European Integration,* ed. Paolo Guerrieri and Pier Carlo Padoan. New York: Harvester Wheatsheaf.

Gowan, Peter. 1995. "Neo-liberal Theory and Practice for Eastern Europe." *New Left Review* 213 (September–October): 3–60.

Grabbe, Heather. 2004. *The Constellations of Europe: How Enlargement Will Transform the EU.* London: Centre for European Reform.

———. 2005. "Regulating the Flow of People across Europe." In *The Europeanization of Central and Eastern Europe,* ed. Frank Schimmelfennig and Ulrich Sedelmeier, 112–134. Ithaca, NY: Cornell University Press.

———. 2006. *The EU's Transformative Power: Europeanization through Conditionality in Central and Eastern Europe.* London: Palgrave Macmillan.

Grabel, I. 2000. "Ideology and Power in Monetary Reform: Explaining the Rise of Independent Central Banks and Currency Boards in Emerging Economies." In *Power, Ideology, and Conflict: The Political Foundations of 21st Century Money.* Ithaca: Cornell University.

Greskovits, Belá. 1998. *The Political Economy of Protest and Patience: East European and Latin American Transformations Compared.* Budapest: Central European University Press.

———. 2006. "The First Shall Be the Last? Hungary's Road to the EMU." In *Enlarging the Euro Area: External Empowerment and Domestic Transformation in East Central Europe,* ed. Kenneth Dyson, 178–96. Oxford: Oxford University Press.

Grzymała-Busse, Anna. 2002. *Redeeming the Communist Past: The Regeneration of Communist Parties in East Central Europe.* Cambridge: Cambridge University Press.

———. 2007. *Rebuilding Leviathan: Party Competition and State Exploitation in Post-Communist Democracies.* Cambridge: Cambridge University Press.

Grzymała-Busse, Anna, and Abby Innes. 2003. "Great Expectations: The EU and Domestic Political Competition in East Central Europe." *East European Politics and Societies* 17 (1): 64–73.

Gutierrez, Brad. 2002. "Defense Reform in Central Europe and the Challenges of NATO Membership: The Case of Hungary." Ph.D. diss., University of California, San Diego.

H. C. 2002. "Premier Accusation: Ambassadors Hunt for the Tenders, and Journalists Shakedown the Firms." *Dnevnik* (22–23 June): 1–2.

Habermas, Jurgen, and Jacques Derrida. 2005. "February 15, or, What Binds Europeans Together." In *Old Europe, New Europe, Core Europe,* ed. Daniel Levy, Max Pensky, and John Torpey, 3–11. London: Verso.

Haggard, S., and C. H. Lee. 1993. "Political Dimensions of Finance." In Haggard, Lee, and Maxfield, 1–20.

Haggard, S., C. H. Lee, and S. Maxfield, eds. 1993. *The Politics of Finance in Developing Countries.* Ithaca: Cornell University Press.

Hall, Peter. 1993. "Policy Paradigms, Social Learning, and the State: The Case of Economic Policymaking in Britain." *Comparative Politics* 25:275–96.

Hanley, Eric, Lawrence King, and István Tóth János. 2002. "The State, International Agencies, and Property Transformation in Postcommunist Hungary." *American Journal of Sociology* 108:129–67.

Harvey, David. 2003. *The New Imperialism.* New York: Oxford University Press.

Hedges, Chris. 1998. "Macedonian's Albanians Are Restive." *New York Times,* 11 May.

Heidenheimer, Arnold J. 1996. "The Topography of Corruption: Explorations in Comparative Perspective." *International Social Science Journal* 48 (3): 337–47.

Heidenheimer, Arnold J., and Michael Johnston, eds. 2002. *Political Corruption: Concepts and Contexts*, 3rd ed. New Brunswick, N.J.: Transaction Publishers.

Helleiner, E. 1994. *States and the Reemergence of Global Finance: From Bretton Woods to the 1990s.* Ithaca: Cornell University Press.

———. 1997. "Braudelian Reflections on Globalization." In *Innovation and Transformation in International Studies,* ed. Gill and Mittleman, 90–105. Cambridge, UK: Cambridge University Press.

Hellman, Joel S. 1998. "Winners Take All: The Politics of Partial Reform in Postcommunist Transitions." *World Politics* 50 (2): 203–34.

Henderson, Jeffrey, ed. 1998. *Industrial Transformation in Eastern Europe in Light of the East Asian Experience.* New York: St. Martin's.

Henderson, Sarah. 2003. *Building Democracy in Contemporary Russia: Western Support for Grassroots Organizations.* Ithaca: Cornell University Press.

Hendrie, A., ed. 1989. *Banking in Comecon: Structures and Sources of Finance.* London: Financial Times Business Information.

Higley, John, and Richard Gunther, eds. 1992. *Elites and Democratic Consolidation in Latin America and Southern Europe.* New York: Cambridge University Press.

Hislope, Robert. 1996. "Intra-Ethnic Conflict in Croatia and Serbia: Flanking and the Consequences for Democracy." *East European Quarterly* 30 (4): 471–94.

———. 2003. "Between a Bad Peace and a Good War: Insights and Lessons from the Almost-War in Macedonia." *Ethnic and Racial Studies* 26:129–51.

Hjartarson [Heatley], J. 2004. "Foreign Banks, Domestic Networks and the Preservation of State Capacity in Internationalized Financial Sectors." Paper presented at the annual meeting of the Canadian Political Science Association, University of Manitoba.

Holdanowicz, Grzegorz. 2005. "Bumar-Dostawy do Iraku za 236 mln USD Raport 01/2005." http://www.altair.com.pl/files/r1014/0105bumar.htm.

Horowitz, Donald L. 1985. *Ethnic Groups in Conflict.* Berkeley: University of California Press.

Hughes, James, Gwendolyn Sasse, and Claire Gordon. 2004. *Europeanization and Regionalization in the EU's Enlargement to Central and Eastern Europe: The Myth of Conditionality.* London: Palgrave.

Human Rights Watch. 1998. *Police Violence in Macedonia* 10 (April). http://www.hrw.org .

———. 2003. "U.S. State Department Trafficking Report Undercut by Lack of Analysis." June, 11, 2003. http://www.hrw.org/press/2003/06/traffickingreport.htm.

Huntington, Samuel P. 1968. *Political Order in Changing Societies.* New Haven, CT: Yale University Press.

———. 1996. *The Clash of Civilizations and the Remaking of World Order.* New York: Simon and Schuster.

Icevska, Gordana. 1999. "Skopje's United Front Holds." *Institute for War and Peace Reporting.* 17 April.

Ikenberry, John G. 2001. *After Victory: Institutions, Strategic Restraint and the Rebuilding of Order after Major Wars.* Princeton, NJ: Princeton University Press.

Interfax. 2003a. "Central Bank Head Járai Urges Budget Reform Ahead of EU Accession." *Hungary Weekly Business Report,* 29 September.

———. 2003b. "Central Bank Governor Pushes 'More Radical' Public Finance Reform." *Czech Republic and Slovakia Weekly Business Report,* 24 January.

———. 2003c. "Entrepreneurs' Alliance Warns against Rush to Euro, Criticizes Tax Regime." *Hungary Weekly Business Report,* 17 November.

———. 2003d. "Klaus Calls Adoption of Euro 'Unwise.'" *Czech Republic and Slovakia Weekly Business Report,* 1 August.

———. 2004a. "Further HUF 100–150 Billion Budget Cuts Needed, Says Járai—Converge Program 'Realistic.'" *Hungary Weekly Business Report,* 17 June.

———.2004b. "Over 50% of Czech's Favor Adopting Euro." *Czech Republic and Slovakia Weekly Business Report,* 9 August.

———. 2004c. "Press—Klaus Prepares Shake-Up at CNB." *Czech Republic Business News Service,* 16 August.

International Crisis Group (ICG). 1998. "The Albanian Question in Macedonia," *ICG Balkans Report,* no. 38 (11 August).

———. 1999. "Macedonia: Towards Destabilization?" *ICG Balkans Report,* no. 67 (21 May).

———. 2002. "Macedonia's Public Secret: How Corruption Drags the Country Down," *ICG Balkans Report,* no. 133 (14 August).

International Organization for Migration (IOM). 2001. *Applied Research and Data Collection on Trafficking in Human Beings to, through and from the Balkan Region.* Geneva: International Organization for Migration.

Jacoby, Wade. 1999. "Priest and Penitent: The European Union as a Force in the Domestic Politics of Eastern Europe." *East European Constitutional Review* 8 (1–2): 62–67.

———. 2000. *Imitation and Politics: Redesigning Modern Germany.* Ithaca, N.Y.: Cornell University Press.

———. 2004. *The Enlargement of the European Union and NATO: Ordering from the Menu in Central Europe.* Cambridge: Cambridge University Press.

———. 2005. "External Incentives and Lesson-Drawing in Regional Policy and Health Care." In *The Europeanization of Central and Eastern Europe,* ed. Schimmelfennig and Sedelmeier, 91–111. Ithaca: Cornell University Press.

———. 2006. "Inspiration, Coalition, and Substitution: External Influences on Postcommunist Transformations." *World Politics* 58 (4): 623–51.

James, Oliver, and Martin Lodge. 2003. "The Limits of 'Policy Transfer' and 'Lesson Drawing' for Public Policy Research." *Political Studies Review* 1:179–93.

Janácková, S. 2002. "Eurozone Enlargement: Some Risks for Catching-Up Countries." *Politicka Ekonomie* 50 (6): 759–79.

Janácková, S., and K. Janácek 2004. "European Monetary Union and Risks for Real Convergence." *Politická Ekonomie* 52 (4).

Janos, Andrew. 2000. *East Central Europe in the Modern World: The Politics of the Borderlands from Pre- to Postcommunism.* Stanford: Stanford University Press.

————. 2001. "From Eastern Empire to Western Hegemony: East Central Europe under Two International Regimes." *East European Politics and Societies* 15 (2): 221–49.

Jelinek, Yeshayahu. 1976. *The Parish Republic: Hlinka's Slovak People's Party 1939–1945*. Boulder: East European Quarterly Monographs.

Jileva, Elena. 2002. "Visa and Free Movement of Labour: The Uneven Imposition of the EU Acquis on the Accession States." *Journal of Ethnic and Migration Studies* 28 (4): 683–700.

Johnson, J. 2002. "Financial Globalization and National Sovereignty: Neoliberal Transformations in Post-Communist Central Banks." Paper presented at American Political Science Association annual meeting, Boston.

————. 2006. "Postcommunist Central Banks: A Democratic Deficit?" *Journal of Democracy* 17 (1): 90–103.

Johnston, Michael. 1986. "The Political Consequences of Corruption: A Reassessment." *Comparative Politics* 18 (4): 459–77.

Jones, Rochelle. 2005. "Prevention as the New Approach to Human Trafficking: AWID Interviews Barbara Limanowska." *Resource Net* 240 (19 August). http://www.awid.org.

Kaelberer, M. (2003). "Knowledge, Power and Monetary Bargaining: Central Bankers and the Creation of Monetary Union in Europe." *Journal of European Public Policy* 10 (3): 365–79.

Kahneman, D., and A. Tversky, eds. 2000. *Choices, Values and Frames*. Cambridge: Cambridge University Press.

Kamm, Henry. 1994. "Macedonia Sees Its Albanians as Its 'Biggest Problem'." *New York Times,* 5 May.

Kapstein, E. 1989. "Resolving the Regulator's Dilemma: International Coordination of Banking Regulations." *International Organization* 46:265–87.

————. 1992. "Between Power and Purpose: Central Bankers and the Politics of Regulatory Convergence." *International Organization* 46 (1): 265–87.

Karatnycky, Adrian. 2005. "Ukraine's Orange Revolution." *Foreign Affairs* 84 (March/April): 35–52.

Kawalec, Stefan, Piotr Rymaszewski, and Slawomir Sikora. 1994. "Polish Program of Bank Enterprise Restructuring: Design and Implementation, 1991–1994." Paper presented at the Central and Eastern European Privatisation Network's Workshop, Budapest.

Keck, Margaret, and Kathryn Sikkink. 1998. *Activists beyond Borders: Advocacy Networks in International Politics*. Ithaca, NY: Cornell University Press.

Kelley, Judith. 2004a. "International Actors on the Domestic Scene: Membership Conditionality and Socialization by International Institutions." *International Organization* 58 (4): 425–57.

————. 2004b. *Ethnic Politics in Europe: The Power of Norms and Incentives*. Princeton: Princeton University Press.

Kelly, Liz. 2005. "'You Can Find Anything You Want': A Critical Reflection on Research on Trafficking in Persons within and into Europe." *International Migration* 43:235–65.

Kenen, P. B., and E. E. Meade. 2004. "EU Accession and the Euro: Close Together or Far Apart?" In *EU Enlargement and the Future of the Euro*, ed. R. Pringle and N. Carver, 79–98. London: Central Banking Publications.

Kennedy, Francis. 1994. "Pope Flies into Cauldron of Balkans." *Sunday Times*, 9 September.

Kennedy, Michael D. 1999. "The Liabilities of Liberalism and Nationalism after Communism: Polish Businessmen in the Articulation of the Nation." In *Intellectuals and the Articulation of the Nation*, ed. Ronald Grigor Suny and Michael D. Kennedy, 345–78. Ann Arbor: University of Michigan Press.

———. 2002. *Cultural Formations of Postcommunism: Emancipation, Transition, Nation, and War.* Minneapolis: University of Minnesota Press.

Kenney, Padraic. 2003. *A Carnival of Revolution.* Princeton: Princeton University Press.

Keohane, Robert O., and Joseph S. Nye. 1977. *Power and Interdependence.* Boston: Little Brown.

Kis, Janos. 1989. *Politics in Hungary: For a Democratic Alternative.* Boulder: Social Science Monographs, distributed by Columbia University Press.

Kitschelt, Herbert. 2003. "Accounting for Postcommunist Regime Diversity: What Counts as a Good Cause?" in Ekiert and Hanson, 49–86.

Klaus, V. 2004. "The Future of the Euro: An Outsider's View." In *EU Enlargement and the Future of the Euro,* ed. R. Pringle and N. Carver. London: Central Banking Publications.

Kontra, Martin, and Jaroslav Špurný. 1998. "Třetí pokus se jmenuje NATO: Ospalost' hlavní překážkou na cestěk diplomatickému úspechu století." *Respekt* 9 (9 March): 9–11.

Koppa, Maria-Eleni. 2001. "Ethnic Albanians in the Former Yugoslav Republic of Macedonia: Between Nationality and Citizenship." *Nationalism and Ethnic Politics* 7:37–65.

Kopstein, Jeffrey. 2006. "The Transatlantic Divide over Democracy Promotion." *Washington Quarterly* 29 (2): 85–98.

Kopstein, Jeffrey S., and David A. Reilly. 2000. "Geographic Diffusion and the Transformation of the Postcommunist World." *World Politics* 53 (1): 1–37.

Kostrzewa-Zorbas, Grzegorz. 1999. "Kameleony I Niezłomni." *Gazeta Polska,* 3 December.

Kramer, Andrew E. 2006. "Russia Cuts Off Gas to Ukraine in Cost Dispute." *New York Times,* 2 January.

Krasnodebski, Zdzislaw. 2004. "Czy miekkie imperium Europa?" *Fakt/Europa,* 21 April.

———. 2005. "Poprzedni i obecny koniec dziejow." *Fakt/Europa,* 19 January.

Krastev, Ivan. 2004. *Shifting Obsessions: Three Essays on the Politics of Anticorruption.* Budapest: Central European University Press.

Krenzler, H., and S. Senior Nello. 1999. "Implications of the Euro for Enlargement: Report of the Working Group on the Eastern Enlargement of the European Union." *RSC Policy Paper* 99 (3).

Kristof, Nicholas D. 2006. "Bush Takes on the Brothels." *New York Times,* 9 May.

Krosta, Andreas, and Tony Major. 2003. "Central Banks Urge Adherence to Pact Budget Deficit Rules." *Financial Times,* 29 August.

Krzeminski, Adam. 2005. "First Kant, Now Habermas." In *Old Europe, New Europe, Core Europe,* eds. Daniel Levy, Max Pensky, and John Torpey, 146–52. London: Verso.

Kubicek, Paul. 2003. "International Norms, the European Union, and Democratization." In *The European Union and Democratization,* ed. Kubicek, 1–29. London: Routledge.

Kubik, Jan, and Amy Linch. 2007. "Justice, Hegemony, and Social Movements: Views from East/Central Europe and Eurasia." Paper presented at the Social Science Research Council Conference "Justice, Hegemony and Social Movements: Views from East/Central Europe and Eurasia," Warsaw University, March.

Kuroń, J. 1991. *Moja zupa.* Warsaw: Polska Oficyna Wydawnicza BGW.

Kurski, Jacek. 2003. "Czy umierać za Niceę?" ("Are we ready to die for Nice?"). *Gazeta Wyborcza,* 10 October.

Kwitny, Jonathan. 1997. *Man of the Century: The Life and Times of Pope John Paul II.* New York: Doubleday.

Kymlicka, Will. 1995. *Multicultural Citizenship: A Liberal Theory of Minority Rights.* Oxford: Clarendon Press.

Laclau, Ernesto, and Chantal Mouffe. 1985. *Hegemony and Socialist Strategy: Towards a Radical Democratic Politics.* London: Verso.

Laczko, Frank, and Marco Gramegna. 2003. "Developing Better Indicators of Human Trafficking." *Brown Journal of World Affairs* 10:186–91.

Laitin, David. 1986. *Hegemony and Culture.* Chicago: University of Chicago Press.

Landay, Jonathan S. 1993. "No Hitch for Truckers Busting Sanctions through Macedonia." *Christian Science Monitor,* 9 July.

Landesmann, M. A., and I. Abel. 1995. "The Transition in Eastern Europe: The Case for Industrial Policy." In Chang and Nolan, 136–62.

Landler, Mark. 2006. "Gas Halt May Produce Big Ripples in European Policy." *New York Times,* 4 January.

Laszlo, Leslie. 1989. "Religion and Nationalism in Hungary." In *Religion and Politics in Soviet and East European Politics,* ed. Pedro Ramet, 286–98. Durham: Duke University Press.

Latham, Robert, and Saskia Sassen, eds. 2005. *Digital Formations: IT and New Architectures in the Global Realm.* Princeton: Princeton University Press.

Leff, Nathaniel. 1964. "Economic Development through Bureaucratic Corruption." *American Behavioral Scientist* 8 (3).

Łętowski, Maciej. 2002. "Polska Prawica o Polskiej Racji Stanu." *Gazeta Wyborcz,* 10–13 October.

Lévesque, Jacques. 1997. *The Enigma of 1989: The USSR and the Liberation of Eastern Europe.* Berkeley: University of California Press.

Levy, D. 1995. "Does an Independent Central Bank Violate Democracy?" *Journal of Post-Keynesian Economics* 18 (2): 189–210.

Leys, Colin. 1965. "What Is the Problem about Corruption?" *The Journal of Modern African Studies* 3 (2): 215–30.

Lijphart, Arend. 1997. *Democracy in Plural Societies: A Comparative Exploration.* New Haven: Yale University Press.

Limanowksi, Barbara. 2005. *Report on Trafficking in Human Beings in Southeastern Europe.* Warsaw and Sarajevo: UNICEF, UNOHCHR, OSCE/ODIHR. http://www.unicef.org/ceecis/Trafficking.Report.2005.pdf.

Linden, Ronald, ed. 2002. *Norms and Nannies: The Impact of International Organizations on the Central and East European States.* Lanham: Rowman and Littlefield.

Lindstrom, Nicole. 2004. "Regional Sex Trafficking in the Balkans: Transnational Networks in an Enlarged Europe." *Problems of Post-Communism* 51:45–52.

———. 2007. "Transnational Responses to Human Trafficking in the Balkans." In *Human Trafficking, Human Security and the Balkans,* ed. Richard Friman and Simon Reich, 61–80. Pittsburgh: University of Pittsburgh Press.

Linz, Jaun J., and Alfred Stepan. 1992. "Political Identities and Electoral Sequences: Spain, the Soviet Union and Yugoslavia." *Daedalus* 121 (2): 123–39.

———. 1996. *Problems of Democratic Transition and Consolidation: Southern Europe, South America, and Post-Communist Europe.* Baltimore: John Hopkins University Press.

Liotta, Peter H., and C. R. Jebb. 2004. *Mapping Macedonia: Idea and Identity.* Westport, CT: Praeger.

Little, Robert. 2004. "U.S. Dollars Wooed Ally in Iraq Coalition." *Baltimore Sun,* 17 October. http://www.informationclearinghouse.info/article7097.htm.

Lorenz, Ryan. 2002. "Conflict Prevention in Macedonia: An Oasis of Pieces?" Master's thesis, School for Oriental and African Studies, University of London.

Lukes, S. 1974. *Power: A Radical View.* London and New York: Macmillan.

Macedonian Information Center. 1994a. "Party Statements." 21 December.

———. 1994b. "Game of Nerves." 5 December.

———. 1994c. "Hard Rock 'Cream.'" 6 December.

———. 1994d. "Intensive Preparations for New Government Cabinet." 29 November.

———. 1994e. "Interview with Kiro Gligorov." 28 December.

———. 2002. "Macedonia Is Exposed to Corruption from Abroad." 24 June.

———. 2006. "Elections as a Source of Corruption." 22 June.

Magyar Nemzet. 2002. Munkaadói kirohanás a jegybankelnök ellen [Employers are criticizing the president of the central bank]. June 12.

Mahlberg, B., and R. Kronberger. 2003. "Eastern Enlargement of the European Monetary Union: An Optimal Currency Area Theory View." In *Institutional, Legal and Economic Aspects of the EMU,* eds. Fritz Breuss, Gerhard Fink, and Stefan Griller, 243–77. New York: Springer.

Makfax. 2001a. "Menduh Thaci—The Albanians Do Not Support the Terrorist Attacks." 7 February.

———. 2001b. "Pavle Trajanov—There Are Witnesses to Confirm the Phone-Tapping Was Conducted in the Interior Ministry." 9 February.

———. 2001c. "We Recognize Macedonia's Territorial Integrity but only as Albanian-Macedonian Federation." 12 March.

———. 2001d. "Xhaferi—Macedonia Is a Stable State After All." 31 January.

Mandelbaum, Michael. 1996. "Foreign Policy as Social Work." *Foreign Affairs* 75 (1): 16–32.

Mann, Michael. 2004. *Incoherent Empire*. London: Verso.

Mansfield, Edward, and Jack Snyder. 2005. *Electing to Fight: Why Emerging Democracies Go to War.* Cambridge: MIT Press.

Marcussen, M. 1998. "Central Bankers, the Ideational Life Cycle, and the Social Construction of EU." *EUI Working Paper RSC* 98 (33).

———. 2000. *Ideas and Elites: The Social Construction of Economic and Monetary Union.* Aalborg: Aalborg University Press.

Mattar, Mohamed. 2003. "Monitoring the Status of Severe Forms of Trafficking in Foreign Countries: Sanctions Mandated under the US Trafficking Victims Protection Act." *Brown Journal of World Affairs* 10:159–78.

Mattli, Walter. 1999. *The Logic of Regional Integration, Europe and Beyond.* New York: Cambridge University Press.

Mattli, Walter, and Thomas Plümper. 2004. "The Internal Value of External Options." *European Union Politics* 5 (3): 307–30.

Maxfield, S. 1997. *Gatekeepers of Growth: The International Political Economy of Central Banking in Developing Countries.* Princeton, NJ: Princeton University Press.

Mazower, Mark. 2002. *Dark Continent*. New York: Vintage.

McDermott, Gerald. 2002. *Embedded Politics: Industrial Networks and Institutional Change in Post Communism.* Ann Arbor: University of Michigan.

McFaul, Michael. 2002. "The Fourth Wave of Democracy *and* Dictatorship: Noncooperative Transitions in the Postcommunist World." *World Politics* 54 (2): 212–44.

McKinsey, Kitty 1999. "Yugoslavia: NATO, US pledge to uphold stability in Macedonia." *Radio Free Europe/Radio Liberty,* 19 April.

McNamara, K. 2002. "Rational Fictions: Central Bank Independence and the Social Logic of Delegation." *West European Politics* 25 (1): 23–47.

Mendelson, Sarah, and John Glenn, eds. 2002. *The Power and Limit of NGOs.* New York: Columbia University Press.

Merritt, Jeff S. 2001. "Coming Apart at the Seams." *Transitions on Line*. http://www.tol.cz.

Meyer, John W. 1989. "Conceptions of Christendom: Notes on the Distinctiveness of the West." In *Cross-National Research in Sociology,* ed. Melvin Kohn, 395–413. Thousand Oaks: Sage.

Meyer, John W., John Boli, George Thomas, and Francisco Ramirez. 1997. "World Society and the Nation-State." *American Journal of Sociology* 103 (1): 144–81.

Michnik, Adam. 1985. *Letters from Prison and Other Essays.* Berkeley: University of California Press.

Milicevic, Aleksandra. 2004. "Joining Serbia's Wars: Volunteers and Draft-Dodgers, 1991–1995." Ph.D. diss., University of California, Los Angeles.

Mitchell, Paul. 1995. "Party Competition in an Ethnic Dual Party System." *Ethnic and Racial Studies* 18 (4): 773–96.

Mongelli, F. P. 2002. "New Views on the Optimum Currency Area: What Is the EMU Telling Us?" *European Central Bank Working Paper Series* 138.

Montalbano, William D. 1994. "Frail Pontiff Urges Croats to Forge Peace." *Los Angeles Times,* 11 September.

Moore, Solomon, and T. Christian Miller. 2005. "Iraq: Before Rearming Iraq, He Sold Shoes and Flowers." *Los Angeles Times,* 6 November.

Moravcsik, Andrew. 1998. *The Choice for Europe: Social Purpose and State Power from Messina to Maastricht.* Ithaca: Cornell University Press.

———. 2000. "The Origins of Human Rights Regimes: Democratic Delegation in Postwar Europe." *International Organizations* 54:217–52.

Moravcsik, Andrew, and Milada Anna Vachudova. 2003. "National Interest, State Power, and EU Enlargement." *East European Politics and Society* 17:42–57.

MTI News. 1991. "Law on Financial Institutions: An Econews Amplifier." 15 November.

———. 1993a. "MKB Managing Director on Future Structure of Banking Sector." 23 November.

———. 1993b. "Preparations for Privatisation at BB and MPB." 19 November.

———. 1999. "Hungarian Central Bank Head Opposes Joining Euro Upon Admission to EU." 1 July.

———. 2004a. "Hungarian Central Bank President Says Early Euro Still Possible." 2 February.

———. 2004b. "Járai Says Substantial Sacrifice Needed for 2008 Euro Zone Entry." 23 February.

Myant, M. R. 1993. *Transforming Socialist Economies: The Case of Poland and Czechoslovakia.* Brookfield, VT: Edward Elgar.

Naaborg, Ilko, Hanneke Bol, Jakob de Haan, Ralph Haas, and Bert Scholtens. 2003. "How Important Are Foreign Banks in the Financial Development of Eastern Transition Countries?" CESifo Working Paper Series, CESifo Working Paper No. 1100, CESifo GmbH.

Naegele, Jolyon. 2001a. "Refugees Flee the Tanusevci Region." *Radio Free Europe/Radio Liberty* 5 (13 March).

———. 2001b. "The Tanusevci Story." *Radio Free Europe/Radio Liberty* 5 (9 March).

National Bank of Poland. 2001. Summary Evaluation of the Financial Situation of Polish Banks. http://www.nbp.pl.

Naumann, Friedrich. 1917. *Central Europe.* New York: Knopf.

Nederveen Pieterse, Jan. 2004. *Globalization or Empire?* New York and London: Routledge.

Nelsen, Brent F., James L. Guth, and Cleveland R. Fraser. 2001. "Does Religion Matter? Christianity and Public Support for the European Union." *European Union Politics* 2: 267–91.

Népszabadság. 2003. "Euró: László elveti Járai érveit [Euro: Laszlo rejects the argument of Jarai]." 8 May.

New York Times. 1993. "The Big Leak in Serbia Embargo: Nervous, Needy Macedonia." 18 July.

———. 2001. "Fighting Flares for 2nd Day as Macedonia Pounds Rebels." 4 May.

Nikolov, Marjan. 2004. "Corruption's Economic and Political Implications in the Republic of Macedonia." Paper prepared for the conference "Macedonia and the Corruption—Conditions and Challenges," 10 November 2004, organized by FOSIM-Skopje.

Nye, J. S. 1967. "Corruption and Political Development: A Cost-Benefit Analysis." *American Political Science Review* 61 (2): 417–27.

Obokata, Thomas. 2003. "EU Council Framework Decision on Combating Trafficking in Human Beings: A Critical Appraisal." *Common Market Law Review* 40: 917–36.

O'Connor, Mike 1998. "Slavs and Albanians Form Unusual Coalition in Macedonia." *New York Times,* 30 November.

O'Donnell, Guillermo, and Philippe C. Schmitter. 1986. "Tentative Conclusions about Uncertain Democracies." In *Transitions from Authoritarian Rule: Prospects for Democracy,* ed. Guillermo O'Donnell, Philippe C. Schmitter, and Laurence Whitehead, 3–78. Baltimore: Johns Hopkins University Press.

O'Dwyer, Conor. 2006a. "Reforming Regional Governance in East Central Europe: Europeanization or Domestic Politics as Usual?" *East European Politics and Societies* 20 (2): 219–53.

———. 2006b. *Runaway State Building: Patronage Politics and Democratic Development.* Baltimore: Johns Hopkins University Press.

OECD. 1997. Convention on Combating Bribery of Foreign Public Officials in International Business Transactions, 21 November, Paris.

———. 2004. *Survey of Hungary.* London: OECD.

Offe, Claus. 1997. *Varieties of Transition: The East European and East German Experience.* Cambridge: MIT Press.

Ordanoski, Saso. 1992. "A Fragile Peace?" *East European Reporter* 5 (6): 10–12.

Orenstein, Mitchell. 2000. "How Politics and Institutions Affect Pension Reform in Three Postcommunist Countries." World Bank Policy Research Working Paper 2310, World Bank, Washington, DC.

———. 2001. *Out of the Red: Building Capitalism and Democracy in Postcommunist Europe.* Ann Arbor: University of Michigan Press.

Orenstein, Mitchell, and Hans Peter Schmitz. 2006. "The New Transnationalism and Comparative Politics." *Comparative Politics* 38 (4): 479–500.

Orenstein, Mitchell, and Umat Ozkaleli. 2005. "The European Union as a Network Actor." Unpublished paper, Syracuse University.

Organisation for Economic Co-operation and Development. 1997. *The New Banking Landscape in Central and Eastern Europe: Country Experience and Policies for the Future.* Paris: OECD.

Orgieva, L. G. 2002. "The State Is Exposed to Corruption from Abroad." *Nova Makedonija* (22–23 June): 1–2.

Ost, David. 2004. "Letter from Poland." *Nation* (4 October).

Ottaway, Marina, and Thomas Carothers, eds. 2000. *Funding Virtue: Civil Society Aid and Democracy Promotion*. Washington, DC: Carnegie.

Packer, Tomos. 2004. "Finance Minister Defies Central Bank Criticism." *Emerging Markets Daily News*, 30 June.

Paltrow, Scott. 1986. "Poland and the Pope: The Vatican's Relations with Poland, 1978 to the Present." *Millennium: Journal of International Studies* 15:1–26.

Papagianni, Katia. 2002. "The Making of Minority Policies in the Context of an Emerging European Regime on Minority Rights." Paper presented at the 13th Conference of Europeanists, Council for European Studies, 14–16 March 2002, Chicago.

Pattanaik, Swaha. 2004. "Newcomers Must Meet Euro Rules Convincingly-ECB." Reuters, 23 April.

Pawlak, Justyna. 2004. "Polish Central Banker—EU Stab Pact Should Stay Intact." Reuters, 19 April.

P. D. 2002. "Imaginations from Reality Are Dangerous. Last Evening at the Organized Conference 'Macedonia and the Corruption—Context and Challenges.'" *Vecer* (22–23): 5.

Pecze, Zoltán. 1998. *Civil-Military Relations in Hungary, 1989–1996*. Groningen, The Netherlands: Centre for European Security Studies.

Perry, Duncan M. 1996. "Macedonia: Balkan Miracle or Balkan Disaster?" *Current History* 95 (March): 113–17.

———. 2000. "Macedonia's Quest for Security and Stability." *Current History* 99 (March): 129–36.

Peto, Sandor. 2002. "Hungary Employers Want Central Bank Chief to Quit." Reuters, 5 December.

———. 2003. "Hungary Central Banker Says EU Entrants Need Euro Targets." Reuters, 26 February.

———. 2004a. "Central Bank Hopes Hungary Keeps 2008 Euro Goal." Reuters, 8 January.

———. 2004b. "Hungary Finance Minister, Central Bank Bickers Over Convergence Plan." Reuters, 29 June.

Petruseva, Ana. 2002. "Macedonia: Threats Follow Corruption Report." *Institute for War and Peace Reporting* 360 (21 August).

Phillips, Ann. 2000. *Power and Influence after the Cold War: Germany in East Central Europe*. Lanham, MD: Rowman and Littlefield.

Philp, Mark. 2002. "Conceptualizing Political Corruption." In Heidenheimer and Johnston, 41–57.

Pinski, Jan, and Krzyszgtof Trebski. 2005. "Prawnik Pierwszego Kontaktu." *Wprost* (13 March): 22–24.

Piroska, D. 2005. "Small Post-Socialist States and Global Finance: A Comparative Study of the Internationalization of State Roles in Banking in Hungary and Slovenia." Ph.D. diss., Central European University, Budapest.

Pope Benedict XVI. 2005. "Angelus." http://www.vatican.va. 24 July.

———. 2007. "Address of His Holiness Benedict XVI to the Participants in the Convention Organized by the Commission of the Bishops Conferences of the European Community." http://www.vatican.va. 24 March.

Pope John Paul II. 1992. *Crisis in Yugoslavia: Position and Actions of the Holy See.* Citta del Vaticano: Libreria Editrice Vaticana.

———. 1995. "Posolstvo (Message)." In *Visit of the Pope John Paul II to Slovakia, June 30–July 3, 1995.* Office of the President of the Slovak Republic.

———. 1997. "True Unity Must Be Based on Gospel." http://www.vatican.va. 3 June.

———. 2003a. "Ecclesia in Europa." http://www.vatican.va. 28 June.

———. 2003b. "Welcome Ceremony at the International Airport of Bratislava: Address of John Paul II." http://www.vatican.va. 11 September.

Pope, Hugh 1994. "A Nation Clinging to Peace." *Los Angeles Times,* 29 March.

Powers, D. V., and Cox, J. H. 1997. "Echoes from the Past: The Relationship between Satisfaction with Economic Reforms and Voting Behavior in Poland." *American Political Science Review* 91:617–33.

Price, Richard. 1998. "Reversing the Gun Sights: Transnational Civil Society Targets Land Mines." *International Organization* 52:613–44.

Pridham, Geoffrey. 2002. "The European Union's Democratic Conditionality and Domestic Politics in Slovakia: The Mečiar and Dzurinda Governments Compared." *Europe-Asia Studies* 54 (2): 203–27.

———. 2005. *Designing Democracy: EU Enlargement and Regime Change in Post-Communist Europe.* London: Palgrave Macmillan.

Pringle, R., and N. Carver, eds. 2004. *EU Enlargement and the Future of the Euro.* London: Central Banking Publications.

Przeworski, Adam. 1991. *Democracy and the Market: Political and Economic Reforms in Eastern Europe and Latin America.* Cambridge: Cambridge University Press.

Quandt, Richard. 2002. *The Changing Landscape in Eastern Europe: A Personal Perspective on Philanthropy and Technology Transfer.* New York: Oxford University Press.

Rabushka, Alvin, and Kenneth A. Shepsle. 1972. *Politics in Plural Societies: A Theory of Democratic Instability.* Columbus, Ohio: Charles E. Merrill.

Radio Free Europe. 1999. "Arben Xhaferi Says Macedonian Albanians Want No Border Change." *Radio Liberty Balkan Report* 3 (19 February).

Ramet, Petra. 1996. *Balkan Babel: The Disintegration of Yugoslavia from the Death of Tito to Ethnic War.* 2nd ed. Boulder: Westview Press.

Raxhimi, Altin. 2001. "Gaining Ground." *Transitions Online* (7 March).

Reed, John. 2000. "Poland: Foreign Presence Proves Controversial." *Financial Times,* 17 April.

Reno, Will. 2002. "Mafiya Troubles, Warlord Crisis." In *Beyond State Crisis Postcolonial Africa and Post-Soviet Eurasia in Comparative Perspective,* ed. Mark R. Beissinger and Crawford Young, 105–27. Washington, DC: Woodrow Wilson Center Press.

Reuters. 2003a. "Czech Central Bank Warns against Delaying Euro Adoption." 14 July.

———. 2003b. "Czech Central Banker Chides Government for Slow Reform Progress." 28 March.

———. 2003c. "Czech Central Banker Warns Reform Delays Threaten Crown." 24 April.

———. 2003d. "Hungary Central Bank Chief Warns of Euro Entry Delay." 9 September.

———. 2003e. "Hungary Central Bank Governor Slams Income Tax Cut Plan." 24 May.

———. 2003f. "Hungary Central Bank Urges Budget Restraint, Eyeing Euro." 10 October.

———. 2004a. "Czech Central Banker Seeks Loose Reading of Euro CPI Test." 5 April.

———. 2004b. "Hungary Central Bank Says Supports New Euro Entry Plan." 13 May.

Riker, W. H. 1996. *The Art of Political Manipulation*. New Haven: Yale University Press.

Risse, Thomas, Stephen Ropp, and Kathryn Sikkink, eds. 1999. *The Power of Human Rights: International Norms and Domestic Political Change*. Cambridge: Cambridge University Press.

Risse-Kappen, Thomas. 1994. "Ideas Do Not Float Freely: Transnational Coalitions, Domestic Structures, and the End of the Cold War." *International Organization* 48:185–214.

———, ed. 1995. *Bringing Transnational Relations Back In: Non-state Actors, Domestic Structures, and International Institutions*. Cambridge: Cambridge University Press.

Ritson, M. 1989. "Commentary." In Hendrie, 98–102.

Rohrschneider, Robert, and Stephen Whitefield. 2006. "Political Parties, Public Opinion, and European Integration in Post-Communist Countries: The State of the Art." *European Union Politics* 7:141–60.

Rosati, D. 2002. "A Fast Track to the Euro Zone for Accession Countries?" *The Euro, EU Enlargement, and the Challenge of Risk Mitigation*. Paris: Promethee.

Rosenau, James. 2003. *Distant Proximities: Dynamics beyond Globalization*. Princeton: Princeton University Press.

Rothschild, Joseph. 1974. *East Central Europe between the Two World Wars*. Seattle: University of Washington Press.

Rubinstein, Alvin Z. 1998. "NATO Enlargement versus American Interests." *Orbis* 42 (1): 37–48.

Rupnik, Jacques. 1999. "The Postcommunist Divide." *Journal of Democracy* 10 (1): 57–62.

Rusi, Iso. 1999. "Macedonia Unravels." *Balkan Crisis Report* (23 April).

———. 2002a. "Albanian Power Struggle Heats Up." *Balkan Crisis Report* 334 (1 May).

———. 2002b. "Macedonia, One Year After: Where Are We Going?" *Lobi* 54 (25 February).

———. 2002c. "Octopus Endangers Macedonia." *Lobi* (5 July).

———. 2002d. "Our Age Hero, Portrait: Menduh Thaci." *Lobi* (10 June).

———. 2003. "Party Alchemy: Can Lead Be Turned to Gold?" *Lobi* 124 (10 July). http://www.pressonline.com.mk.

Rustow, Dankart. 1991. "Transitions to Democracy: Toward A Dynamic Model." *Comparative Politics* 2 (3): 337–63.

Sachs, Jeffrey. 1993. *Poland's Jump to the Market Economy.* Cambridge, MA: MIT Press.

Sájo, András. 1997. "Universal Rights, Missionaries, Converts, and 'Local Savages.'" *East European Constitutional Review* 6 (1): 44–49.

———. 1998. "Corruption, Clientelism, and the Future of the Constitutional State in Eastern Europe." *East European Constitutional Review* 7 (2): 37–46.

Salome, Louis J., and Bob Deans. 1994. "Survival Comes First: Macedonia Winks at Smuggling into Yugoslavia." *Atlanta Journal and Constitution,* 12 June.

Sandholtz, W. 1993. "Choosing Union: Monetary Politics and Maastricht." *International Organization* 47 (1): 1–39.

Sartori, Giovanni. 1976. *Parties and Party Systems: A Framework for Analysis.* Cambridge: Cambridge University Press.

Sasse, Gwendolyn. 2007. "Minority Protection and EU Enlargement: Constructing and De-Constructing an EU Condition and Its Effects." Working paper, Oxford University.

Schimmelfennig, Frank. 2001. "The Community Trap: Liberal Norms, Rhetorical Action, and the Eastern Enlargement of the European Union." *International Organization* 55 (1): 47–80.

———. 2003. *The EU, NATO and the Integration of Europe: Rules and Rhetoric.* Cambridge: Cambridge University Press.

———. 2005. "Strategic Calculation and International Socialization: Membership Incentives, Party Constellations, and Sustained Compliance in Central and Eastern Europe." *International Organization* 59 (4): 827–60.

Schimmelfennig, Frank, Stefan Engert, and Heiko Knobel. 2003. "Costs, Commitment and Compliance: The Impact of EU Democratic Conditionality on Latvia, Slovakia and Turkey." *Journal of Common Market Studies* 41 (3): 495–518.

———. 2005. "The Impact of EU Political Conditionality." In Schimmerlfenning and Sedelmeier, *The Europeanization of Central and Eastern Europe,* 29–50. Ithaca: Cornell University Press.

Schimmelfennig, Frank, and Ulrich Sedelmeier. 2005. "Introduction: Conceptualizing the Europeanization of Central and Eastern Europe." In Schimmelfennig and Sedelmeier, *The Europeanization of Central and Eastern Europe,* 1–28. Ithaca: Cornell University Press.

———. 2005. *The Europeanization of Central and Eastern Europe.* Ithaca: Cornell University Press.

Schneider, Ondrej. 2003. "The Fine Print of EU Membership Reveals Unpleasant Fiscal Accounting." *Prague Business Journal* (23 June).

Schoppa, L. J. 1993. "Two Level Games and Bargaining Outcomes: Why *Gaiatsu* Succeeds in Japan in Some Cases and Not Others." *International Organization* 47:353–86.

———. 1997. *Bargaining with Japan: What American Pressure Can and Cannot Do.* New York: Columbia University Press.

———. 1999. "The Social Context in Coercive International Bargaining." *International Organization* 53:307–42.

Schwellnuss, Guido. 2005. "The Adoption of Non-Discrimination and Minority Protection Rules in Romania, Hungary, and Poland." In Schimmelfennig and Sedelmeier, 51–70.

Scott, James C. 1967. "An Essay on the Political Functions of Corruption." *Asian Survey* 5:501–23.

———. 1972. *Comparative Political Corruption.* Englewood Cliffs, NJ: Prentice-Hall.

Sedelmeier, Ulrich. 2005. *Constructing the Path to Eastern Enlargement: The Uneven Policy Impact of EU Identity.* Manchester, UK: Manchester University Press.

———. 2006. "Europeanisation in New Member and Candidate States." *Living Reviews in European Governance (LREG).* http://www.livingreviews.org/lreg-2006-3.

Šević, Ž., ed. 2002. *Banking Reforms in South-East Europe.* Cheltenham, UK: Edward Elgar.

Sewell, William H., Jr. 2005. "A Theory of Structure: Duality, Agency, and Transformation." In *Logics of History: Social Theory and Social Transformation,* 124–51. Chicago: University of Chicago Press.

Shelton, Eleanor. 2004. "Two Polish Visitors Take Sides over Coalition of the Willing." *Journal of the International Institute* (Spring/Summer).

Sheppard, E. 2002. "The Spaces and Times of Globalization: Place, Scale, Networks, and Positionality." *Economic Geography* 78 (3): 307–30.

Shields, S. 2003. "The 'Charge of the Right Brigade': Transnational Social Forces and the Neoliberal Configuration of Poland's Transition." *New Political Economy* 8:225–44.

Shleifer, Andrei, and Robert Vishny. 1993. "Corruption," In *Quarterly Journal of Economics* 108 (3): 599–617.

Simmons, Beth, and Zachary Elkins. 2004. "The Globalization of Liberalization: Policy Diffusion in the International Political Economy." *American Political Science Review* 98 (1): 171–89.

Simon, Jeffrey 2003. *Hungary and Nato: Problems in Civil-Military Relations.* Lanham, MD: Rowman & Littlefield.

———. 2004. *Poland and NATO.* Lanham, MD: Rowman & Littlefield.

Sisk, Timothy D. 1996. *Power Sharing and International Mediation in Ethnic Conflicts.* Washington, DC: United States Institute of Peace.

Sissenich, B. 2005. "The Transfer of EU Social Policy to Poland and Hungary." In Schimmelfennig and Sedelmeier, 156–77.

————. 2007. *Building States without Society: European Union Enlargement and the Transfer of EU Social Policy to Poland and Hungary.* Plymouth, UK: Lexington Books.

Slaughter, Anne-Marie. 2004. *A New World Order.* Princeton: Princeton University Press.

Smith, Karen E. 2003. "The Evolution and Application of EU Membership Conditionality." In *The Enlargement of the European Union,* ed. Marise Cremona, 105–39. Oxford: Oxford University Press.

Smith, R. Jeffrey. 2001. "Birth of New Rebel Army." *Washington Post,* 30 March.

Smolar, Aleksander. 2002. "Guliwer i Lilipuci." *Gazeta Wyborcza,* 28–29 September.

————. 2004. "Interes narodowy w polskiej polityce zagranicznej od 1989 roku." Res Publica (April). http://respublica.onet.pl/1157133,0,druk.html?u=http%3A%2F%2Frespublica.onet.pl%2F1157133%2Cartykul.html.

Snyder, Jack. 2000. *From Voting to Violence: Democratization and Nationalist Conflict.* New York: Norton.

Snyder, Jack, and Karen Ballentine. 1996. "Nationalism and the Marketplace of Ideas." *International Security* 21 (Fall): 5–40.

State Statistical Office. 2003. Census of Population, Households and Dwellings in the Republic of Macedonia, 2002 Final Data. Skopje, Republic of Macedonia.

Steinmetz, George. 2005. "Return to Empire: The New US Imperialism in Comparative Historical Perspective." *Sociological Theory* 23 (4): 339–67.

Stiglitz, J. 1998. "Central Banking in a Democratic Society." *De Economist* 146 (2): 199–226.

————. 2003. *Globalization and Its Discontents.* New York: Norton.

Stone, Randall. 2002. *Lending Credibility: The International Monetary Fund and the Post Communist Transition.* Princeton: Princeton University Press.

Strąk, Michał. 2002. "Lilipuci i dwóch Guliwerów." *Gazeta Wyborcza,* 26–27 October.

Strang, David. 1991. "Adding Social Structure to Diffusion Models: An Event History Framework." *Sociological Methods and Research* 19:324–53.

Strang, David, and Sarah Soule. 1998. "Diffusion in Organizations and Social Movements: From Hybrid Corn to Poison Pills." *Annual Review of Sociology* 24:265–90.

Stylinski, Andrzej. 2003. "Poland Signs Multibillion-Dollar Deal to Buy F-16 Fet Fighters." *Detroit News,* 19 April.

Surtees, Rebecca. 2005. "Second Annual Report on Victims of Trafficking in South-Eastern Europe." Geneva: International Organization for Migration. http://www.iom.int//DOCUMENTS/PUBLICATION/EN/Second_Annual_RCP_Report.pdf.

Szajkowski, Bogdan. 1983. *Next to God . . . Poland: Politics and Religion in Contemporary Poland.* New York: St. Martin's Press.

Tanner, Norman P. 1990. *Decrees of the Ecumenical Councils.* Washington, DC: Georgetown University Press.

Tarrow, Sidney. 2006. *The New Transnational Activism.* Cambridge: Cambridge University Press.

Taylor, Brian. 2006. "Law Enforcement and Civil Society in Russia." *Europe-Asia Studies* 58 (2): 193–213.

Thelen, K. 1999. "Historical Institutionalism in Comparative Politics." *Annual Review of Political Science* (2): 369–404.

Theobold, Robin. 1990. "So What Is Really the Problem about Corruption?" *Third World Quarterly* 20 (3): 491–502.

Tilly, Charles. 1986. "War Making and State Making as Organized Crime." In *Bringing the State Back In,* ed. Peter Evans, Dietrich Rueschemeyer, and Theda Skocpol, 169–91. Cambridge: Cambridge University Press.

Trebski, Krzysztof, Ludwik M. Bednarz, and Marlgorzata Zdiehowska. 2005. "Woz albo Airbus: LOT wybiera nie tylko samoloty ale I sojusznikow dla Polski." *Wprost* (13 March): 40–43.

Tsantis, Andreas. 1997. "Developments in the Romanian Banking Sector." In *The New Banking Landscape in Central and Eastern Europe: Country Experiences and Policies for the Future,* 167–216. Paris: Organization for Economic Co-operation and Development.

Tupanchevski, Nikola. 2002. "Macedonians and Albanians Make a Coalition of Corruption in the Government." Debate on the Research of Dr. Robert Hislope. *Vest* (23 June): 5.

United Nations. 2000. *Protocol to Prevent, Suppress and Punish Trafficking in Persons, Especially Women and Children, Supplementing the United Nations Convention Against Transnational Organized Crime.* Geneva: United Nations.

United Nations Development Program. 2001. *National Human Development Report 2001: Social Exclusion and Human Insecurity in FYR Macedonia.* Skopje: Skenpoint.

U.S. Department of State. 2003. "U.S. Government Assistance to Eastern Europe under the Support for East European Democracy (SEED) Act, FY 2002." http:// www.state.gov/p/eur/rls/rpt/23586.htm.

———. 2005a. "First Polish Rail Cars Delivered to Iraq." http://poland.usembassy .gov/poland/rail.htm.

———. 2005b. "Iraqi Reconstruction News." http://poland.usembassy.gov/poland/ iraq_reconstruction_page.html.

———. 2005c. "Trafficking in Persons Report, 2005." http://www.state.gov/g/tip/ rls/tiprpt/2005/46606.htm.

U.S. Institute of Peace. 2001. "The Future of Macedonia: A Balkan Survivor Now Needs Reform." http://www.usip.org.

University of Cambridge. 2003. "A New Security Paradigm: The Cambridge Security Seminar, 30 and 31 July, C-SIS and Cambridge Review of International Affairs." http://www.cambridgesecurity.net/pdf/new_security_paradigm.pdf.

Vachudova, Milada Anna. 2005. *Europe Undivided: Democracy, Leverage, and Integration after Communism.* Oxford: Oxford University Press.

———. 2006. "Democratization in Postcommunist Europe: Illiberal Regimes and the Leverage of International Actors." Center for European Studies Working Paper

Series #139, Harvard University. http://www.ces.fas.harvard.edu/publications/docs/pdfs/Vachudova.pdf.

Vachudova, Milada Anna, and Liesbet Hooghe. 2006. "Postcommunist Politics in a Magnetic Field: How Transition and EU Accession Structure Party Competition on European Integration." http://www.unc.edu/~hooghe/parties.htm.

Vachudova, Milada Anna, and Timothy Snyder. 1997. "Are Transitions Transitory? Two Types of Political Change in Eastern Europe since 1989." *East European Politics and Societies* 11 (1): 1–35.

Vallier, Ivan. 1971. "The Roman Catholic Church: A Transnational Actor." In *Transnational Relations and World Politics,* ed. Robert O. Keohane and Joseph S. Nye. Cambridge: Harvard University Press.

Van Evera, Stephen. 1994. "Hypotheses on Nationalism and War." *International Security* 18 (4): 5–39.

Verdier, D. 2000. "The Rise and Fall of State Banking in OECD Countries." *Comparative Political Studies* 33: 283–318.

Verdun, A. 1998. "The Increased Influence of EU Monetary Institutions in Determining National Policies: A Transnational Monetary Elite at Work." In *Autonomous Policy Making by International Organizations,* ed. Bob Reinalda and Bertjan Verbeek, 178–94. London and New York: Routledge.

Vintrová, R. 2004. "The CEE Countries on the Way into the EU—Adjustment Problems: Institutional Adjustment, Real and Nominal Convergence." *Europe-Asia Studies* 56 (4): 521–41.

Vishny, Robert W. 1993. "Corruption." *Quarterly Journal of Economics* 108 (3): 599–617.

Volkov, Vadim. 2002. *Violent Entrepreneurs: The Use of Force in the Making of Russian Capitalism.* Ithaca: Cornell University Press.

Wade, Robert. 2002. "US Hegemony and the World Bank: The Fight over People and Ideas." *Review of International Political Economy* 9 (2): 215–43.

Wallace, H., and A. Mayhew. 2001. *Poland: A Partnership Profile.* OEOS Policy Paper 4/01. Sussex: University of Sussex, Sussex European Institute.

Warsaw Business Journal. 1995. "BPH Consolidation Stuns Investors, Analysts, State Officials" (8 December): 3.

Warsaw Voice. 2004. "Investing—Money in the Bank" (21 November).

Watson, M. 2004. "Challenges for Central Banks in the New Member States." In *EU Enlargement and the Future of the Euro,* ed. R. Pringle and N. Carver, 53–63. London: Central Banking Publications.

Wedel, Janine. 1998. *Collision and Collusion: The Strange Case of Western Aid to Eastern Europe, 1989–1998.* New York: St. Martin's Press.

———. 2001. *Collision and Collusion: The Strange Case of Western Aid to Eastern Europe.* Rev. ed. New York: St. Martin's.

Weigel, George. *Witness to Hope: The Biography of Pope John Paul II.* New York: Cliff Street Books.

Williams, Abiodun. 2000. *Preventing War: The United Nations and Macedonia.* Lanham, MD: Rowman & Littlefield Publishers.

Williams, Michael C. 2007. *Culture and Security: Symbolic Power and the Politics of International Security.* London: Routledge.

WMRC Daily Analysis. 2004. "Renewed Tensions Emerge between Hungary's Government and Central Bank" (29 June).

Woodruff, David. 2000. "Rule for Followers: Institutional Theory and the New Politics of Economic Backwardness in Russia." *Politics and Society* 28 (4): 437–82.

Woodward, Susan. 1995. *Balkan Tragedy: Chaos and Dissolution after the Cold War.* Washington, DC: Brookings Institution.

World Bank. 1993. *The East Asian Miracle.* New York: Oxford University Press.

———. 2000. *Anticorruption in Transition: A Contribution to the Policy Debate.* Washington, DC: World Bank.

Yarrington, Doug. 2003. "Cattle, Corruption, and Venezuelan State Formation during the Regime of Juan Vicente Gomez, 1908–35." *Latin American Research Review* 38 (2): 9–33.

Young, D. G. 1989. "Commentary." In Hendrie, 71–73.

Zielonka, Jan, and Alex Pravda, eds. 2001. *Democratic Consolidation in Eastern Europe: International and Transnational Factors.* Oxford: Oxford University Press.

Życie Warszawy. 1995. "Strategie bankowych fuzji" (29 November): 8.

Życie Warszawy. 1996. "Konsolidacja banków—tak, ale z głową" (14 March): 9.

LIST OF CONTRIBUTORS

Stephen Bloom received his Ph.D. in 2004 from the University of California, Los Angeles, and is currently assistant professor of political science at Southern Illinois University. He has conducted extensive fieldwork in Ukraine and Latvia on ethnic politics and postcommunist transitions. His article "Competitive Assimilation or Strategic Non-Assimilation? The Political Economy of School Choice in Latvia" is forthcoming in *Comparative Political Studies.*

Timothy A. Byrnes is professor of political science at Colgate University in Hamilton, New York. His most recent book, edited with Peter Katzenstein, is *Religion in an Expanding Europe*. He is currently working on a book on the role of transnational Catholicism in the making of U.S. foreign policy.

Rachel A. Epstein is assistant professor at the Graduate School of International Studies at the University of Denver. Her work has appeared in *Comparative Political Studies*, *East European Politics and Societies,* and *Security Studies.* Her forthcoming book is *In Pursuit of Liberalism: The Power and Limits of International Institutions in Postcommunist Europe.*

Robert Hislope is associate professor of political science at Union College. He writes and teaches on Macedonian politics and the intersection of ethnicity, organized crime, and corruption. His work has been published in journals such as *Problems of Post-Communism, Journal of Democracy*, and *Ethnic and Racial Studies.*

Wade Jacoby is professor of political science and director of the Center for the Study of Europe at Brigham Young University. His writings on postcommunism include *The Enlargement of the EU and NATO: Ordering from the Menu in Central Europe* and *Imitation and Politics: Redesigning Modern Germany*. His recent articles on those topics have been in *World Politics, Review of International Organizations*, and *International Studies Review*. Jacoby has been a German Marshall Fund fellow and was recently winner of the DAAD Prize for his scholarship on Germany and the European Union.

Juliet Johnson is associate professor of political science at McGill University. She is the author of *A Fistful of Rubles: The Rise and Fall of the Russian Banking System* and coeditor of the *Review of International Political Economy.* She has served as both a research fellow in foreign policy studies at the Brookings Institution and the A. John Bittson National Fellow at the Hoover Institution. Her forthcoming book is entitled *Priests of Prosperity: The Transnational Central Banking Community and Post-Communist Transformation.*

Michael D. Kennedy is professor of sociology and director of the Center for Russian and East European Studies and the Center for European Studies/European Union Center at the University of Michigan. He is the author of *Cultural Formations of Postcommunism*. His current scholarship focuses on the articulation of cultural and global transformations through social movements, globalizing knowledge, and energy security in Europe and Eurasia.

Nicole Lindstrom is a lecturer in the Department of Politics at the University of York. She has taught at the Central European University in Budapest and held visiting positions at the New School and the University of Warwick. Her forthcoming book analyzes how elites in Estonia, Croatia, and Slovenia have navigated problems of state building during the process of European integration.

Mitchell A. Orenstein is S. Richard Hirsch Associate Professor of European Studies at the Johns Hopkins University School of Advanced International Studies in Washington, DC. He was director of the Maxwell European Union Center at Syracuse University during the preparation of this project. Orenstein is the author of *Out of the Red: Building Capitalism and Democracy in Postcommunist Europe* and other books and articles on postcommunist political economy. His new book is *Privatizing Pensions: The Transnational Campaign for Social Security Reform*.

David Ost, professor of political science at Hobart and William Smith Colleges in Geneva, New York, has written extensively on political economy, democratization, and labor in Eastern Europe. His most recent book, *The Defeat of Solidarity: Anger and Politics in Postcommunist Europe*, was awarded the 2006 Ed Hewett prize for the best book in the political economy of postsocialism, and came out in a Polish edition in 2007. He has published articles in numerous journals and is on the editorial boards of *Politics and Society* and *Studie Socjologiczne*.

Milada Anna Vachudova is associate professor of political science at University of North Carolina, Chapel Hill. Her book *Europe Undivided: Democracy, Leverage, and Integration after Communism* was awarded the twelfth biennial Stein Rokkan Prize for Comparative Social Science Research of the European Consortium for Political Research.

INDEX